'Indian Wars' and the Struggle for Eastern North America, 1763–1842

'Indian Wars' and the Struggle for Eastern North America, 1763–1842 examines the contest between Native Americans and Anglo-Americans for control of the lands east of the Mississippi River, through the lens of native attempts to form pan-Indian unions, and Anglo-Americans' attempts to thwart them.

The story begins in the wake of the Seven Years' War and ends with the period of Indian Removal and the conclusion of the Second Seminole War in 1842. Anglo-Americans had feared multi-tribal coalitions since the 1670s and would continue to do so into the early nineteenth century, long after there was a credible threat, due to the fear of slave rebels joining the Indians. By focusing on the military and diplomatic history of the topic, the work allows for a broad understanding of American Indians and frontier history, serving as a gateway to the study of Native American history.

This concise and accessible text will appeal to a broad intersection of students in ethnic studies, history, and anthropology.

Robert M. Owens is Professor of History at Wichita State University, USA. He is the author of *Red Dreams, White Nightmares: Pan-Indian Alliances in the Anglo-American Mind, 1763–1815* (2015).

Introduction To The Series

History is the narrative constructed by historians from traces left by the past. Historical enquiry is often driven by contemporary issues and, in consequence, historical narratives are constantly reconsidered, reconstructed and reshaped. The fact that different historians have different perspectives on issues means that there is often controversy and no universally agreed version of past events. *Seminar Studies* was designed to bridge the gap between current research and debate, and the broad, popular general surveys that often date rapidly.

The volumes in the series are written by historians who are not only familiar with the latest research and current debates concerning their topic, but who have themselves contributed to our understanding of the subject. The books are intended to provide the reader with a clear introduction to a major topic in history. They provide both a narrative of events and a critical analysis of contemporary interpretations. They include the kinds of tools generally omitted from specialist monographs: a chronology of events, a glossary of terms and brief biographies of 'who's who'. They also include bibliographical essays in order to guide students to the literature on various aspects of the subject. Students and teachers alike will find that the selection of documents will stimulate the discussion and offer insight into the raw materials used by historians in their attempt to understand the past.

Clive Emsley and Gordon Martel
Series Editors

'Indian Wars' and the Struggle for Eastern North America, 1763–1842

Robert M. Owens

LONDON AND NEW YORK

First published 2021
by Routledge
2 Park Square, Milton Park, Abingdon, Oxon OX14 4RN

and by Routledge
52 Vanderbilt Avenue, New York, NY 10017

Routledge is an imprint of the Taylor & Francis Group, an informa business

© 2021 Robert M. Owens

The right of Robert M. Owens to be identified as author of this work has been asserted by him in accordance with sections 77 and 78 of the Copyright, Designs and Patents Act 1988.

All rights reserved. No part of this book may be reprinted or reproduced or utilized in any form or by any electronic, mechanical, or other means, now known or hereafter invented, including photocopying and recording, or in any information storage or retrieval system, without permission in writing from the publishers.

Trademark notice: Product or corporate names may be trademarks or registered trademarks, and are used only for identification and explanation without intent to infringe.

British Library Cataloguing-in-Publication Data
A catalogue record for this book is available from the British Library

Library of Congress Cataloging-in-Publication Data
Names: Owens, Robert M. (Robert Martin), 1974- author.
Title: 'Indian Wars' and the struggle for eastern North America, 1763-1842 / Robert M. Owens.
Description: New York : Routledge, 2020. | Series: Seminar studies | Includes bibliographical references and index. | Identifiers: LCCN 2020024537 (print) | LCCN 2020024538 (ebook) | ISBN 9780367492052 (paperback) | ISBN 9780367492076 (hardback) | ISBN 9781003045021 (ebook)
Subjects: LCSH: Indians of North America–Wars–East (U.S.) | Indians of North America–Wars–Historiography. | Woodland Indians–Government relations–Sources. | Indians of North America–Government relations–1789-1869–Sources. | Indians of North America–East (U.S.)–History.
Classification: LCC E81 .O835 2020 (print) | LCC E81 (ebook) | DDC 970.004/97–dc23
LC record available at https://lccn.loc.gov/2020024537
LC ebook record available at https://lccn.loc.gov/2020024538

ISBN: 978-0-367-49207-6 (hbk)
ISBN: 978-0-367-49205-2 (pbk)
ISBN: 978-1-003-04502-1 (ebk)

Typeset in Sabon
by KnowledgeWorks Global Ltd.

Contents

List of Figures   ix
Chronology   x
Who's Who   xvii
Glossary   xxx
Map   xxxiv

PART I
Analysis and Assessment   1

Introduction: Clashing Cultures   3

Competition and Conquest: How Europeans Saw America 3
For the Love of God 4
Gender and Colonization 4
To be "Civilized" 5
Forming an Imperfect Union 9
The Tyranny of Terminology 10

1 Britain's Tenuous Empire   12

The European Contest for North America 12
Penny-wise and Pound-foolish: Pontiac's War 14
Efforts in Diplomacy 19
Bleeding Pennsylvania 21
War's End? 23
Murder and Real Estate: Lord Dunmore's War 26

2 Revolting Americans   29

Many Problems and Few Solutions 29
Factionalism among the Cherokees 30

    The British-Indian Alliance Stumbles in the North 33
    Southern Discomfort 35
    Violence Surges in the West 42

3 Confederations   46
    Patriotic Paternalism 48
    Creeks, Cherokees, and Southerners 53
    Elusive Peace on the Frontier 58

4 Dueling Unions   63
    Harmar's Campaign 63
    The St. Clair Disaster 65
    Wayne Takes Command 70
    The Treaty of Greenville 76
    Bowles Bows Out 78

5 Jeffersonians and Indians   81
    Jefferson's Indian Land Policy 81
    Tecumseh: The Greatest Pan-Indianist 84
    A Civil War Among the Creeks 91
    Americans Take Aim at Canada 92
    Red Sticks and Old Hickory 95

6 Indian Wars in the Age of Jackson   100
    The Question of Florida 100
    The First Seminole War 102
    The Black Hawk War 106
    The Second Seminole War 109

Conclusion: Making Sense of History   116
    Indian Wars in Memory 116
    "Heroes" Need "Villains" 117
    Professors and Producers 118

PART II
Documents 121

1. George Croghan at Fort Pitt to Sir William Johnson, 31 March 1762 — 123
2. Sir William Johnson at Johnson Hall, 18 March 1763, to Gen. Jeffery Amherst — 124
3. Speech of Pontiac, 27 April 1763 — 124
4. Proclamation of Gov. Josiah Martin, North Carolina, 18 May 1774 — 125
5. *Virginia Gazette,* 17 August 1776 — 125
6. *Virginia Gazette,* 14 September 1776 — 126
7. *Virginia Gazette,* 30 May 1777 — 126
8. Extract of a letter from Silver Bluff, 28 October 1779 — 126
9. *The Royal South Carolina Gazette,* 9 May 1782 — 127
10. Alexander McGillivray at Little Tallassee, 15 September 1788, to Richard Winn, Andrew Pickens, and George Mathews, Commissioners for treating with the Southern Nations of Indians — 127
11. Richard Winn, Andrew Pickens, George Mathews, to Alexander McGillivray, Esq. and the head men and warriors of the Creek nation. Hopewell on Keowee, 28 November 1788 — 128
12. *Kentucky Gazette,* 12 April 1788 — 130
13. General Joseph Martin, Agent to Cherokees, to Sec. War Knox, 2 February 1789 — 130
14. "For the Indian Department," *Boston Gazette,* 2 January 1792 — 132
15. Sec. of War Knox to Gov. William Blount, Southwest Territory, 31 January 1792 — 133
16. Hanging Maw's Talk, *Kentucky Gazette,* 17 November 1792 — 135
17. Memorial from the Widow of a Cherokee Chief, submitted to Congress, 17 January 1797 — 136
18. Piomingo in the Chickasaw Nation to General James Robertson, 17 June 1793 — 137
19. *Kentucky Gazette,* 1 September 1800, story from Savannah, Georgia — 139
20. Pres. Jefferson to Gov. Harrison, 27 February 1803 — 139
21. Tecumseh's speech to Gov. Harrison, 20 August 1810 — 141
22. Lydia Bacon's journal, 30 November 1811 — 143

23 Indian Removal Act of 1830 — 144
24 *Baltimore Patriot,* 21 July 1831, "The Indian Disturbances" — 146
25 *Pittsfield Sun* (MA), 4 August 1831, from the St. Louis Beacon — 146
26 *New Hampshire Sentinel,* 11 February 1836, "A second Tecumseh" — 147
27 *The Floridian,* 21 May 1836 — 147

Guide to Further Reading — 148
References — 153
Index — 158

Figures

Maps

Key tribes, towns, and battles, 1763–1842   xxxiv

Illustrations

1.1 Sir William Johnson, (c.1715–1774)   15
3.1 William Augustus Bowles (1763–1805)   55
5.1 Tecumseh (1768–1813)   85
5.2 Andrew Jackson (1767–1845) and William Weatherford,
     a.k.a. Red Eagle (c.1781–1824)   98
6.1 Black Hawk (1767–1838)   107
6.2 Osceola (1804–1838)   110

Chronology

1763

10 February	Peace of Paris signed, ending Seven Years' War
9 May	Pontiac launches his assault on Detroit
2 June	Fort Michilimackinac taken by Ojibwas and Sauks
24 June	Captain Simeon Ecuyer tries to introduce smallpox among the Delawares and Shawnees
5 August	Battle of Bushy Run
7 October	King issues Royal Proclamation of 1763
14–27 December	Paxton Rioters murder peaceful Indians in Pennsylvania

1764

August	Col. John Bradstreet declares end to Pontiac's war

1766

Creek-Choctaw War begins

1768

17 October	Treaty of Hard Labor
5 November	Treaty of Fort Stanwix

1774

26 April	Lord Dunmore's War
11 July	Sir William Johnson dies
10 October	Battle of Point Pleasant

1775

| 19 April | Battles of Lexington and Concord, MA |
| 14 March | Treaty of Muscle Shoals/Treaty of Watauga |

1776

| April | Pan-Indian conference at Chota |
| 2–4 July | Declaration of Independence endorsed |

1777

| 27 July | Jane McCrea murdered |
| 10 November | Chief Cornstalk murdered at Fort Randolph |

1778

| 7 February | Daniel Boone captured by a Shawnee war party |
| 3 July | "Wyoming Massacre" |

1779

| 25 February | George Rogers Clark re-takes Vincennes |
| June–Oct. | Sullivan's Iroquois campaign |

1780

| 22 June | Massacre at Ruddle's Station |
| 8 August | Battle of Piqua |

1781

| 1 April | Battle of Fort Nashborough |
| 26 July | Overhill Cherokees sign the Treaty of Holston |

1782

8 March	Gnadenhütten Massacre
11 July	Colonel William Crawford executed by Delawares
19 August	Battle of Blue Licks

1783

| January | St. Augustine conference of British agents and southeastern Indians |

3 September	Peace of Paris ends Revolutionary War (ratified 1784)
22 October	Treaty of Fort Stanwix concluded

1784

23 August	"State" of Franklin declared

1785

21 January	Treaty of Fort McIntosh concluded
20 May	Land Ordinance of 1785 adopted
28 November	Treaty of Hopewell marked by Cherokees

1786

31 January	Treaty of Fort Finney
6 October	Logan's attack on Maquachack, murder of Chief Moluntha

1787

13 July	Northwest Ordinance adopted
17 September	Constitutional Convention adjourns in Philadelphia

1788

June	John Sevier invades Cherokee territory Murder of Old Tassel

1790

22 July	Trade & Intercourse Act passed
7 August	Creeks and U.S. sign Treaty of New York
19–22 October	Battles of Kekionga

1791

4 November	Battle of the Wabash

1792

25 February	William Bowles captured by Spanish
29 February	Dragging Canoe dies

1793

17 February	Alexander McGillivray dies
12 June	John Beard's militia attack Hanging Maw's village
August	Northwestern Indians reject American proposals to buy Ohio lands
August	John Sevier and James Ore invade Cherokee towns again
25 September	Cherokees retaliate against Cavett's Station

1794

April–June	Britain builds Fort Miami in Ohio Country
30 June	Northwest Indians attack Fort Recovery, repulsed with losses
20 August	Battle of Fallen Timbers
19 November	John Jay's Treaty w/Britain signed

1795

May–August	Treaty of Greenville

1796

29 June	Creeks reaffirm peace with U.S.

1798

June	William Bowles escapes Spanish custody

1803

27 February	President Thomas Jefferson orders Indiana Governor William Henry Harrison to run Indian chiefs into debt and purchase their lands
30 April	U.S. buys Louisiana Territory for $15 million
27 May	Upper Creeks capture William Bowles to hand him over to Spanish

1805

November	Tenskwatawa, the Shawnee Prophet, begins preaching Indian unity
23 December	William Bowles dies in prison

1807

22 June   *Chesapeake-Leopard* Affair

1808

May   Tenskwatawa establishes Prophetstown on the Tippecanoe River

June   Tecumseh and Tenskwatawa reject military alliance with Britain

1809

Aug–Sept.   Fort Wayne Treaties

1810

Summer   Tecumseh asks Britain for aid in a war with the U.S.

1811

August   Conferences between Illinois Territory and Illinois Indian tribes in Peoria

7 November   Battle of Tippecanoe

1812

12 May   Red Sticks attack Crawley family on Duck River in Tennessee

18 June   U.S. declares war on Britain, officially starting War of 1812

16 August   General William Hull surrenders Detroit to General Isaac Brock

1813

23 January   River Raisin Massacre

5 October   U.S. wins Battle of the Thames/Moraviantown, Canada. Tecumseh dies.

27 July   Battle of Burnt Corn Creek, Alabama – initiates U.S. war against Red Sticks

30 August   Fort Mims Massacre, spurring Tennessee's invasion of Creek territory

1814

27 March	Battle of Horseshoe Bend/Tohopeka
9 August	Treaty of Fort Jackson signed by U.S. and Creeks
24 December	U.S. and Britain sign Treaty of Ghent (Belgium)

1815

8 January	British defeated in the Battle of New Orleans
17 February	U.S. Senate ratifies Treaty of Ghent, officially ending War of 1812

1816

27 July	Maroon fort at Prospect Bluff (FL) destroyed

1818

15 March	Andrew Jackson invades Spanish Florida
9 April	Jackson hangs Seminole prophet Hillis Hadjo/Josiah Francis
29 April	Jackson executes two British subjects accused of aiding the Seminoles

1819

22 February	Spain cedes Florida to the U.S.

1823

18 September	Treaty of Moultrie Creek signed between U.S. and Seminoles

1828

21 February	*Cherokee Phoenix* (newspaper) first published, in both English and Cherokee

1829

4 March	Andrew Jackson becomes president of the U.S.

1830

28 May	President Jackson signs Indian Removal Act into law

1831

30 June	Sauk leader Black Hawk marks the "Corn Treaty," agrees to move to Iowa
21–23 August	Nat Turner's slave rebellion in Southampton County, VA

1832

5 April	"British Band" of Sauks return to their former village of Saukenauk, IL
9 May	Some Seminole chiefs mark Treaty of Payne's Landing, agreeing to removal west
2 August	Battle of Bad Axe River, Wisconsin, ends Black Hawk War

1835

26 November	Osceola kills Charley Emathla
28 December	Osceola kills agent Wiley Thompson; "Dade Massacre"
29 December	Unauthorized Cherokees sign the Treaty of New Echota, promising Removal west

1837

21 October	Osceola captured under flag of truce
25 December	Battle of Lake Okeechobee

1838

30 January	Osceola dies in custody, Fort Moultrie, SC

1839

22 June	All Cherokee signers of the Treaty of New Echota, except Stand Watie, murdered

1842

14 August	U.S. declares end to Second Seminole War

Who's Who

Indian nations/groups

Catawbas – From South Carolina, they formed a strong alliance with that colony, which became ever more important as their numbers shrank in the eighteenth century.

Cherokees – Originally claiming much of the Carolinas, and parts of Georgia, Tennessee, and Virginia, the Cherokees were culturally similar to the Iroquois League, though often at odds with them. They were important allies for the English from 1730 until the Cherokee War of 1759–61; they renewed that bond until the end of the American Revolution. From the 1770s onward they saw increased factionalism, particularly between the Overhill towns and the Lower/Chickamaugas, the latter of whom were particularly militant in resisting American encroachment.

Chickasaws – Numerically one of the smaller Southern nations, they lived in western Tennessee and northern Mississippi, but hunted far and wide. They had a fierce reputation as warriors, and often fought much larger nations, like the Creeks, to a stalemate. First allied to Britain, after the Revolution they became important allies of the U.S.

Choctaws – A large nation living along the Mississippi River in Mississippi, they allied themselves first with France, then Britain, and eventually the U.S. After they had abandoned the French alliance, their relations with the Chickasaws to their north improved considerably.

Creeks – They call themselves the Muskogee Nation. Muskogean speakers, the Creeks occupied exceptionally fertile farmlands in Georgia and Alabama, and had two main groups, the Upper and Lower Creeks. Often the most numerous of the Indian nations in the South – about 20,000 – European and American officials often found them troublesome.

Delawares – Originally from Pennsylvania, New Jersey, and southern New York, the Delawares call themselves Lenni Lenape. They spoke an Algonquian language related to Shawnee, and practiced hunting, gathering, and trading. By the early nineteenth century they had been largely pushed out of Pennsylvania, and many lived in southern Indiana at the invitation of the Miamis.

Iroquois League – From upstate New York, they call themselves the Haudenosaunee. Beginning in the sixteenth century, the Iroquois comprised – from west to east – the Senecas, Cayugas, Onondagas, Oneidas, and Mohawks. In the early 1700s, they were joined by the Tuscaroras, who migrated from the Carolinas, making the Five Nations into the Six Nations. They supplemented their women's farming with hunting, fishing, and trading, and were key allies for the British in the wars of the eighteenth century.

Kickapoos – Algonquian speakers, they lived across much of central Illinois and southern Wisconsin. Like the Shawnees, they were well traveled and had a reputation as warriors, and many fought against American expansionists.

Mesquakies – Detested by the French, who called them "Les Renards" (Foxes), they are closely associated with the Sauk nation. Many allied themselves to the British in imperial conflicts, and the War of 1812. They made their home in Illinois and southern Wisconsin.

Miamis – A confederacy that originally included the Wea, Piankeshaws, Eel River, and "Miamis Proper," they call themselves the Twightwee. Algonquian speakers, they primarily lived in rich farm lands of Indiana and western Ohio. Like the Shawnees, they were among the leading opponents to American expansion prior to 1795.

Mingos – An offshoot of the Iroquois League who moved west into the Ohio Country. They tended to ally themselves with the British.

Ojibwas – Sometimes rendered "Chippewas," they are related to the Ottawas and Potawatomis. Algonquian speakers from the Great Lakes region, they hunted and gathered extensively, and often allied with France.

Ottawas – From the Great Lakes region, sometimes rendered "Odawas," these Algonquian speakers hunted extensively, and became known as feared warriors in the late seventeenth century, allied to France. The war chief Pontiac was an Ottawa. They are related to the Ojibwas and Potawatomis.

Potawatomis – Algonquian speakers from the Great Lakes region, and later the prairie of Illinois, they are related to the Ottawas and Ojibwas – collectively known as the Anishinabeg peoples.

Sauk – Algonquian speakers, they lived in western Illinois and southern Wisconsin. In the early eighteenth century, they became closely associated with the Mesquakies, or Fox. Chief Black Hawk was a Sauk.

Seminoles – From Florida, the Seminoles are thought to be the result of a number of refugee peoples, many of them Muskogean speakers, who coalesced in the Spanish colony in the eighteenth century. While related to the Creeks, they also relished their independence. By the early nineteenth century, American plantation owners in the Southeast saw them as a threat to their slaves and security.

Shawnees – Sometimes formerly spelled "Savannas" or "Sawanoes" or "Shawanese," they are an Algonquian-speaking, patrilineal group originally from southern Ohio. They dispersed in the bloody seventeenth century, and bands made contacts with many different groups. They largely returned to Ohio in the eighteenth century. Though many Shawnees would move west of the Mississippi during the Revolution, those who remained gained a reputation as fierce opponents of American expansion into the Ohio Country.

Individuals

Sir Jeffery Amherst (1717–1797) – Britain's commander-in-chief of North America in the wake of the Seven Years' War. His decision to cut costs by no longer giving diplomatic gifts, particularly arms, to Indians, enraged them, and helped bring on Pontiac's War in 1763.

Attakullakulla (c.1708–1777) – Cherokee chief – called Little Carpenter by the English. He had been part of a Cherokee delegation that went to England in 1730. He spent much of his adult life as an advocate for the British alliance, and once saved the life of British officer (and future Indian affairs superintendent) John Stuart. An Overhill Cherokee who usually sought to accommodate the British, including selling them Cherokee land, he increasingly came into conflict with his son, Dragging Canoe, who became the leader of militant Cherokee resistance to whites. Attakullakulla was the uncle of Nancy Ward, the Cherokee Beloved Woman who repeatedly urged peace with the Americans.

Black Fish (c.1729–1779) – Shawnee chief of Chillicothe. Blackfish led the party that captured Daniel Boone's salt-making party in Kentucky, and briefly adopted Boone as his son. After Boone's escape, Blackfish led other raids against the Kentucky stations. In 1779, when Kentuckians attacked Chillicothe, Blackfish was mortally wounded defending the town.

Blue Jacket (c.1743–1810) – Principal war chief of the Shawnees. Blue Jacket helped engineer the great Indian victory against Arthur St. Clair in 1791, but was among the defeated at Fallen Timbers in 1794. He marked the Treaty of Greenville, and did not fight the Americans again.

Henry Bouquet (1719–1765) – Swiss-born colonel serving in the British Army during the Seven Years' War, Bouquet had a reputation as a skillful field officer, and was credited with relieving Fort Pitt during Pontiac's War, after winning the Battle of Bushy Run. He also communicated via letter with his commander, Jeffery Amherst, speculating about the utility of using large war dogs or smallpox as ways to defeat Pontiac and his Indian allies.

Daniel Boone (1734–1820) – Famous Kentucky "longhunter," Boone fought in Lord Dunmore's War and the American Revolution, and was captured and briefly adopted by the Shawnee chief Black Fish.

William Augustus Bowles (1763–1805) – Maryland Tory and British officer in Florida during the Revolution, Bowles married a Creek woman and became increasingly interested in forming an independent Creek state, which he of course would lead. Calling himself the "Director General of the Creek Nation," Bowles was as much a huckster as a pan-Indianist, and never had the Indian following or British authority he repeatedly claimed. After repeatedly antagonizing the Spanish, he died in prison in Havana, Cuba.

Joseph Brant/Thayendanegea (1743–1807) – Mohawk war captain and chief. Brant, brother-in-law to Sir William Johnson, was a staunch British ally his entire adult life, and fought in the Seven Years' War and the Revolution. In the latter conflict, he was so feared that Americans sometimes credited him with attacks where he had not been present. In his later years he tried to assert leadership of native resistance to American encroachment, but was increasingly ignored by more militant Indians in the Ohio Country.

Richard Butler (1743–1791) – American brigadier general, Indian trader, Indian treaty commissioner. From Pennsylvania, Butler spent the 1760s and early 1770s as trader with the Ohio Indians, reputedly fathering a child with Nonhelema, the sister of Shawnee chief Cornstalk. Serving in the Continental Army during the war, in the 1780s, he was one of the commissioners at the treaties of Fort McIntosh and Fort Finney, which cost him much of the goodwill he had earned with Ohio natives previously. He died at the Battle of the Wabash in 1791, the first American general to die in combat since the Revolution.

George Rogers Clark (1752–1818) – Virginia militia officer, U.S. Indian treaty commissioner. Credited with "conquering" the Northwest

Territory during the Revolution, he gained a reputation as a brutal but effective fighter. Clark also helped found Louisville, Kentucky. In the 1780s he served as a commissioner to the Fort McIntosh and Fort Finney treaties, where he advocated a hardline, bullying stance with the Indians. For his wartime service, Virginia gave him "Clark's Grant," 150,000 acres of southern Indiana. But crushing debts and heavy drinking soured his later years. His younger brother William explored the Louisiana Purchase with Meriwether Lewis from 1803 to 1805.

George Croghan (c.1718–1782) – Pennsylvania Indian trader and later Indian Agent, he worked closely with Sir William Johnson, and like Johnson, speculated heavily in Indian lands. Unlike Johnson, he lived long enough to see the American Revolution wreck his finances.

William Crawford (1732–1782) – Colonel, Continental Army. A surveyor and friend of George Washington's prior to the war, in 1782, Crawford was tapped to lead an invasion of the Ohio Country. He had the misfortune of doing so in the wake of widespread native outrage after the murder of the Moravian Delawares at Gnadenhütten. Though they had no role in the massacre, when Crawford and a number of his men were captured, they were tortured and executed. Crawford's death took two hours, and his gruesome end was widely publicized in the American media.

Dragging Canoe/Tsi.yu.gansi.ni (c.1738–1792) – Leader of the Chickamauga Cherokees. Frustrated by the accommodation and land sales to whites practiced by older chiefs, including his father, Attakullakulla, Dragging Canoe advocated violently resisting all white encroachment if necessary. His name derived from a boyhood incident, wherein he was told he could not join a war party if he could not carry a canoe himself. The spirited youngster dragged the too heavy craft for some distance. As leader of the Lower (later Chickamauga) Cherokees, he distinguished himself not only for his willingness to fight against encroachment, but his openness to pan-Indian allies from both north and south to do so. It is thought he died of a heart attack after a vigorous night of dancing in celebration of an alliance with the Creeks.

Lord Dunmore (1730–1809) – John Murray, the 4th Earl of Dunmore, was the last royal governor of Virginia. The Scotsman was briefly popular in the colony when he championed a war against the Shawnees and Mingos in 1774 that bears his name. The war ended with the Shawnees ceding their claims to what would become Kentucky to Virginia, which began referring to the land as its "Western District." Months later, American rebels drove Dunmore out of office.

Simeon Ecuyer (c.1720–?) – Veteran Swiss soldier/mercenary, he served as a captain in the British Army in North America during the Seven Years' War. When approached by Delaware embassies during the early days of Pontiac's War, he declined their offer to let him evacuate his command at Fort Pitt, and gifted them two blankets and a handkerchief from the smallpox ward of the post's hospital. While he may or may not have succeeded in introducing the disease, his attempt at biological warfare was most deliberate.

Sir Thomas Gage (1718–1787) – A combat veteran of the Seven Years' War in North America, General Gage was promoted to commander-in-chief of North America after Jeffery Amherst's recall in 1764. He spent the next eleven years trying to manage unruly colonists and complex Indian affairs with an ever-shrinking budget. Gage held the post until 1775, when he was recalled in the wake of the disastrously costly British victory over rebels at Breed's Hill.

Simon Girty (1741–1818) – Captured by Indians as a teenager, Girty spent several years with the Senecas, and while he eventually returned to his Pennsylvania community, he spent the rest of his years as an interpreter and agent, with a great affinity for Indians. When the Revolution broke out he originally served the Americans at Fort Pitt, but later ran off to take up with his Seneca relations. Fighting as a British ally, he was loathed by Americans as a "renegade" who had joined the Indians against them. Girty fought against the U.S. in many engagements, including Blue Licks and the defeat of St. Clair at the Battle of the Wabash. He also secured the release of many American prisoners, though was unable to see Colonel Crawford spared in 1782.

Henry Hamilton (c.1734–1796) – British army colonel, commander of Fort Detroit. During the early years of the Revolution in the West, Hamilton was charged with recruiting Indian allies for Britain. When these Indians attacked white settlers in Kentucky and presented Hamilton with scalps or prisoners, he rewarded them with various gifts. Americans charged, unfairly, that he was a "Hair-buyer." Hamilton retook Vincennes after George Rogers Clark captured it in 1778, but then was himself captured by Clark in February 1779 when he returned. Hamilton was shipped to Virginia in chains, but was eventually exchanged and became Lt. governor of Quebec, then governor of Bermuda.

Josiah Harmar (1753–1813) – American brigadier general. A veteran of the Revolution, Harmar led an American force of Regulars and militia to attack the Miami towns in 1790. Though his army burned some Miami towns and cornfields, they took heavy casualties, and afterwards he was court martialed – at his own request – and cleared of wrongdoing.

William Henry Harrison (1773–1841) – First governor of Indiana Territory. Harrison negotiated numerous Indian land cession treaties, often deliberately ignoring tribes who had the best claims to the land in question, and never paying more than three cents per acre. When Tecumseh and the Shawnee Prophet opposed further land sales to the U.S., Harrison marched an army to destroy the village of Prophetstown in 1811. As a general in the War of 1812, he led the army that killed Tecumseh in 1813. He later served (very briefly) as president of the U.S.

Black Hawk (1767–1838) – Sauk war chief. An ally of Tecumseh's in the War of 1812, Black Hawk and his followers resisted leaving their village in western Illinois. When they left Iowa to reoccupy it in 1832, they were met by great numbers of militia and Regular troops. Black Hawk hoped to forge a pan-Indian union with British aid that would intimidate the Americans into backing down, but instead his band was crushed. Captured, Black Hawk was sent on a tour of the eastern U.S. to impress upon him the power of the nation.

Benjamin Hawkins (1754–1816) – Senator from North Carolina, and an Indian agent in the 1780s, he was appointed Superintendent of Southern Indian Affairs from 1796 to his death, and was a leading proponent of the "civilization" program. Hawkins resided in the Creek Indian Agency, and took a Creek woman for his common law wife. Hawkins denounced Tecumseh's visit in 1811, and survived several assassination attempts when civil war broke out among the Creeks. He was widely regarded as the most knowledgeable man in the American government regarding Indian affairs.

Hokolesqua/Cornstalk (c.1720–1777) – Shawnee chief. Hokolesqua opposed Shawnee involvement in Lord Dunmore's War, but when the majority of them called for action, he led a spirited by failed attack at the Battle of Point Pleasant. Later, during the Revolution, he tried desperately to keep his people out of the conflict, but was taken hostage by Americans while on a diplomatic embassy to Fort Randolph, Virginia. While confined there, he and several other Shawnees were murdered by vengeful American militia, which spurred many more Shawnees to join the war as British allies.

Sir William Johnson (c.1715–1774) – Known as the "Mohawk Baronet," Sir William rose in colonial New York society in part because of his close ties to the Iroquois Confederacy, in particular the Mohawks. He took a prominent Mohawk woman, known as Molly Brant, as his common-law wife, and worked closely with her brother Joseph Brant, a Mohawk chief. Johnson was named Superintendent for Northern Indian Affairs in 1755, a post he held until his death. He strongly advised against General Amherst's decree against diplomatic gifts to Indians, and was also an avid land speculator, directing the Fort Stanwix cession of what would become Kentucky by the Iroquois.

Junaluska (c.1775–1868) – Cherokee warrior and leader. He rejected Tecumseh's call for an alliance against the U.S. in 1811, and served in Andrew Jackson's army against the Red Sticks. At Tohopeka/Horseshoe Bend, he killed a Red Stick prisoner who lunged at Jackson with a knife. Years later, when Jackson refused to meet with him over the Indian Removal Act, Junaluska wished he had killed Jackson rather than the Red Stick.

Henry Knox (1750–1806) – Continental Army general. Knox served as Secretary of War both before and under the Federal Constitution. Charged with Indian affairs, Knox tried to avoid wars with Indians, for reasons both financial and humane. However, like President Washington, Knox remained committed to eventually American expansion into the West, and used military force (or its threat) to convince Indians to make peace and sell land to the United States.

Benjamin Logan (1742–1802) – Kentucky militia colonel. Logan led several invasions of Indian lands north of the Ohio River during and after the Revolutionary War. Most infamously, it was his 1786 raid that led to the murder of the aged Shawnee chief Moluntha, despite Logan's having ordered that prisoners would be spared. Logan later served in the Kentucky House of Representatives.

John Logan (c.1723–1780) – Mingo chief. Long known for his friendship to whites, Logan became enraged when a party of Virginians led by Daniel Greathouse murdered most of his family in the Yellow Creek Massacre in 1774. Logan announced to Virginia authorities that he would exact revenge on Virginia frontiersmen. These attacks were used as a pretext for Lord Dunmore's War in 1774.

Jane McCrea (1752–1777) – Engaged to a New York Loyalist, McCrea was mistakenly captured by British Indian auxiliaries during the Saratoga Campaign during the Revolution, and shortly thereafter killed. In a propaganda windfall, American officers and newspapermen spun her death into a lurid tale of British/Indian "savagery." Her death was even used in Parliament by the opposition to criticize the American war.

Alexander McGillivray/Hoboi-Hili-Miko (1750–1793) – Muskogee Beloved Man. The son of a Scottish trader and an adopted Creek woman of the Wind Clan, McGillivray was a Loyalist during the Revolution and a Creek nationalist after it. In the 1780s the calculating McGillivray emerged as a leading member not only of the Creeks – despite his weakness with the language – and of pan-Indian efforts to resist white encroachment. He skillfully played off Spanish and American officials against each other – at one point he was receiving secret salaries from both governments. However, his increasing materialism eventually cost him credibility with some Creeks. He died on his plantation at age 42, thought to be a victim of (then incurable) syphilis.

William McIntosh (1775–1825) – Métis Creek chief. A slave owner and enemy of the Red Sticks, McIntosh led his men as American allies in the Creek War, and then in Andrew Jackson's Florida incursions – partly because Jackson promised McIntosh he could keep every slave he captured. Later, McIntosh would be executed by his fellow Creeks for the crime of selling Creek land without authorization.

Alexander McKee (1735–1799) – British Indian Agent. Son of a Scots-Irish father and Kispoko Shawnee mother, McKee spent four decades in the Indian service, starting in the Seven Years' War. Initially working for the Americans at Fort Pitt during the Revolution, like Simon Girty, he ran off to join the Ohio Indians after witnessing the Americans treating them poorly. He eventually achieved the rank of Colonel.

Hanging Maw (c.1710–c.1795) – Overhill Cherokee chief. Though sometimes a combatant, by the 1790s Hanging Maw routinely called for peace with the Americans. In 1793, Tennessee militia under John Beard attacked his village, wounding Hanging Maw and killing other innocent Cherokees, including Nancy Ward's daughter Betsy. Yet the next year, Hanging Maw sent a party of warriors to capture a Creek who had murdered a white man, and handed him over to the Americans.

Moluntha (c.1692–1786) – Shawnee chief. A signer of the Treaty of Fort Finney, Moluntha had long advocated for peace with the Americans. When his town was invaded by Kentuckians under Benjamin Logan in 1786, he met the militia holding his copy of the treaty. When Hugh McGary asked him if he had been at Blue Licks, the confused chief nodded in the affirmative, and McGary murdered him with a tomahawk.

Neolin (18th century, exact dates unknown) – Delaware religious prophet, he preached in the wake of the Seven Years' War that the Great Spirit was angry with Indians for adopting too many European ways. All Indians, not just the Delawares, he insisted, needed to purify themselves of these outside influences. When the Ottawa war chief Pontiac began a great war against the English in 1763, using Neolin's prophecy as inspiration, Neolin himself condemned the war.

Edward Nicholls (1779–1865) – Officer of the Royal Marines. In the War of 1812, Nicholls was charged with raising, training, and leading an army of Indians and former slaves in the Southeast to punish the United

States. Yet he arrived several months after Horseshoe Bend, and so found relatively few Indian volunteers. A fervent abolitionist, Nicholls hoped to start a war of slave liberation in the American South, and at war's end made sure that he left an impressive, well-armed fort – Prospect Bluff – for the use of his native and maroon allies.

Osceola/Billy Powell (1804–1838) – Métis Seminole chief. Osceola became the most famous of the Seminole chiefs who resisted Removal in the Second Seminole War. At times ruthless, he killed Seminoles whom he considered traitors for agreeing to leave Florida. He was captured under a flag of truce in 1837. Already suffering from malaria, he died in the prison at Fort Moultrie, South Carolina.

Paxton Boys (1763–64) – Known also as the Paxton Rioters, these Scots-Irish Pennsylvanians reacted to Pontiac's War by murdering twenty peaceful Indians who were under the protection of the Pennsylvania government, in December 1763. The Paxton Boys, in addition to hating all Indians, vented their anger at the colony government that had failed to protect their neighbors, and even briefly threatened to invade Philadelphia. They were never prosecuted for the murders.

Andrew Pickens (1739–1817) – South Carolina militia officer and Congressman. Pickens fought in the Revolution, and against the Cherokees. In the 1780s he was frequently called to serve as an Indian treaty commissioner. Though a committed nationalist, Pickens eventually ceased serving as a commissioner, becoming disenchanted when he felt that the Federal government was not honoring its treaty commitments.

Piomingo/Mountain Leader (eighteenth century) – Chickasaw war chief. Piomingo called repeatedly for an alliance with the Americans beginning in the 1780s, knowing that his people needed supplies to ward off their native enemies, especially the far more numerous Creeks. Piomingo personally led his warriors against the Northwest Confederation in the 1790s.

Pontiac (c.1714–1769) – Ottawa war chief and enthusiastic French ally in the Seven Years' War. Pontiac, significantly tweaking the vision of the Delaware prophet Neolin, inspired a great war to drive the English out of the Great Lakes region, hoping for a return of French influence. His effort ultimately failed, and he eventually made peace with the English. He was assassinated in 1769 by a Peoria Indian.

Shawnee Prophet/Tenskwatawa (1775–1836) – Shawnee religious leader. Tecumseh's younger brother, the Prophet preached a message of Indian unity and separation from American political and cultural influences, including alcohol. With his brother, he called for all Indians to reject further land sales to the government. He lost some clout after Governor Harrison's army destroyed Prophetstown in 1811, but remained part of the movement even after his brother's death. He died on a reservation in Kansas.

James Robertson (1742–1814) – Militia general, founder of Nashville. Robertson and his wife Charlotte helped defend Fort Nashborough from the Chickamaugas in 1782, and later was much beloved by the Chickasaws as their Agent from the U.S.

John Ross (1790–1866) – First elected principal chief of the Cherokee Nation. Ross served against the Red Sticks in the Creek War, and as chief of the Cherokees presided over an era of rapid assimilation. He opposed Indian Removal, but found his old ally Andrew Jackson deaf to his pleas. Ross's wife and son later died on the Trail of Tears.

Arthur St. Clair (1737–1818) – American general, governor of the Northwest Territory. St. Clair led the disastrous invasion of the upper Wabash region that was nearly annihilated by the Northwest Confederacy on Nov. 4, 1791. Having lost 630 men and all of the artillery, it was the worst defeat the U.S. ever suffered at Indian hands, and St. Clair was the subject of the first ever Congressional investigation. He was officially absolved of blame, but his military career was over.

Charles Scott (1739–1813) – Kentucky militia general. A veteran of the Revolution, Scott was ordered to invade the Miami heartland in 1791 to distract the Northwest Confederacy. Attacking villages near modern Lafayette, Indiana, Scott's army specifically targeted native women (for capture) and their capacity as food producers. He fought again at Fallen Timbers, and was later elected governor of Kentucky.

John Sevier (1745–1815) – Militia leader. Sevier was a hero of the Southern backcountry during the Revolution, and later helped lead the breakaway state of Franklin and its numerous raids against Cherokees. He somehow survived Franklin's collapse, likely because his reputation as an "Indian fighter" kept him popular among backcountry whites. He became Tennessee's first governor in 1796.

John Stuart (1718–1779) – British army officer captured during the Cherokee War in 1760, he was spared when the Cherokee chief Attakullakulla (Little Carpenter) purchased him and returned him to South Carolina. Later, after Attakullakulla endorsed him for the post of Indian agent, Stuart was appointed Superintendent for Southern Indian Affairs. Prior to the Revolution, Stuart was charged with preventing anti-British coalitions cheaply, which often meant quietly encouraging Indians to fight each other, as with the Creek-Choctaw war of the mid-1760s–1775. Stuart remained loyal to the King when the Revolution broke out, and died in exile in Florida.

General John Sullivan (1740–1795) – American army officer from New Hampshire. In 1779, General George Washington ordered Sullivan to "scourge" the Iroquois League's heartland in upstate New York as punishment for their aiding the British. Sullivan's campaign burned over forty Iroquois towns, including some that had aided the U.S. While Sullivan's men certainly punished the Iroquois, the campaign did not knock the Iroquois out of the war, but actually drove them deeper into the British alliance, as they now desperately needed food and supplies.

Tecumseh (1768–1813) – Shawnee war chief. Son of a principal war chief, Tecumseh fought against American encroachment in the 1780s and 1790s, including at Fallen Timbers. In the early nineteenth century he joined the religious movement of his brother, Tenskwatawa/the Shawnee Prophet. Originally hoping to be at peace with the U.S., after the Fort Wayne treaties of 1809, Tecumseh saw war as inevitable if Indians were to have any hope of independence. Considered the greatest advocate for pan-Indian resistance, he tried (unsuccessfully) to recruit the Southern nations to join his coalition. A natural, skillful leader, his multi-tribal followers fought very well in the War of 1812 until he was killed at the Battle of the Thames in 1813.

Teedyuscung (c.1700–1763) – Delaware chief. Colorful and hard-drinking, Teedyuscung alternately fought and tried to appease Pennsylvanians in an effort to keep Delaware territory. He was murdered when persons unknown – likely white land speculators – set fire to his cabin while he slept. His murder inspired many Delawares, including his son, Captain Bull, to lash out at Pennsylvania's settlers during Pontiac's War.

Little Turtle (c.1747–1812) – Miami war chief. He fought against the U.S. in the Revolution, and was a principal leader in the defeats of both the Harmar and St. Clair expeditions. He fought at Fallen Timbers, and reluctantly signed the Treaty of Greenville in 1795. After that, he increasingly worked with American officials, and eventually opposed Tecumseh and the Prophet.

Nancy Ward/Nanyehi (c.1738–1824) – Cherokee Beloved Woman. First recognized as a teenager as a War Woman for taking up her dying husband's gun during a battle with the Creeks, she later became known as an advocate for peace. Repeatedly she warned white settlers of impending attacks during and after the Revolutionary War. Through her daughter, Betsy, she became mother-in-law to U.S. Agent to the Cherokees, Joseph Martin.

Anthony Wayne (1745–1796) – American general in the Revolutionary War, the brash but effective Wayne, once nicknamed "Mad" Anthony, proved the first American capable of defeating the Northwest

Confederacy, which he did in 1794 at Fallen Timbers. In 1795, he directed the treaty council at Fort Greenville (Ohio), which ended the fighting in the west for the first time since 1775, promised annuities to the tribes that signed, and secured the cession of ¾ of future Ohio to the U.S. The treaty became a model for future U.S.-Indian treaties.

William Weatherford (c.1781–1824) – Métis Upper Creek/Red Stick chief. Weatherford fought at Fort Mims and other engagements in the Creek War, but after the devastating loss at Tohopeka, he surrendered to Andrew Jackson personally. Impressed, Jackson released him.

William Wells (1770–1812) – American soldier, Indian agent, translator. Adopted by Miamis after a raid into Kentucky, Wells assimilated, fighting for the Northwest Confederates against St. Clair and marrying the daughter of Chief Little Turtle. But in 1792 he returned to his white family, and served Anthony Wayne as "chief of spies." He later served as an Indian agent at Fort Wayne, and died trying to protect his American relatives from Potawatomi attackers in the Fort Dearborn Massacre.

David Williamson (1752–1814) – Colonel, Pennsylvania militia. Williamson led the party that committed the infamous Gnadenhütten Massacre of almost 100 Christian Delaware Indians in March of 1782. He was never prosecuted for the mass murder, and was later elected sheriff of Washington County, PA.

Glossary

Annuity – An annual payment made by the U.S. government to Indians, often in the form of trade goods, food, or agricultural implements, and usually as payment for a cession of land.

Cumberland Gap – A slight lowering of the height of the Appalachian Mountains, located near the intersection of the modern states of Kentucky, Tennessee, Virginia, and North Carolina. The gap was a preferred route for whites who wanted to move into the western country, as it was somewhat easier to pass through the gap than the nearly unbroken stretches of high mountains to both the north and south.

Ethnocentrism – The belief that one's own culture is superior to other cultures.

Fathers **and** ***children*** – Native diplomacy often relied upon creating fictive kin relationships with outsiders. Indians called Europeans, and later Americans, "father," and themselves "children." Europeans slowly realized, however, that rather than giving them coercive authority over Indians, it actually implied they would provide paternal protection over Indians. When Indians and whites wished to stress a more equal, if still fictive, kin relationship, they used the term *brother*.

Franklin – A quasi-legal state formed from the eastern counties of what would become Tennessee, in 1784. Franklin's founders hoped to become a state of the union, and then an independent republic, but finally dissolved in 1789. In addition to fighting skirmishes with North Carolina militia, the Franklinites had numerous bloody battles with the Cherokees and other Indians.

Genocide – A term created in the 1940s, it refers to one culture group's assault on another, designed to destroy them. The United Nations defines genocide as (a) Killing members of the group; (b) Causing serious bodily or mental harm to members of the group; (c) Deliberately inflicting on the group conditions of life calculated to bring about its physical destruction in whole or in part; (d) Imposing measures intended to prevent births within the group; (e) Forcibly transferring children of the group to another group.

Gifts – In the context of North American Indian diplomacy, the giving of gifts was tremendously important, as native peoples felt that words unaccompanied by some tangible symbol were empty, and meaningless. While Europeans often bristled at the idea of providing blankets, firearms, or other trade goods to Indians, seeing them as essentially bribes, native peoples insisted upon reciprocal gift-giving when conducting official business.

Iroquois League – Culturally related tribes in what became upstate New York – the Five Nations were the Senecas, Cayugas, Onondagas, Oneidas, and Mohawks, had joined in a confederacy in the sixteenth century, and were joined in the early eighteenth century by the Tuscaroras, making the "Five Nations" the "Six Nations." Called "Iroquois" by the French, they called themselves the Haudenosaunee.

Loyalists – American colonists who refused to rebel against King George III during the American Revolution, they were also known as Tories, a reference to the British political party that favored royal power. Most Loyalists suffered tremendous property losses (or worse) during the Revolution.

Maroons – Escaped slaves who forged their own societies, often in mountains, swamps, or other hard to access regions. While the most famous maroon groups lived on Caribbean islands like Jamaica, recent scholarship demonstrates that maroon societies also existed in mainland North America.

Matrilineal descent – A system of reckoning one's kin through the mother's side of the family.

Mercantilism – The dominant economic theory of western Europe during the era of colonization – c.1500–1890 – mercantilism stressed the need for countries to acquire as much gold as possible, which would then be used to fund great armies and navies, marrying economics with national defense. Mercantilist nations sought to control supplies of natural resources for their manufactures, and also to control markets for selling them. By definition, mercantilists did not believe in free trade zones, but strictly regulated their trade to benefit their own economies through placing protective tariffs on foreign goods, banning direct sales of strategic products to rivals, etc. Britain, for example, used a series of laws known as the Navigation Acts to enforce mercantilism on its colonies.

Mestizo – Spanish – A person with one Indian and one white parent. The French equivalent is métis. While contemporary sources referred to such people as "half breeds," this term lost favor in the twentieth century. Scholars moved to using "mixed blood," but now mestizo and métis are considered preferable terms. In the eighteenth and nineteenth centuries, mestizos were invaluable as cultural go-betweens and translators for diplomacy with Indians, though they often – especially from whites – remained objects of suspicion regarding their loyalties.

Métis – The French equivalent of mestizo. In Canada, when capitalized – Métis – the term refers to a recognized ethnic group of mixed indigenous and European ancestry.

Militia – Usually defined as able-bodied men between their teens and early sixties, militia were called up in emergencies for defense of their colonies/territories/states. While often romanticized in the wake of the American Revolution, militia tended to be poorly trained, poorly disciplined, ill-equipped, and often ineffective or even counterproductive.

Muskogees – The native name for the loose confederacy the English later dubbed the Creeks.

Nationalist – In the context of early American history, someone who viewed the good of the entire nation as being more important than the benefit of one region, faction, or state.

Northwest Confederacy – This multi-tribal coalition rose in the mid-1780s to oppose American expansion into the Ohio River Valley, and fought until the Treaty of Greenville in 1795. Principal members included the Miamis, Potawatomis, Shawnees, Delawares, Kickapoos, Wyandots, Ottawas, and Ojibwas.

Pan-Indianism – A twentieth-century term for a broad alliance of Indians, stressing native unity. In the context of the eighteenth and nineteenth centuries, it represents the fearsome spectacle of a multi-tribal alliance resisting encroachment from whites. Contemporary whites used the term "general Indian war," meaning a war against all or many different Indian groups.

Paternalism – The practice of one group of adults essentially treating another group of adults as if they were children, ostensibly for the latter's benefit, but usually for self-serving purposes.

Patrilineal descent – A system of reckoning one's kin through the father's side of the family.

Proclamation of 1763 – Issued in October of that year, King George III's royal proclamation sought to ban – indefinitely, but not permanently – white settlement west of the Appalachians. The move was intended to prevent future wars with Indians, which were both bloody and expensive. American colonists despised it, as they hoped to sell and settle upon Indian lands in the West.

Regulars – Paid, professional soldiers, in theory they were better trained and disciplined than militia or short term volunteers.

Ruse de guerre – From the French, "trick of war." By the eighteenth century, European land armies considered such ruses – a false flag of truce, for example – unacceptable, and "uncivilized." Oddly, they were still considered legitimate in naval warfare. For Indians, who generally lacked siege weapons, a *ruse de guerre* was often the only reasonable chance they had of capturing a large fortification.

Wampum belt – Great belts woven together from beads made from sea shells (and eventually glass copies), natives used wampum belts as pneumonic devices to recall terms made in treaties by weaving different colored beads into specific patterns, which could then be taken among and between Indian nations. Wampum belts served as documents for establishing peace, forging alliances, or calling for a war.

Whitehall – Short for Whitehall Palace, the London location of much of the British government's offices, including the War Office (now Ministry of Defence) and the cabinet ministers.

Whitewash – A modern term for the practice of white people writing non-whites out of the historical record.

Map

Key tribes, towns, and battles, 1763–1842.

Source: Adapted from "Key peoples, towns and battled, 1763–1815," from *Red Dreams, White Nightmares*, University of Oklahoma Press (2015).

Part I
Analysis and Assessment

Introduction: Clashing Cultures

Competition and Conquest: How Europeans Saw America

When Europeans first stumbled into the Americas in the late fifteenth century, they were in the midst of a tremendous international struggle. Operating under an economic theory known as *mercantilism*, Spain, France, and Britain sought to accumulate vast reserves of gold, which would allow them to build larger armies and navies than their rivals. To acquire and keep that gold, they sought a vast network of raw materials, favorable markets, and economic independence. Especially for a small island nation like Britain, with few natural resources, overseas colonies proved key as a source for materials, and, through colonists, a favorable market for manufactured goods. Spain and France engaged in colonization for similar reasons. Much like an arms race, at some point mercantilism seemed more like an obligation than a choice.

Once one's rivals began scrambling for greater wealth, not playing the game left one's nation extremely vulnerable. If the British did not acquire an empire, it seemed, Spain or France would accrue so much wealth that they could invade and defeat them. Indeed, Spain was so successful in stealing literally tons of gold from the indigenous peoples of the Americas, like the Aztecs and Incas, that for over a century they terrified the rest of Europe, invading the Netherlands and twice threatening to do the same to England. Locked in an escalating competition for resources, financial strength, and powerful militaries for both protection and conquest, Britain, Spain, and France hoped to harness the vast raw materials of the Americas for their benefit. Financial success became inextricably tied to military readiness and national survival.

Aside from their perceived economic/military needs, Europeans in the era of mercantilism – which lasted well into the nineteenth century – also possessed high levels of what anthropologists would later call *ethnocentrism*, that is, the belief that one's own culture was obviously superior to others. All peoples have a certain amount of ethnocentrism – we all speak a native language, for example - but the soldiers, explorers and conquerors who invaded the Americas were especially ethnocentric. The idea of *cultural relativism*, of judging peoples' lifeways by their own merits, rather than your own preferences, was an unknown concept. Native peoples were themselves ethnocentric, though by the time Europeans arrived north of Mexico, they rarely showed much interest in conquering large numbers of outsiders and forcing them to accept native cultures.

For the Love of God

Part of what made Europeans so intent upon conquering outside cultures – part of what made them feel so justified in imposing their will upon native peoples – was their unshakeable belief in their respective religions. By the early sixteenth century, as Christendom faced a brutal schism between Catholics and Protestants – the Reformation – this religious certitude took on extra weight. In an era when almost all Europeans believed in eternal paradise in Heaven or eternal damnation in Hell as literal concepts, the idea of "live and let live" was largely unthinkable. Christians of whatever denomination, it was held, were required by God to seek out and convert the heathen. Those who did not practice Christianity – and of course one's own denomination – were condemned to Hell. This would repeatedly serve as a justification for killing or enslaving nonbelievers.

The jealous Abrahamic God – for Jews and Muslims also utilized the Old Testament – forbid the worship of "false idols," or other deities, and further made significant demands upon His followers. They were to be fruitful and multiply their numbers, and to cultivate the earth. Most of the crops consumed by natives in Eastern North America were grown and managed by women, who used hoes and digging sticks rather than draft animals and plows. The differences in farming – Europeans saw tilling the soil as a man's occupation – would be frequently used to dismiss native agriculture. (Only recently have scholars begun eschewing the term "horticulture" when used for Indians' farming techniques. While technically correct, because of the lack of draft animals and plows, the term horticulture almost implies a hobbyist in a garden, rather than a serious subsistence strategy.) Because Indians did not "farm correctly" – with men, plows and draft animals – argued British colonists, they did not farm at all, and therefore antagonized God and forfeited a right to the land. Europeans (and later Americans) proved highly successful at creating self-serving arguments to justify taking Indian lands and possessions (Sleeper-Smith, 2018).

Gender and Colonization

European ethnocentrism also colored how they went about interacting with native peoples. In the sixteenth century, indigenous peoples in the Americas had gendered divisions of labor – women farmed and men hunted, for example – but did not exclude women from political decisions. Most tribes had women's councils, who had to be consulted on any major decision, especially regarding their crop fields, and men who dismissed their will did so at their own peril. For example, men made war, but if the village's women disagreed, they could refuse to provide the spare moccasins and dried corn that would be essential for a war party. Men who made war without the consent of women would be footsore and hungry within a day or two – not nearly enough time to reach most traditional enemies. And in some native cultures, like the Iroquoians, it would often be female elders – clan matrons – who called for a war party comprised of their male relatives (Axtell, 1981).

For Europeans, war and politics were male concerns. They tended to be shocked when confronted with the idea of Indian women weighing in on such matters, and increasingly sought to exclude women from these activities when Europeans were involved. That did not happen overnight, but from the beginning of diplomacy with native peoples, European men downplayed the importance of women in major decisions, and by the early nineteenth century Euro-American attitudes about a "woman's place" had made significant inroads among native peoples. Perhaps more frustrating for scholars, even before native women were being shouldered out of those traditional roles, whites tended to ignore or downplay women's influence in making peace and war, leaving us precious little written data with which to reconstruct their contributions.

To be "Civilized"

Perhaps the greatest iteration of Europeans' ethnocentrism came from the concept of "civilization." They prided themselves on being civilized – of living in highly stratified, organized, complex societies, with numerous professional specialties and refined standards of behavior. They did not consider that "civilized" is a highly subjective term, and when they encountered native peoples in the Americas, who did not practice Christianity, live in crowded urban areas, or cover their bodies from head to toe in clothes, the natives were deemed "uncivilized." While well-intentioned (if self-righteous) Europeans hoped to "improve" native peoples by leading them to civilization, it would just as often be used as a justification for demeaning or attacking native peoples. In fairness to them, anthropologists and historians into the twentieth century held to a very basic, equally presumptuous model. This model held that humans passed through three stages of social organization; "savagery," defined by an emphasis on hunting and gathering, with no agriculture; "barbarism," a village-level society with some agriculture and animal husbandry; and "civilization," the aforementioned stratified, economically diverse society with complex agriculture, animal husbandry, and (for elites, at least) literacy.

Even a cursory glance at the record reveals numerous flaws to that argument. European and native societies functioned in significantly different ways, not in qualitatively better or worse ones. The peoples of North America organized themselves in great tribes or nations, and sometimes in even larger confederacies. In day to day life, however, the village would be the more important civil unit. Villages were divided among several clans – groups who claimed kinship to a distant, often fictional ancestor. Native peoples usually had clans named for different important animals – deer, bears, turtles, etc., and the eldest man or woman in the clan carried considerable influence, though not dictatorial power. Most natives who spoke languages of the Algonquian language family were *patrilineal*, that is, the most important kinship derived from one's father. Iroquoian and Muskogean speakers reckoned kinship *matrilineally*, that is, through one's mother. Usually, clans were exogamous, meaning one was expected to marry outside one's own clan; doing otherwise would be considered incestuous, even if there were no biological kinship.

From Columbus' first encounter with the Taino natives of the Caribbean in 1492, he immediately noted their relative lack of clothing, and the absence of draft animals, metal tools and weapons, and Christian houses of worship, and concluded that they were meek and deserving of colonization. Famously convinced that he had reached India, he labeled them as "Indians," and claimed their lands for the Spanish Crown. For better or worse, the name stuck.

Aside from ethnocentrism and a strong sense of generalized superiority, Europeans also brought diseases then unknown in the Americas. Illnesses like smallpox, measles, and influenza wreaked havoc in the Americas. The millennia of isolation from Europe, Asia, and Africa, meant that the peoples of the Americas had, on a genetic level, remarkably similar immune systems. Once a malevolent virus like smallpox mutated enough to conquer one native, it was practically custom made to infect others. Estimates vary, but the native populations of the Americas fell somewhere between 60 and 90% in the century and a half after Columbus. Though native populations had somewhat stabilized by the seventeenth and eighteenth centuries, they had in no way recovered. While steel weapons and gunpowder played their parts in the conquest of the Americas, infectious disease did the heavy lifting. Typical of their worldview, Europeans tended to see the waves of epidemic disease – which killed Europeans, but on a much smaller scale – as God's will (Taylor, 2002; Fenn, 2001).

When it came to warfare, native and European fighters exercised different standards. Neither was necessarily better or worse, but reflecting the socio-cultural realities of their practitioners. While Europeans periodically engaged in large scale wars, for most native peoples it was almost an annual event, where traditional enemies might be attacked to gain honors and restore spiritual/cultural balance. Europeans initially evinced great contempt for what they considered frivolous, low-casualty affairs, not understanding that the frequency of combat in the Americas did actually lead to significant losses (Keeley, 1997).

Native warriors, while often highly skilled, were not *professionals.* That is, they drew no salary, and could not depend upon a massive state to supply them with provisions and equipment. Europeans blanched when they saw Indians scalp dead enemies, and saw the taking of articles from dead opponents as looting (though many European soldiers committed the latter). This view failed to consider that Indian warriors fought for honor and social standing – which also influenced many whites – rather than a salary or a land grant. The scalp of a vanquished foe, or his coat, musket, etc., all served as evidence of the warrior's valor. A native man who agreed to join a war party and then came home without any type of trophy risked becoming a laughing stock in his community. Indeed, he might have joined that war party at the behest of the eldest woman in his clan, the clan matron, and his failure would reflect poorly upon her as well. Further, while he had been away, his family had been denied his labor in the form of hunting, and he certainly felt he deserved some compensation for his time and risk.

Indians also put great value on taking prisoners, though they often treated them in ways Europeans found shocking. Chivalrous Europeans, through mutual agreement, tended to consider the lives of prisoners of war as sacrosanct, in theory if not always in practice. In part they did so in the hopes that they could eventually exchange their prisoners for their captive countrymen. Indians, lacking the type of infrastructure that would allow them to hold large numbers of prisoners in confinement indefinitely, felt differently. Women of child-bearing age and children were frequently adopted by their captor's village, and might even become members of the family. Infants, or those too weak or sickly to make the journey back to the victor's country, might be dispatched quickly. Better a swift death than an arduous one that might also imperil the raiders by slowing them down in the face of inevitable pursuit by the targeted village, reasoned most Indians. Men of military age, however, if they survived the journey, would often be tortured to death, slowly and publicly, by entire clans or villages, and usually clan matrons took the lead.

Though European sensibilities detested this, they missed the cultural function of such executions, which provided a community outlet for their grief at the death of their own loved ones. The subject of the torture saw the process as a last opportunity to display his courage and resiliency in the face of pain. (Europeans also used public executions as a crude form of moral instruction and community grief venting, though by this era they usually did so with criminals, rather than prisoners of war.) Europeans decried the brutality of burning a prisoner of war to death, though for centuries they had shown little such compassion for those accused of witchcraft or religious heresy. At the same time, most Indians considered hanging, then thought by Europeans to be a more humane form of execution, as a particularly cruel way to kill someone. When Indians were condemned among themselves to die, the subject was usually tomahawked in the head, often by a kinsman.

One other Indian captivity practice tended to surprise Europeans. While Indian raiders might exercise shocking brutality on captives, especially on the forced march back to the villages, Europeans and later Americans repeatedly expressed amazement that warriors rarely if ever committed sexual assaults on captives. (This probably reflected a tacit admission that European warriors did sometimes consider women's bodies part of the spoils of war.) Natives of the Eastern Woodlands, that is, the nations east of the Mississippi River, had two basic reasons to avoid such behavior. First, captives might be adopted into the tribe, and in fact might become kin, and therefore sexual activity of any kind would violate incest taboos. Further, warriors tended to abstain from sex while on the warpath, as sex would be considered spiritually *polluting* for a warrior until he had undergone the proper post-combat cleansing rituals. [Not all Indians of the Trans-Mississippi West shared these taboos] (Axtell, 1981).

Numerous wars between natives and newcomers meant large numbers of prisoners taken. For whites, perhaps the only thing more distressing than having loved ones taken away in Indian raids was the fact that, with an alarming frequency, those who were adopted into native families often preferred to stay, even once peace had resumed. Treaties ending wars with Indians often stipulated that peace could only be had if all captives were returned. Yet young boys and girls adopted by Indians had numerous incentives to stay. Boys found their native counterparts' roles – to learn to hunt, fish, and fight – far preferable to toiling behind a plow and performing seemingly endless chores around the homestead. Girls found that their new life required even more physical toil than that among whites, but this was accompanied by a significant appreciation of their cultural and subsistence contributions, and even some political say. Further, once adoptees were old enough to marry and have children, their ties to their Indian families only strengthened. It was not unheard of for white adoptees to eventually return to the society of their birth, but it proved far less frequent than adopted Indians choosing to return to their native villages (Steele, 2013).

Native peoples proved very keen on the idea of kinship. In diplomacy, Indians often referred to Europeans as *father* and themselves as *children*. The French, for example, initially applauded that notion, assuming that, as in Europe, fathers were unquestioned patriarchs whom children obeyed. They were quite crestfallen to eventually learn that Indians saw that relationship as emphasizing a parental benevolence and protection for the *children*, not their forced obedience (White, 1991).

flawed, but any honest appraisal would note that, from the mid-eighteenth century on, Indians were far more frequently the targets, not perpetrators, of massacres.

One other semantic point deserves attention. In the latter twentieth century, it became increasingly common to refer to the dispossession of Indians as an "ethnic cleansing," or even a "genocide." While an old concept, the term genocide was coined in the wake of the Holocaust and World War II. For years I mistakenly taught students that, while it behaved deplorably, the U.S. government had not technically been guilty of genocide toward Indians, insofar as the government had never actually sought to completely exterminate them. (Individual American citizens were an entirely different matter.) However, when one reads the United Nations' definition of genocide, it includes not only complete physical extermination, but also:

> (a) Killing members of the group; (b) Causing serious bodily or mental harm to members of the group; (c) Deliberately inflicting on the group conditions of life calculated to bring about its physical destruction in whole or in part; (d) Imposing measures intended to prevent births within the group; (e) Forcibly transferring children of the group to another group (United Nations Office on Genocide Prevention).

Under that definition, the United States – both the government and individual civilians – have been repeatedly guilty of genocide against Indians.

By the time Andrew Jackson became president in 1829, many American whites would state that Indians simply could not coexist near white Americans. These poor creatures would go extinct, the argument went, if they could not be removed to a safe distance – say, across the Mississippi River. In so doing, it would open up vast tracts of valuable farmland for sale to Americans. It proved the latest iteration of whites' seeking a justification for taking Indian lands for their own use. But in the mid-eighteenth century, Anglo-Americans voiced little concern for Indians' survival. They were far too worried about their own.

1 Britain's Tenuous Empire

The European Contest for North America

Since the late fifteenth century, Europeans had looked to the Americas as a source of wealth and national power. While Spain seemed untouchable in Central and South America, there was actual competition for what would become the United States and Canada. Spain held tenuous colonies in what would be the southeastern U.S., but France and especially Britain had made significant inroads to the immediate north. In all of these colonial efforts, relations with local Indians proved crucial. France and Spain never managed to put nearly enough colonists into North America, and were absolutely dependent on Indians as economic partners in the fur and skin trade. The need for Indian friends became most apparent during wartime, when the undermanned colonies of New France and New Spain desperately relied upon Indians as allies to make up the difference.

The British mainland colonies had far larger populations, and their strong interest in agricultural lands – whether for small farmers or great commercial plantations – brought considerably more friction with local Indians. Yet the British nevertheless saw Indians as important trading partners and useful allies in times of war. By the eighteenth century, Indian allies came to be incredibly useful assets when Europeans fought for North America.

To a lesser and variable extent, Europeans could convince themselves that they were simultaneously bringing *civilization*, especially Christianity, to Indians.

For a long time, native peoples managed to play Europeans off against each other. When British merchants proved reluctant to sell them firearms, Indians could look to French, Spanish, or sometimes Dutch merchants to do so. If Spanish diplomats displeased natives, they might strike a deal with their French or British counterparts. Really clever tribes managed to maintain peaceful trading relations with two or more European nations at the same time.

By the mid-eighteenth century, the European competition had grown acute. After a series of wars between Britain, its (usually Protestant) allies, and France and/or Spain and their (usually Catholic) allies, by the 1750s, many people had died, but the tendency for peace treaties to simply call for a return to *status quo antebellum*, that is, to the way things were prior to the outbreak of war, did little to actually end the competition. When war broke out again between Britain and France in 1755, the immediate cause was control of the Ohio River Valley. But the conflict that became known as the Seven Years' War (1756–1763) was really about global imperialism, and who would dominate trade not just in North America and the Caribbean, but in Africa, India, and beyond. With characteristic myopia, British colonists in America called it the "French and Indian War," because once more they fought against the French and their native allies. The fact that a number of Indians fought alongside British forces, like the Iroquois League in the North, and the Cherokees and Catawbas in the South, was left out of the rhetoric (Taylor, 2002).

When British forces under General Jeffery Amherst captured Montreal in September of 1760, it marked the end of major combat operations between France and Britain in North America. The Peace of Paris in 1763 starkly demonstrated the British victory in the Seven Years' War. France no longer claimed any significant territory on the North American mainland, and had further lost many valuable colonies in the Caribbean, Africa, and India. What former Secretary of State William Pitt had called Britain's "Great War for Empire" had succeeded in a stunning fashion. Yet the great strains that effort had placed upon the empire opened dangerous fault lines in North America, and they began shifting almost immediately (Anderson, 2000).

When Anglo-American forces finally drove the French from the forks of the Ohio River – the site of the war's start – they almost immediately began building a much larger, more permanent-looking fort on the ruins of Fort Duquesne. Local Shawnees and Delawares – both groups had been British allies until the early 1750s – looked upon the construction of Fort Pitt, the eventual site of Pittsburgh, with alarm. To the south, their traditional enemies, the Cherokees, themselves stalwart allies of Britain since the 1730s, were now engaged in a bloody war against British troops and colonists in the western Carolinas. After a series of insults and attacks from white colonists, the Cherokees destroyed Fort Loudoun, in what would become Tennessee – a fort they themselves had insisted that Britain build (Ingram, 2014).

The Cherokee War ended in 1761, only after British armies invaded Cherokee country. The Cherokees largely withdrew before them, and avoided combat casualties. But the invaders burned a number of villages and cornfields, striking at native sustenance. Years of imperial warfare in America had placed considerable strain on native peoples, and also forcefully demonstrated the importance of European trade goods, especially firearms. Prior to the Cherokee War, the Cherokees had numbered over 20,000 people – on par with the Creeks and Choctaws. By 1775, they had dropped to about 12,000 people. Further, with the ouster of the French in 1763, Cherokees and other native peoples had lost an important counterbalance to Britain. Whereas before native peoples could force three European powers – Britain, France, and Spain – to compete for their loyalties, now they were increasingly dependent upon British aid (Schmidt, 2014).

Penny-wise and Pound-foolish: Pontiac's War

Thus, the appointment of General Amherst, now Sir Jeffery, as commander-in-chief for all of His Majesty's forces in North America, proved unfortunate for all concerned. An excellent field commander, Amherst lacked the requisite skillset for a peacetime administrator, particularly regarding Indian affairs. He sincerely loathed Indians, even Britain's Indian allies (Dowd, 2002). He considered them culturally inferior and also annoyingly insubordinate. The fact that they had functioned as allies, rather than servants of His Majesty, does not seem to have registered with Sir Jeffery. He still carried a considerable grudge against the Iroquois League of New York, for example, because they insisted upon being consulted, rather than simply ordered about.

When major combat operations ended, financial austerity became the government's watchword. William Pitt's financial strategy had been to borrow as much money as needed to vigorously prosecute the war, costs be damned - later generations of Americans would call that "deficit spending," - and then reap the financial windfall of snatching away French and Spanish colonies. In the short term, the policy was wildly successful – French efforts in North America soon crumbled. However, Britain's national debt had more than doubled to £133 million, and interest payments kept the number growing. (Britain's understandable efforts to economize in North America would have negative ramifications in both the near and long term.) In this new political climate, Amherst saw an opportunity to combine his disdain for Native Americans with imperial penny-pinching. He would cease the giving of diplomatic *gifts* to Indians, and the reduction in expenditures would surely curry favor with his superiors (Anderson, 2000).

While Amherst was aware that French operatives had long before decided that dealing with Native Americans meant that any meaningful diplomacy would be accompanied with giving copious quantities of trade goods, particularly guns and ammunition, he felt it unnecessary. Had Britain not conquered North America, he reasoned? If Indians wanted such things, they could purchase them through the fur trade. He does not seem to have considered that those goods were also increasingly important tools for natives' hunting and trapping efforts. By the 1760s, many Indians were losing their skill with the bow and arrow, while becoming excellent marksmen with firearms. And he completely discounted just how insulting this cessation would be for Indians, who regarded speeches and gestures unaccompanied by gifts as insincere (Dowd, 2002; White, 1991).

Amherst certainly should have known better. Far more knowledgeable men, like New York's Sir William Johnson, the "Mohawk land baronet," and his ally, Indian agent George Croghan of Pennsylvania, warned Amherst about his literally "penny wise and pound foolish" policy. They knew how insulting it would be to the King's Indian allies, not to mention his recent Indian foes, who certainly had no reason to see themselves as conquered or subject peoples. If sufficiently angered, they could start a war that would cost far more than the relatively paltry savings of shutting down gift-based diplomacy. Amherst waved off their concerns (Dixon, 2014). [**See Docs. 1–2**]

Figure 1.1 Sir William Johnson (c.1715–1774). An adopted Mohawk chief, land speculator, and brigadier general, Johnson was appointed Britain's first Superintendent for Northern Indian Affairs.

Johnson and Croghan were not, nor did they really claim, to be disinterested parties. In the eighteenth century, few if any held to the idea that those in the public service should avoid enriching themselves, or that such a thing as "conflict of interest" even existed. Both men would spend much of their time engaged in quasi-legal speculation in Indian lands and trade. Indeed, when Amherst's plans spectacularly blew up in his face, Johnson and Croghan took considerable measures to destroy him in their correspondence to the ministers at Whitehall. But they had been quite correct. Amherst's haughty policies helped spark Indian anger in the Great Lakes/Ohio region and threatened to spread it even wider (Hinderaker, 1997).

The Ottawa war chief Pontiac, an enthusiastic ally of France before and during the war, fumed at the news that his French *father* would be leaving the continent. Amherst's policies only fueled his rage. He was not the only one angered by the notion of Britain's supposed hegemony. A Delaware religious prophet named Neolin preached in the early 1760s that Indians' distressed situation – a poor economy, alcoholism, and the intrusion of whites onto Indian lands – arose because of the Great Spirit's displeasure with his Indian children. Neolin and other native religious leaders were preaching, by the mid-eighteenth century, a view of race that paralleled that of Europeans. Where earlier generations of natives had seen a broad spectrum of common humanity, increasingly popular was the idea that Indians, whites, and blacks had been separate creations of the Great Spirit. In the native version, Indians were the Creator's favorite people, but currently, they disappointed him (Dowd, 2002).

The Great Spirit's disappointment came, Neolin said, from Indians – not just his own Delawares, but all Indians – becoming too enamored with the European intruders and their corrupt material culture. Alcohol, European clothing, domesticated livestock, and all the other features of the fur trade had caused Indians to lose their way. (Neolin himself was a reformed alcoholic.) Pontiac seized on Neolin's message, but tweaked it considerably. He argued that the Great Spirit's anger sprang from Indians' failure to keep their French *father* in place. Once the British were driven out, Pontiac insisted, the French, and happy prosperity, would return (Dowd, 2002). [See Doc. 3]

Whether Native Americans genuinely believed Pontiac's prophecy, or whether he actually believed it himself, is probably beside the point. He provided a rallying point for the thousands of Indians who resented Britain's presence and policies in their country, and they welcomed the opportunity to strike back. While they lacked siege weapons, they hoped a series of well-coordinated *ruses de guerre* – tricks of war – would allow them to capture or destroy Britain's posts in the western country.

Later Anglo-American accounts overemphasized Pontiac's role in the conflict – calling it *Pontiac's Rebellion*. Natives recognized no role equivalent to a commander-in-chief. While Pontiac led efforts among his Ottawas and the Ojibwas in what would become Michigan, particularly in the siege of Fort Detroit, many other Indians lashed out at British troops and colonists, with little or no direction from the Ottawa. Guyasuta, a prominent Seneca chief, led the fight against British troops outside of Fort Niagara in western New York. Seneca efforts in the war proved especially unnerving for Britain. They were the westernmost nation of the Iroquois League, who had been perhaps the most stalwart members of the British alliance.

Yet the Senecas had always listened to the French far more than their eastern cousins did. They had in fact circulated war belts since at least 1761, calling for a multitribal defensive alliance against an anticipated war of extermination by the British. Further, their participation made it more difficult for Sir William Johnson, an adopted Mohawk, to recruit other Iroquois to help put down the western Indians. The Iroquois League had been founded upon the principle that the Five (later Six) Nations would not fight each other. Most Iroquois would decline to fight when their brother Senecas might be engaged (Dowd, 2002).

Aside from the Anishinabeg peoples of the Great Lakes – the Ottawas, Ojibwas, and Potawatomis – other Algonquian-speaking peoples in the Illinois Country took up the fight. Miamis, Weas, Mascoutens, Piankeshaws, and Kickapoos attacked the British. Further east in the Ohio Valley, Shawnees, Delawares, and Mingos – an offshoot of the Iroquois League – cut off Fort Pitt. We should also note that while members of all these tribes took up the fight, none of the nations did so unanimously. Even the Ottawas saw only a faction that favored Pontiac take part (Dixon, 2014).

The first shots of the war came at Detroit in May of 1763. Pontiac led the first attempt personally. Knowing he had little chance of taking the fort in a formal siege – lacking artillery, etc., he planned a surprise attack on the garrison. During a planned parley, he would flip a great wampum belt in his hands to signal his men to begin the attack. But when Pontiac and some picked men entered the fort, they found its commander, Major Henry Gladwin, and the entire garrison on full alert. They had been tipped off by a native woman, the partner of one of the soldiers. Pontiac awkwardly ended the parley, and once outside the closing gates, his men soon began to cut off and besiege the garrison (Dowd, 2002).

They had no hope of taking the place by storm, but could cut off landward communications and resupply. (They also tried, via canoe, to stop British communications via the Great Lakes, but eventually well-armed ships did break through the Indian blockade.) Anti-British warriors throughout the region held some key advantages in the opening weeks.

Aside from numerical superiority, by cutting off word from Detroit, they knew a war had started long before many hapless British soldiers did. Fort Michilimackinac, located at the strategic straits between Lake Michigan and Lake Huron, fell to local Ojibwas and some Sauks in a spectacular ruse in June.

The Ojibwas engaged the visiting Sauks – from Wisconsin and northern Illinois – in a grand game of stickball, similar to lacrosse, and dozens of warriors from both tribes played outside the open gates of the fort. As their wives, wearing blankets over their shoulders, milled about casually inside the fort's walls, the ball suddenly sailed towards the gate. The players followed swiftly, but ignored the ball and rushed to the women, who suddenly produced weapons from under the blankets slung on their shoulders. The warriors fell upon the unsuspecting garrison, dispatching them swiftly. Other posts fell in less spectacular, if equally gory, fashion. Some would simply be abandoned. Of the thirteen British forts/outposts in the Trans-Appalachian West, only the three largest – Detroit, Fort Pitt, and Fort Niagara – survived what came to be known as Pontiac's War (Dixon, 2014).

Shawnee and Delaware embassies tried to convince the commander of Fort Pitt, the Swiss-born Captain Simeon Ecuyer, to peacefully abandon his strategic post at the forks of the Ohio. They promised him safe passage if he did so. While their sincerity might have been up for debate, Ecuyer's brutal determination to hold out was not. Before dismissing his visitors, he gifted them some blankets and handkerchiefs. He neglected to mention that he had drawn them from the smallpox ward of the fort's hospital. Ecuyer's attempt to practice biological warfare often stuns students, but his thinking was very much in line with his contemporaries and direct superiors. In correspondence with his officers, General Amherst had extolled the possible benefits of introducing smallpox among the Indians, while Ecuyer's direct superior, another Swiss-born officer, Colonel Henry Bouquet, thought that the pox, or possibly great war dogs (as used by the Conquistadors), might be set upon the Indians (Dowd, 2002).

Not long after Ecuyer made his deadly gift, an epidemic did sweep through many of the villages in southern Ohio, killing hundreds at a minimum. Smallpox has a known incubation period, and the dates of Ecuyer's deadly gift and the outbreak do not quite match up, as historian Elizabeth Fenn has demonstrated (Fenn, 2000). Regardless of its effects, the attempt was indisputable. Angry at the termination of their hard-won peace, and terrified of the potential of a great coalition of Indians to wreck their corner of the Empire, desperate British officers had tried to unleash the deadliest disease then known upon the Indians.

Fort Pitt would eventually receive reinforcements, when a column led by Colonel Bouquet marched west to the forks of the Ohio. Bouquet's men were primarily Scots Highlanders of the 42nd and 77th Foot regiments, who had been pressed into this emergency action – they had just completed a withering tour in the West Indies and had been declared unfit for duty. As the Highlanders neared the fort, they were surrounded in the woods by Shawnee and Delaware warriors, at a place called Bushy Run. Unbeknownst to Bouquet, these were the men who had been laying siege to Fort Pitt. Cut off and facing disaster, Bouquet's men made impromptu barricades from the flour and supplies their mule train was carrying, but seemed doomed. Bouquet, however, made a desperate gambit and managed to catch his overeager opponents in a pincer maneuver, and a fierce "Highland charge" by sword and bayonet-wielding Scots drove them off. Bouquet's force managed to limp into Fort Pitt, but they had lost nearly all of the supplies the beleaguered garrison needed. Though of questionable impact on the war, the Battle of Bushy Run would be remembered as a British victory, a rare occurrence in 1763 (Dowd, 2002).

The combination of fear and rage continued to play out over the summer, as word of the extent of the war finally began reaching Amherst and others in the east. Worse still was the pervasive knowledge that the war could easily spread. Though Amherst's letters from this time betray much bluster and a thirst for vengeance, he was also terrified. In August, he wrote to praise the British garrison on Nova Scotia – a thousand miles away from the war – for being on alert. The civilian press, meanwhile, grew increasingly alarmed, and some openly questioned if this war with tribes in the Great Lakes/Ohio region might not become a dreaded general Indian war against all the nations (Owens, 2015).

Efforts in Diplomacy

That concern had considerable merit. During the Cherokee War, Cherokee diplomats had sought aid from the Ohio Valley nations, regardless of their old quarrels. Along the Mississippi River, the numerous Choctaws – long-time allies of France – also sought help from their old enemies to the north to fend off the British. These embassies failed, partly because of old animus, but largely because most of the peoples north of the Ohio had come to peace with Britain between 1758 and 1760. Still, British agents knew of these efforts, and their mere possibility had terrified them (Dowd, 2002).

Britain would benefit more from dumb luck than skill, then, when Ohio Indians reached out to the Cherokees in 1762 and 1763. While angry with Anglo-Americans, the Cherokees did not relish another fight with the English when they were still recovering from the punitive campaigns launched against them to end the Cherokee War. Further, they had for some time beseeched Sir William Johnson to pressure the

Iroquois League to stop their periodic raids into Cherokee Country, and hoped their forbearance would finally bear fruit.

By the end of 1763, most of the fighting had paused. Indian warriors had little patience for long sieges to begin with, and their cultures and economies did not lend themselves to that type of sustained effort. By the fall, they knew they were needed back home to hunt for their families. Some may well have assumed that their point had been made. Indeed, they would have had some reason to think that was so. Jeffery Amherst was recalled to London, not, as he had hoped, to receive further congratulations for the conquest of Canada, but to explain the Indian affairs debacle which he had largely precipitated. Still a national hero, he was technically reassigned, rather than fired. General Thomas Gage, a less talented field officer but significantly better administrator, would take over the North American command. Parliament also created two Indian affairs superintendents. In the North, Sir William Johnson proved to be the obvious choice. In the South, John Stuart – a former army officer and captive of the Cherokees – took the post. Indeed Stuart, who had survived the Cherokee War because Cherokee chief Attakullakulla, or Little Carpenter, adopted him, took great pains to discourage the Southern nations from joining in the fray. The King himself also weighed in directly on American affairs (Dowd, 2002; Alden, 1966).

Though he had been considering it for some time, perhaps two years prior, the King's Royal Proclamation of 1763 seemed even more sensible with the outbreak of Pontiac's War. Issued in October, the Proclamation drew an imaginary line down the crest of the Appalachian Mountains, and forbade English subjects – at least civilians – from settling west of it. Those who had already settled across the line were demanded to return. The King saw this as equal parts humanitarian gesture towards his Indian *children*, and pragmatic, cost-saving policy. Even a novice realized that white settlers barging onto Indian lands caused considerable friction and could bring warfare. (They also squatted on land that prominent officials hoped to sell for profit.)

Long convinced that colonists did a poor job defending themselves, the Crown and Whitehall reasoned that preempting such conflicts would save the Treasury vast sums by avoiding military campaigns. The logic on that point was sound. Indians, upon learning of the Proclamation, generally applauded. American colonists, however, grew furious. What had been the point of defeating the French, land speculators like Virginia's George Washington and Pennsylvania's Benjamin Franklin, might ask, if not to open the Ohio Valley to land sales? The fact that the Proclamation was never intended to permanently ban such sales offered little comfort. Greater comfort came when, in the years after 1763, it became abundantly clear that the Crown would never put enough men or resources on the frontier to actually enforce the Proclamation (Anderson, 2000).

Regardless of the Proclamation, Whitehall and the army felt another campaign would be necessary to reestablish (or just establish) control in the West. Others saw a need to continue to hinder pan-Indian sentiments. As early as November 1763, Sir William Johnson advocated recruiting warriors from the Southern nations – the Cherokees, Creeks, Choctaws, and Chickasaws – to fight against the Ohio tribes. Not only would they bring their expertise in irregular warfare, but, as Johnson noted, their participation would help intensify old feuds and lessen the chances that they might join the Northern tribes in fighting the British. The concept of encouraging intertribal conflict to stave off pan-Indianism, a sound if not especially honorable tactic, would be repeated over and over again (Owens, 2015).

Bleeding Pennsylvania

Pennsylvania, which had enjoyed perhaps the least violent relations with Indians prior to the Seven Years' War, became a brutal war zone in 1755. In western and central Pennsylvania, the colony's settlers, largely Scots-Irish and German-speaking immigrants, increasingly came under attack by Native American groups. The brazen land acquisition policies of William Penn's sons, the most infamous example being the so-called Walking Purchase of 1737, brought considerable anger from the colony's Indian population, especially Lenni Lenape, or Delawares, and Shawnees. Pennsylvania's social and political dynamics made the situation worse (Silver, 2007).

While the colony government was dominated by largely Quaker populations in the east – who disliked raising taxes or funding warlike operations – the settlers to the west bore the brunt of Indian anger. As recent scholarship demonstrates, Indian war parties made the most of killing settlers in as public and horrifying a manner as possible to magnify their numbers and frighten the settlers into abandoning Pennsylvania. When the war came to an end, the Scots-Irish and Germans had not forgotten the searing images of their friends and relatives killed and mutilated, often left at crossroads or other public areas for maximum impact. Nor did they forget the Penn government's lackluster response in defending them (Dowd, 2002; Silver, 2007).

The month before Pontiac attacked Detroit, unknown whites attacked a Delaware village in the Wyoming district – later to become Wilkes-Barre, Pennsylvania. In addition to twenty other homes burned, the arsonists burned down the cabin of Teedyuscung, a Delaware chief and ally of the colony. The colony had in fact built the cabin for him. Teedyuscung died in the blaze. The attackers may well have been from Connecticut, members of the Susquehanna land speculation company, whose supporters did soon colonize the area. At any rate, the chief's gruesome death proved to be another example of Pennsylvania's inability to offer protection, even to its friends. While the Delawares had multiple well-earned grudges against the colony, Teedyuscung's murder was likely the most direct cause of their attacking the colony in 1763 (Wallace, 1990).

When Pontiac's War came in 1763, a large Delaware war party led by Captain Bull – Teedyuscung's son – attacked the new settlers at Wyoming. As war parties once more lashed out at the frontier, and once more the colony showed little zeal or competence in defending them, westerners came to hate their government nearly as much as they did their Indian enemies. In a shamefully common pattern in American Indian affairs, some disgruntled colonists lashed out at innocent Indians living nearby.

Among the first militia to respond to the Wyoming attack had been men from Paxton, Pennsylvania. (Paxton was a corruption of the Lenni Lenape word *Paxtang*.) They took grim note of the mutilated men and women, some found with farming implements thrust through their bodies. On December 14, 1763, a group of these Paxton men, mostly Scots-Irish, armed themselves with muskets and knives and tomahawks – the preferred weapons of Indian warriors – and attacked the village of Conestoga. They murdered and mutilated six friendly Indians – Delawares who had lived in peace with the colony for decades. When alarmed colony officials moved the survivors – at public expense – and locked them in the workhouse at Lancaster for safe-keeping, more than fifty Paxton Boys rode there two days after Christmas, broke into the workhouse, and murdered fourteen more Indians – three married couples and their eight young children. Once again, they scalped and mutilated their victims in broad daylight, and no whites dared or bothered to intervene (Silver, 2007).

Second only to the horror of the killings was the fact that the colony government seemed too inept or powerless to stop them. A group of British soldiers from the 42nd Highlanders – the famed Black Watch Regiment – had been sent to the town to protect the Indians, but they had not been posted adjacent to them, and offered no resistance to the riotous Paxton men. Philadelphia's (largely Quaker) population grew terrified that January, when hundreds of Paxton men rode toward the city, hoping to murder the few remaining friendly Indians being sheltered by the government there. Finally, the Penn government mounted a response – the city's inhabitants, even many of the Quakers, armed themselves for defense against their fellow colonists. Benjamin Franklin, a political rival of the Penn family, was nevertheless dispatched to meet the mob outside of the city. He managed to dissuade them from attacking Philadelphia with vague promises to consider their grievances, and so averted disaster (Anderson, 2000).

Though the outright violence of the Paxton Riots had ended, a war of words, in the form of pro and anti-Paxton pamphleteers, began.

Franklin and other critics of the killers rightly noted the horrific violence the Paxton Boys visited on twenty innocent men, women, and children, and that such attacks could bring retaliation from their native relatives, including the powerful Iroquois League. Pro-Paxton writers tended to focus on the weakness of the Penns' governance, and their land speculation policies on the frontier, which had led to widely scattered – and therefore more vulnerable – settlements. They largely ignored the fact that the rioters' brutal violence had fallen upon those who had no role in their grievances. It would not be the last time that whites insisted that consequence-free murdering of Indians was their fundamental right.

War's End?

Pontiac's War brought still more killings to other parts of the frontier, especially western Virginia. The raids, largely by Shawnees, helped create a new generation of angry people, Indian and white, who would seek revenge in the coming years. In one particularly infamous raid into Pennsylvania in 1764, Delaware warriors killed and scalped ten schoolchildren and their teacher. Pennsylvania officials, shocked, furious, and desperate to seem politically relevant, resorted to an old colonial tactic that managed to answer all those needs. They reinstituted a bounty for the scalps of "hostile" Indians over the age of ten, regardless of sex (Dixon, 2014). The fact that such bounties never actually stopped Indian attacks, but did lead to the murder of innocent, often allied Indians, was once again overlooked.

In 1764, though the siege of Detroit had been lifted, General Gage felt it was necessary to send two armies into the Ohio country to end the war. Some scholars argue that they in fact might have prolonged the war, by giving native peoples a point of unification and resistance. Colonel John Bradstreet was ordered to proceed west via the Great Lakes, while Colonel Henry Bouquet – who had survived the bloody encounter at Bushy Run – was to march west from Pittsburgh. Bradstreet's campaign proved the more unintentionally comical. Authorized to march into the Ohio Valley and impose a truce, he negotiated several peace treaties – exceeding his authority – and did little chastising of the enemy, angering his superiors. He even agreed to halt Bouquet's march before it started – something he had no right to do. While he did manage to relieve and resupply some British posts in the region, he primarily damaged his career. Bouquet, irked with Bradstreet's efforts, finally began his march west in October (Dixon, 2014).

Neither force saw much actual fighting – Indian warriors preferred to attack isolated settlers and avoid large-scale engagements when possible – but Bouquet in particular did manage to force the return of white prisoners. Even that exercise proved complex. While Native

Americans sometimes tortured and executed war captives, often they adopted them into their families and many *captives* resisted leaving their Indian families. These heart-rending scenes perplexed and troubled Bouquet and Anglo-American officials, who had assumed that any British subject would be overjoyed to leave such a *savage* existence (Steele, 2013).

In all, the war killed about 2,000 British subjects, three fourths of them civilians. Indian combat losses, while difficult to quantify, were significantly less, and probably the bulk of Indian deaths came from smallpox outbreaks that may or may not have been directly caused by the war.

For Pontiac, 1763 proved the highwater mark of his influence. He had long insisted that a grand French army would come to the aid of his Indian friends once the war began. Whether or not the Ottawa actually believed that, British officials applied significant pressure on French officers remaining in North America to put an end to the rumor in no uncertain terms. The commander of Fort De Chartres on the Mississippi, near what is now Prairie du Rocher, Illinois, reluctantly explained the true situation to a delegation of Indians. The Great French Father had made peace with the British, he insisted, and wished for his native children to fight them no more (Anderson, 2000).

While Pontiac's influence did not immediately disappear, it withered considerably as time went on. His failure to deliver on his promise of French aid battered the trust many warriors had placed in him, as well as the inability to achieve any lasting victory. When he officially made peace with the British in 1766, it was probably the last straw for most. Pontiac had become increasingly bitter in the years since 1763, and an apparent uptick in his drinking did not mellow his sour, even quarrelsome nature. At one point in 1767, his argument with a Kaskaskia chief – the Kaskaskias were part of the Illinois Confederacy – ended with the Ottawa's knife in the chief's ribs. He died a slow, painful death. Two years later, a Peoria man – another member of the Illinois Confederacy – assassinated Pontiac as they were leaving a trading post in the village of Cahokia, Illinois. Pontiac's legend grew in the years after his death, partly from the fanciful depictions of him by those who supposedly knew the chief – like famous colonial ranger Robert Rogers, and later historians, like Francis Parkman in the nineteenth century. Parkman's magisterial *The Conspiracy of Pontiac* (1851), which drastically overestimated the chief's sway over other tribes, helped shape the narrative for generations (Owens, 2015).

Assigning a date for the end of Pontiac's War proves challenging, in large part because Britain's Indian department seemed to have no idea themselves. While they knew of Pontiac making peace and his demise, every summer after 1764, wild rumors flew that multitribal coalitions had formed, or were forming, and might at any moment bring destruction to British soldiers and settlers along the frontier. Agent George Croghan reported more than once that Fort Pitt had been "cut off," only to learn that it had not. The Proclamation of 1763 could never be properly enforced, officials knew, without a massive number of regular troops on the frontier. Yet the Proclamation had been issued, they also knew, because the Treasury did not have the money to do that. Further, it became increasingly clear that even those charged with seeing the boundary line enforced, like Superintendent Sir William Johnson, had little desire to maintain a boundary that would constrain their own profits (Owens, 2015).

In the years after 1763, as Britain's national debt ballooned, and continued to rise with interest payments to creditors, the Empire had never been larger, nor more financially precarious. Having fought so hard to "win" the western territories of North America, the King's men quickly began to abdicate any role there, largely from cost concerns. Once-crucial forts, like De Chartres on the Mississippi and even Fort Pitt, would before long be abandoned, as their upkeep was deemed too costly (Griffin, 2007).

In these dire circumstances, it perhaps should not surprise that British officials chose to minimize financial costs and ignore the human ones. Thomas Gage bluntly asserted that it would be far too expensive to keep all the Indian nations happy with Britain. Better then, to keep a few key groups complacent, and encourage the others to kill each other to preclude their ganging up on His Majesty's colonies. In particular, the numerous Creeks proved, in British eyes, troublesome and recalcitrant. While Gage and John Stuart did not start the bitter war between the Creeks and Choctaws that began in 1766, they were willing to quietly encourage it for the next decade, as a cost-effective means of distracting Creeks from attacking British colonists. "Divide and Conquer" would prove a common tactic for British (and later American) Indian policy. Meanwhile, officials did not relent in their own schemes for getting rich off Indian lands (Alden, 1966; Corkran, 1967).

In October of 1768, John Stuart and others concluded the Treaty of Hard Labor, which asserted that the Cherokees had sole ownership of the land that would become Kentucky. Of course, it was not to protect the Cherokees, though Shawnees and others claimed Kentucky as a hunting ground. The purpose of the treaty was to facilitate future land purchases there by allowing officials to deal with just one tribe. Stuart's northern counterpart in the Indian service had similar notions, but he did Stuart one better, and did not consult with him beforehand.

In November of 1768, Sir William Johnson orchestrated a great Indian council at Fort Stanwix (modern Rome, New York). Together with other colonial officials, including Agent Croghan and New Jersey's Governor William Franklin (son of Benjamin), he arranged for the Iroquois League to sell their claims to the land south of the Ohio River all the way west to modern Paducha, Kentucky. The parcel would later become the state of Kentucky. Iroquois rights to that land were sketchy at best. Both the Shawnees to the north and the Cherokees to the south had far more realistic claims – the Cherokee claim even had the Treaty of Hard Labor to support it - and they both depended on Kentucky for its rich (and intentionally well-preserved) hunting grounds. But the Iroquois had long boasted of *conquering* the Ohio Valley and its peoples, and British and colonial officials found supporting these fictitious claims to their advantage. The Iroquois agreed to part with Kentucky for £10,000 in cash and trade goods – by far the largest sum the English had ever paid Indians for a land cession. The most affected tribes, the Shawnees and Cherokees, received nothing. Sir William and the other colonial officials, meanwhile, made sure to include large (illegal) private grants for themselves (Holton, 2011; Calloway, 2013; Campbell, 2012).

Though no open war broke out for several years, as the revelation of the extent of the Fort Stanwix Treaty made its way to the Ohio Valley tribes, it did impact pan-Indian aspirations. Though the Iroquois had long enjoyed a position of at least honorary leadership for many tribes, who referred to the League as their *uncles*, the cash grab at Fort Stanwix disqualified them in the minds of many Ohio natives (Dowd, 1992). The Shawnees, in particular, grew increasingly militant as white "longhunters," like Daniel Boone, poured through the Cumberland Gap of the Appalachian Mountains into Kentucky. While such hunters were already unwelcome for killing what the Shawnees and Cherokees considered their deer, and the theft of their pelts, it became increasingly obvious that the longhunters were also scouting for places to settle. [See Doc. 4] While the first such intruders, including Boone, were initially captured and relieved of their deerskins, but paroled home, increasingly Indian warriors killed them whenever they could. The cycle of frontier violence and retaliation grew steadily worse (Holton, 2011).

Murder and Real Estate: Lord Dunmore's War

In the spring of 1774, a party of whites led by Daniel Greathouse encountered a group of Mingo and Shawnee Indians. The Mingos, Iroquois who had moved into the Ohio Valley, frequently intermarried with its other peoples. The Greathouse party feigned friendship, plied the Indians with alcohol, and invited them to partake in a marksmanship contest. When the Indians had emptied their rifles, the whites attacked brutally, killing all the adults and the unborn child of a pregnant woman. Only one infant was spared and sent away to be raised by whites. Many of the victims were the family of a Mingo chief named John Logan, who had long been known for his friendship towards settlers. Learning of the death of his family, Logan sent word to authorities in western Virginia that he would take to the warpath for revenge. Shawnee relatives joined him in this campaign. Once he had killed one settler for each of his murdered family, he noted, his attacks would cease. While this was not the only way Ohio Indians might handle such a terrible loss, it was certainly not unreasonable to them (White, 1991).

Virginia authorities used Logan's revenge killings, brutal but measured, as a pretext for a war against the Shawnees. Virginia hoped to take the lands of Kentucky, directly to their west, as their own. Murder and revenge killings with the Cherokees also took place around this time, and Virginia could have easily had a war with the Cherokee Nation. But the Cherokees significantly outnumbered the Shawnees, and while the Old Dominion chose diplomacy with the Cherokees, they sought war with the Shawnees (Owens, 2015).

Virginia's royal governor was the Scotsman John Murray, the fourth Earl of Dunmore. Lord Dunmore may have initially been duped into fighting the Shawnees, as there is evidence that frontier officials downplayed the provocation of Logan and his Shawnee relatives. But once joined, the governor seized the opportunity to fight the Ohio peoples and extract a land cession from them. The conflict began in earnest in the summer of 1774, and would be known as Lord Dunmore's War. Much of the fighting took the form of small-scale skirmishes in western Virginia and eastern Kentucky. Some of the white veterans, including Daniel Boone, and his hulking friend Simon Kenton, would become famous among frontier whites. The only large-scale encounter came from a desperate, but very logical, attack by the Shawnees in October of 1774 (Holton, 2011).

Virginia's plan called for two separate militia armies to rally at Point Pleasant on the Kanawha River, in what is now West Virginia. By early October, only one, led by Andrew Lewis, had arrived. The Shawnees, led by the chief Hokolesqua, or Cornstalk, and their principal war chief, Puckesinwa, were already outnumbered by at least two to one. They reasoned that their best hope was to defeat Lewis' force before the second army, led by Dunmore himself, arrived, and so launched their attack on October 10. The Virginians were camped on a narrow spit of land between forks of the river, and the Shawnees tried desperately to drive them into the acute angle. Virginians remembered the fight as one of unusual intensity, with the Indians showing a tremendous willingness to hold their ground and exchange fire. Eventually, though, they began to exhaust their ammunition, and had to abandon the field. Lewis' men actually took the worst of it, losing about seventy-five killed and one hundred and forty wounded. The Shawnees lost between thirty and forty men, but among them was Puckesinwa. His widow would be left to raise their children, including a six-year-old boy named Tecumseh (Holton, 2011; Sugden, 1998).

Though the Shawnees had fought hard, they knew that Virginia held the upper hand. An embittered Cornstalk, who had argued against fighting, now sought peace from the Virginians, or *Long Knives*, as the Shawnees called them. As expected, Dunmore and the Virginians insisted, at the Treaty of Camp Charlotte, that the Shawnees cede their claims to Kentucky, which had served as one of their primary sources of food and deerskins. Cornstalk knew, however, that Dunmore's threat to march into southern Ohio and burn the Shawnee towns was likely no bluff. He marked the treaty, though many Shawnees considered it illegitimate and had no intention of abiding by it.

Despite the heavy casualties at Point Pleasant, the war easily proved to be Dunmore's most popular action as Virginia's governor. The House of Burgesses was still formally thanking him as late as March of 1775. Events far from the frontier, however, and his reactions to them, would soon make Dunmore *persona non grata* in his own colony (Holton, 2011).

2 Revolting Americans

Many Problems and Few Solutions

Having replaced Jeffery Amherst as commander-in-chief for British forces in North America, Thomas Gage continued in that post for more than a decade. While personally brave, Gage was not the greatest combat officer at His Majesty's disposal, but he had proven himself to be a perfectly competent administrator. In peacetime, that would be far more important. This was especially true given the limited resources available to him. Reading Gage's correspondence reveals a hardworking bureaucrat trying to tackle a nearly impossible mission. In addition to his day job of commander-in-chief, he was also made royal governor of Massachusetts in 1774 – a thankless job if ever there were one. The Crown tasked Gage to maintain control of half the continent with a continually shrinking force (and budget), and to promote peace among all of His Majesty's children – Indian and white. By the spring of 1775, that no longer seemed possible.

As gunfire erupted on the common green at Lexington, Massachusetts, it soon became apparent that the differences between royal authorities and colonists would be settled only by extensive bloodshed. British officers and agents, like their rebel counterparts, initially feared the role Indians might play, and sought to discourage their taking part in this Anglo-American quarrel. Most native peoples had little interest in joining the fray, but the idea that they could remain universally neutral proved farfetched for all parties. As Pontiac's War had demonstrated, any significant disruption in the flow of trade goods (particularly firearms and gunpowder) to Native Americans would put enormous economic, cultural, and diplomatic strains upon them. As one American noted, those who could continue to supply Indians with gunpowder would continue to count them as allies (Owens, 2015).

Within months of Lexington, Indians were taking sides in the conflict. American and British officials, in a pattern they would repeat in the War of 1812, sought to preemptively recruit Indian warriors before their opponents did the same. While later generations of Americans sought to *whitewash* them from the historical record, a great many Native Americans did fight alongside the rebels. Generally speaking, they tended to come from smaller nations, who perhaps sought to differentiate themselves from larger tribes who aligned themselves with Britain. Groups who now numbered only in the hundreds, like the Catawbas of South Carolina, and the Mohicans of Massachusetts, nevertheless sent warriors who fought alongside George Washington's men. The Kaskaskias of the Illinois Country had seen their numbers plummet so far, fewer than eight hundred by 1775, that they dared not risk men in combat. Yet they provided invaluable help to American forces as scouts and hunters for isolated American outposts. Though the bulk of the Iroquois League, especially the Mohawks, adhered to the British alliance, the Oneidas and some of the Tuscaroras cast their lot with the Americans. The painful schism in the League would reverberate for years, in some ways to the present day (Owens, 2015).

Britain and its colonies were not the only ones contesting the meaning of nationhood. A cultural and generational struggle was taking place among the Cherokees. There had long been physical and cultural divides between the Overhill Towns, located in what is now eastern Tennessee, and the Lower Towns in Georgia and South Carolina. They were in many ways farther apart than they appear on maps because of the barrier imposed by the rugged Appalachian Mountains. The Lower Towns tended to have closer contacts with the Creeks than some of the other Cherokees, and this would impact their political and military thinking (Boulware, 2011).

Factionalism among the Cherokees

Older Overhill chiefs, like Attakullakulla, or Little Carpenter, hoped to maintain friendship with whites by selling them parcels of land. In the 1775 Treaty of Sycamore Shoals (also known as the Treaty of Watauga), the chief and others had indeed sold much of what would become Kentucky and some of what would become eastern Tennessee – a valuable Cherokee hunting ground. They sold to a group of North Carolina land speculators known as the Transylvania Company, led by Richard Henderson. In addition to about £10,000 worth of welcome trade goods, including gunpowder, the chiefs hoped that this Sycamore Shoals Conference would bring peace with their white neighbors (Boulware, 2011; Finger, 2001).

Attakullakulla's son, *Tsi.yu.Gansi.Ni*, or Dragging Canoe, led a faction of younger warriors and hunters who bitterly opposed the sale. (They were not the only ones who opposed the sale. Colonial authorities decried it, as there had been no permission from the Crown – violating the Proclamation of 1763 – and also disliked that much of the payment was given in the form of ammunition, at a time when Cherokee loyalties might be in doubt.) Before storming out in protest, Dragging Canoe noted that the land was a "bloody ground," meaning that it was hunting land, and valuable, and that Henderson would find it a "dark, and difficult" place to settle. The phrase would later be somewhat distorted as "a dark and bloody ground" (Finger, 2001; Schmidt, 2014:26).

Younger Cherokees, who still hoped to make use of their hunting grounds, tended to follow Dragging Canoe, and this would lead to a further bifurcation of the Cherokees. Dragging Canoe would lead the Lower Cherokees (they would later become known as Chickamaugas, for the river where they would build their towns), while his father's group would be known as the Overhill/Upper Cherokees. The Lower Cherokees/Chickamaugas, eventually settling near modern Chattanooga, Tennessee, in the early 1780s, would prove key players in the resistance to American encroachment into the 1790s. While most of the Cherokee Nation hoped to remain at peace with whites, rebel or otherwise, Dragging Canoe wanted all the invaders gone. He attended a conference at the Cherokee town of Chota in the spring of 1776, and met with Shawnee, Ottawa, and Mohawk emissaries, who sought a pan-Indian alliance to defend Indian lands (Dowd, 1992; Calloway, 1995).

The Lower Cherokees feigned peace towards their white neighbors until July of 1776, when they launched a furious assault on the frontiers of North and South Carolina. They killed almost sixty South Carolinians, and burned up perhaps fifty miles of North Carolina's settlements and planted fields. They attacked both Loyalists and Patriots, and the assaults pushed a number of the former into the latter camp. Despite Dragging Canoe's hopes, however, the Creeks declined to join his war, and he sorely missed their numbers. [See Doc. 5] Meanwhile, as an unintended consequence, white Carolinians now had a pretext to invade Cherokee country and extort more land cessions. South Carolina offered a bounty of £75 for Cherokee scalps, and a series of invasions by militia armies from Virginia and the Carolinas, with aid from Continental troops, brought destruction to Cherokee towns.

The Americans made a point of destroying the vast cornfields and orchards that Cherokee women had so painstakingly cultivated, and found once more that destroying Cherokee sustenance was the key to defeating them. By late fall of 1776, only Dragging Canoe's diehards refused to surrender. The other Cherokees marked treaties that gave away almost all of their claims to South Carolina and Virginia. The war cost the Cherokees about five million acres of territory, and hundreds of lives (Schmidt, 2014; Ward, 1995). [See Doc. 6]

Dragging Canoe, however, remained unbowed. A veteran of the Cherokee War of 1759–61, he now led raids that would aid the British. His warriors joined Redcoats in capturing Savannah and Augusta in Georgia. Meanwhile, they further separated themselves from other

Cherokees, settling along the Chickamauga River, and began to be called Chickamaugas. Dragging Canoe also sent numbers of his men to join war parties of Shawnees, Choctaws, and Delawares against the Americans. As one scholar notes, the war relieved Indians of having to distinguish between British authorities, who might offer at least some protection of their land rights, and British colonists, who had proven rapaciously interested in taking Indian land. "It is therefore little wonder that pan-Indian militancy surged throughout America as the war commenced" (Boulware, 2011:156).

The Cherokees provide an excellent case study of the perils of over-generalizing Indian loyalties. *Nanyehi*, later known as Nancy Ward, originally rose to prominence among the Cherokees in 1755 when, as a teenager, she saw her husband mortally wounded in battle with the Creeks, and took his musket and joined the fight. She became known as a "War Woman" among the Cherokees. Yet the obviously courageous Ward – she adopted her English name after marrying an English trader – repeatedly advocated for peace, and went out of her way on several occasions to warn her white neighbors of impending attacks. In that role, she used her status as a Cherokee "Beloved Woman" – appointed to serve as a negotiator with outsiders. In the Cherokee War of 1776, warriors captured Mrs. William Bean, who was among the illegal white squatters on Cherokee lands along the Holston River. Nancy Ward personally rescued Bean, sentenced to be burned alive, from that cruel fate, and she later returned the captive to her family. Ward did not, however, intervene to spare a young boy, who was burned at the stake shortly after (Finger, 2001).

In 1781, trying desperately to restore peace – and end the punitive invasions of Cherokee country – Ward repeatedly engineered the surreptitious escapes of white captives from Cherokee towns, and also provided intelligence warning the Virginians of Dragging Canoe's plans to attack them. For some Cherokees, she had committed treason. Even her own kinship ties were complicated. As the niece of Attakullakulla/Little Carpenter, she was a cousin of Dragging Canoe, the most famous Cherokee militant, but was also the mother-in-law of American Indian agent Joseph Martin. Indeed, even after her daughter Betsy – Martin's wife – was murdered by American militia in 1793, Ward continued to advocate for peace with the Americans. But, like the vast majority of Cherokees, in the nineteenth century she would later oppose further land cessions to the U.S. Despite Ward's numerous efforts on behalf of the Americans, white squatters flooded into Cherokee territory after the Cherokees made peace in 1781. The suffering of the Cherokees because of this became so manifest that even Isaac Shelby, a hero to frontiersmen, called for Virginia to aid its recent enemies (Finger, 2001; Perdue, 1998; Conley, 2007; Calloway, 1995).

The British-Indian Alliance Stumbles in the North

To the north, Britain's Iroquois allies were to figure prominently in General John Burgoyne's campaign of 1777. Burgoyne hoped to make use of New York Loyalists and numerous Indian allies, along with two British armies – his own from Canada and Lord Howe's from New York City – to trap much of the rebel army in a three-pronged assault. Burgoyne would march south through the Hudson River Valley in New York, while Howe would move north to meet him. This grand plan assumed that everything would work out perfectly, and almost none of it did. An early stumble came in the British-Indian alliance in western New York, where Loyalists and native warriors were to terrify or at least distract Americans from the pincer movement converging on the Hudson Valley. Some of the Crown's native allies, apparently from the Great Lakes, took an American woman named Jane McCrea captive. As she was engaged to marry a Loyalist officer, her capture was likely a mistake. The tragic error was irretrievably compounded when two warriors disputed who had the rights to this honor of war. The dispute became so intense that one of the warriors simply murdered her.

While few solid facts arose from the incident, the American press ran wild. Glossing over, or ignoring entirely, her presumed Loyalist leanings, American officials, soldiers, and editors flogged the story as yet another example of the evils of Indian warfare, made worse by its association with the hated British. It caught General Burgoyne in a diplomatic crossfire; he scolded his Indian allies for the indiscriminate killing of a civilian, which annoyed a number of them so much that they abandoned the campaign and went home. (They were allies, after all, not employees.) Yet many Loyalists were so enraged by the murder of one of their own that they lambasted Burgoyne for not bringing the killers to justice – something that would have been extremely difficult and delicate, if not impossible, for him to do. Loyalist participation in the wake of the murder flagged noticeably, at a time when the departure of some of the western Indians made them even more desperately needed (Schmidt, 2014; Bickham, 2005).

The fallout from McCrea's murder carried across the Atlantic. In Parliament, the opposition party made great political hay out of the death of one of the King's loyal subjects at the hands of a supposed ally. Edmund Burke, the master orator and staunch opponent of the American war, exploited the general public's distaste for attacking their American cousins, especially with Indian allies and their perceived inhumane tactics. It was one thing to unleash Indians upon the hated French, felt many in Britain, but quite another to do so against their own kind. The political storm became so great that, as a long-term consequence, the government grew increasingly reluctant to employ significant numbers of native warriors, despite the obvious tactical advantage Indian allies provided to the King's men in the West (Bickham, 2005).

But at least the Iroquois contingent, led by the Mohawk chief Thayendanegea, also known as Joseph Brant, remained with Burgoyne's army. Brant and his Mohawks, together with some Senecas and other native allies, as well as a few British, Hessians, and Loyalists, laid an ambush for Joseph Herkimer's Tryon County, NY (rebel) militia near the village of Oriskany in August of 1777. Herkimer, with some 700 men, augmented by about 100 Oneida (Iroquois) warriors, came under fire in a steep ravine. Brant's ambush was well planned, and Herkimer's force initially took the worst of the encounter. Then a hard rain fell, precluding gunfire. When the skies cleared, the fight began anew, and Herkimer's men and the Oneidas rallied, though the general himself was mortally wounded.

When the exceedingly bloody fighting ended, both sides would claim victory. Tactically, it was an American defeat, as the 500 in Brant's force had inflicted more than 400 casualties, including 385 killed, while losing less than 100 themselves. However, when Brant's men returned to their camp, they found that while they were engaged at Oriskany, their British allies had failed to safeguard their camp, which had then been ransacked by another party of Americans. Having ended the day noticeably poorer than they had begun it, not to mention their own heavy losses, many of Britain's Indian allies walked out in disgust. The loss of many natives and Loyalists did not outright doom Burgoyne's campaign, which had been a long shot to begin with. But when Burgoyne was captured, along with nearly 7,000 men at Saratoga that October, it certainly deflated any hopes that the rebels would be subdued quickly (Ward, 1995; Glatthaar and Martin, 2006).

Joseph Brant led more raids on rebel settlements in the spring of 1778, particularly in the Mohawk Valley of New York. Brant's name came to be so terrifying that he was sometimes credited with attacks he had not made, like the attack on the Wyoming (PA) cabins that Americans later dubbed the "Wyoming Massacre" in July of 1778. (This attack should not be confused with the one that killed Teedyuscung in 1763.) Seneca warriors, acting with Loyalist Colonel Walter Butler, did kill a number of noncombatants in the aftermath of the battle, but Brant had not in fact been present. Later, Brant and his Mohawks did join with Butler's British-Seneca force for an attack on Cherry Valley, Pennsylvania. Perhaps 30 noncombatants died at the hands of the Senecas, though Brant had actually tried to stop them. (The Senecas probably did not welcome any criticism from their Mohawk cousin.) He had become so infamous among American rebels, however, that he was thereafter known as "Monster Brant." Once again, Americans demonstrated great skill, if not accuracy or honor, in messaging and propaganda (Kelsay, 1984:221).

As outraged Pennsylvanians and New Yorkers protested to Congress, so that body impressed upon General Washington the need to act against the Iroquois. Washington, overlooking that most Oneidas and a number of Tuscaroras were active allies of the rebels, unleashed General John Sullivan to scourge the Iroquois homeland in 1779. Sullivan's campaign met very few Iroquois in combat, as the warriors largely withdrew before his sizable force. But the American army proved quite effective at destroying Iroquois villages, including some belonging to neutralists and even allies. Diarists in the army noted with admiration the enormous Iroquois grain fields, meticulously maintained apple orchards, and orderly towns. They also gleefully noted their destruction. Some 40 Iroquois towns were set ablaze in the late summer and early fall of 1779. As part of another recurring pattern, Anglo-Americans felt that destroying Indian homes and food sources proved safer and more effective than trying to defeat them on the battlefield (Ward, 1995).

Still, as Colin Calloway notes, if the idea had been to knock the Iroquois out of the war, Sullivan's destructive campaign had actually done the opposite. With their homes and food stores gone, most Iroquois had little choice but to double down on the British alliance. They fled west to the British fort at Niagara, desperately in need of British blankets, clothing, and food (Calloway, 1995).

Southern Discomfort

Far to the south, the Muscogees, or Creeks, between their upper and lower towns, numbered perhaps twenty thousand people, meaning they could field as many as five thousand warriors. Had they been employed at once, upon a common foe, they could have tipped the balance in the Southern theater. But not unlike the Cherokees, Creeks saw significant differences between their Upper and Lower villages when it came to political and military decisions, as well as diversity of thought within those regions. While some Creeks, angry at the continual waves of Georgians barging onto their lands, did join the fight against the rebels, many chose to bide their time. American Indian agent George Galphin saw success in keeping the Lower Creeks out of the fight. [See Doc. 7] Upper Creeks, led by Indian agent (and later a Creek *beloved man*) Alexander McGillivray, joined the pro-British fight early, while Lower Creeks did so half-heartedly only after the British captured Savannah, Georgia, – a key port city – in 1779. In 1782, the fierce Upper Creek war chief Emistisiguo was killed in a fight with General Anthony Wayne's Continental troops while he was leading warriors to Savannah (Schmidt, 2014; Ethridge, 2003; Morris, 2014). [See Doc. 8]

British agents, like Superintendent John Stuart, had to walk a fine line between supporting Indian allies, who sought to hold their territory, and trying to keep Loyalists in frontier areas loyal. Whenever Indians used British-made muskets or tomahawks against white interlopers, regardless of provocation, it proved a net propaganda victory for rebels, who soon became experts at conflating British *tyranny* with Indian *savagery*. As historian Peter Silver notes, Americans' "violent self-pity" became a highly effective propaganda tool, minimizing or ignoring white Americans' own brutality while emphasizing that of their enemies. Essentially, Americans painted their opponents as so evil that it justified most any retaliation, at least in their minds (Silver, 2007:94).

Later generations of Americans would go to significant lengths to downplay their ancestors' crimes, while highlighting those of British-allied Indians. In the Ohio Country, the war brought great schisms and anguish for the Shawnees and Delawares. The former, still furious over the forced cession of their Kentucky hunting grounds, found themselves slowly drawn in to the conflict, as whites from Virginia and the Carolinas poured into the West. Led by longhunters like Daniel Boone, they shot game with reckless abandon, but also made clear their intention to remain, building palisaded villages they called "stations." Though nominally in the rebel camp, the Kentuckians were not particularly interested in British tax policies. They opposed the King because he armed their native rivals. Some Shawnees responded to this threat by attacking the interlopers when they could, but the nation as a whole had great misgivings. Perhaps a third of the Shawnees removed west, and settled in Missouri (Edmunds, 1983; Calloway, 1995).

Beginning in 1775, a steady stream of pioneers invaded the lush Bluegrass region of central Kentucky by way of the Cumberland Gap, and also the Ohio River. By 1776, Kentucky had a half-dozen settlements or stations, with the main sites being Harrodsburg on the Dix River, and, to the east, Boonesborough on the Kentucky River. By 1777, Virginia claimed Kentucky as its westernmost county. Indians in southern Ohio feared both the depletion of their game in Kentucky, and that settlers would cross the Ohio. 1777 proved a particularly bloody year (Brown, 2008).

Shawnee and Delaware Indians raided Kentucky at will. Harrodsburg and Boonesborough endured successive attacks during the spring and early summer. During the assault on Boonesborough on April 24, 1777, Simon Kenton saved the life of fellow frontiersman Daniel Boone. Shot through the ankle, Boone was trapped outside the fort's gate, and about to be overtaken by Shawnee pursuers. The hulking Kenton, who stood over six feet tall and weighed more than two hundred pounds, ran to his friend, and killed two Shawnees at close quarters. He then threw the average-sized Boone over his shoulder, and ran into the fort as bullets whizzed by (Ward, 1995).

Reflecting the desire of many Shawnees to avoid war, their chief Hokolesqua, or Cornstalk, had ventured to Fort Randolph in (now West) Virginia. The fort's commander foolishly held Cornstalk's embassy hostage, hoping it would prevent further attacks. Instead, on November 10, 1777, the chief, another Shawnee headman named Red Hawk, and Cornstalk's son (who had come to visit his father) were murdered by

Virginia militia. The militiamen were furious because one of their fellows, hunting outside the fort without authorization, had been murdered and scalped by a party unaffiliated with Cornstalk. Knowing that there were Shawnee hostages – unarmed – held inside Fort Randolph, they stormed in with their weapons drawn. The fort's commander, a Continental Army captain, briefly tried to stop them, but they threatened to shoot any man who interfered.

The wife of the post's interpreter, herself a former Indian captive, ran to warn the Shawnees. Knowing escape was impossible, Cornstalk and his son faced the murderous militia stoically, while their companion died trying to climb up the chimney. The militia emptied their guns into him, Cornstalk, and his son. Rather than reload, they then hacked a fourth Shawnee captive to death with their tomahawks and knives. Cornstalk's murder would prove part of a depressing pattern in Indian-white relations: natives who tried to keep the peace were often among the first victims of violence. Though Cornstalk had been held hostage in an ill-conceived attempt to keep the Shawnees from getting further involved in the war, with his murder the Shawnees remaining in Ohio became implacable foes of the Americans (Calloway, 1995).

Regardless of both the British and the Americans' defensive strategies, they eventually realized that the West HAD to be won. Both sides sent troops on a limited scale into the West. Brutality in the conflict came as much from American frontiersmen as it did Indians. Indian militants came to see the war as an opportunity to staunch the flow of white settlers onto their lands, or even roll the settlements back. Likewise, many Americans saw fighting the King's Indian allies as a way to secure the Indian lands they had long coveted.

By the end of 1777, Indian attacks had destroyed all but three American stations in Kentucky – Boonesborough, Harrodsburg, and Logan's Fort, though the flood of settlers would soon build more. In February 1778, the Shawnees captured Daniel Boone – now a captain in the Virginia militia, while he and his party were making salt at the Blue Licks. Knowing that resistance would be futile, he struck a deal with the Shawnees – he would negotiate the peaceable surrender of his party in return for their lives, and they agreed. Most of his men would be turned over to the British at Detroit, where they could eventually be exchanged. But the Shawnees wanted to hang on to Boone (Brown, 2008).

Boone understood his opponents' warrior ethos. He maintained a cheerful, seemingly fearless attitude while on the march back to Shawnee country, which impressed his captors. Boone was so respected by the Shawnees as a warrior, and so personally charming, that instead of putting him to death, he was adopted by Chief Black Fish himself. Boone's agility and footspeed inspired his joking nickname *Sheltowee*, or Big Turtle. Boone lived with the Shawnees for several months in seeming contentment, and in fact both he and Shawnee men loved to hunt. But he still had a wife, family, and friends back in Kentucky, and when he learned of a planned attack on Boonesborough, he escaped and made a mad dash in time to warn the settlers. Black Fish was apparently quite hurt by his adopted son's betrayal. In running away after adoption, Boone knew he would be marked for death if caught again (Ward, 1995; Brown, 2008).

Boone's escape had been in enough time for 100 Virginia and 50 North Carolina riflemen to rush to reinforce Boonesborough. Black Fish led a party of 400 Shawnees and French Canadians loyal to the Crown in a ten-day siege of Boonesborough in September 1778. A single cannon would have easily reduced the fort, but lacking one, they attempted to set fire to the fort and tunnel under the walls, but failed. The continued Indian raids aroused Kentucky settlers and the state of Virginia, to launch a counterattack, in the form of an invasion by Virginian George Rogers Clark, a young lieutenant colonel in the Virginia militia. Governor Patrick Henry authorized Clark to raise 350 men to protect Kentucky, and issued secret orders to take the French villages north of the Ohio, and, if possible, attack the British at Detroit. Doing so would not only help the American war effort, but firm up Virginian's claims to the southern Ohio Valley (Griffin, 2007; Ward, 1995).

In late June of 1778, Clark's militia force began the 125-mile march from the mouth of the Tennessee River to the village of Kaskaskia on the Mississippi. They made it in less than two weeks, entering at dusk on July 4th. The town was taken completely by surprise, and when Clark announced the French-American alliance, signed in early 1778, the local militia commander, Phillipe de Rocheblave, surrendered without a shot. Elements of Clark's force made similar bloodless conquests of Prairie du Rocher, and Cahokia, and also Fort Sackville at Vincennes, on the Wabash, in what is now southern Indiana. In December, though, British Colonel Henry Hamilton launched a counterattack from Detroit and retook Fort Sackville (Ward, 1995).

Clark determined to recapture Vincennes, and in February of 1779 set out from Kaskaskia overland with 170 men, passing though the cold, flooded plains and rivers that lay in his path. Most would have considered such a march at that time of year as foolhardy or impossible, and indeed some of Clark's men would never regain their former health after the campaign. Yet they did survive the march, and arrived at Vincennes on February 22nd. Clark arrayed his men on the hills carefully, giving the impression of a much larger force. Hamilton had only 79 soldiers and militia in Ft. Sackville, and half were French settlers who refused to fight the Americans. Hamilton's Indian allies did not like the odds, and most fled, while the townspeople gave Clark gunpowder that they had hidden from the British. The next morning, Clark paraded five captives – four Indians and a Frenchman in Indian dress, in front of the fort. Clark and some of his men then tomahawked them in sight of the horrified garrison.

Hamilton surrendered the next day, and he and two dozen other prisoners were sent in irons to Williamsburg, Virginia. Hamilton would not be paroled until 1780, and eventually returned to Canada as Lieutenant Governor of Quebec. He never forgave Clark for his imprisonment, or for the brutality shown to his native allies (White, 1991; Griffin, 2007).

Clark had achieved a stunning victory, but unlike his admirers, he knew he had not actually "conquered" the Northwest. He built forts at what is now Louisville, Kentucky – the Falls of the Ohio – and just below the mouth of the Ohio River – Forts Nelson and Jefferson, respectively. He spent the next three years hoping to raise a force which might lay siege to Detroit. In 1779, Congress voted $932,743 for raising a force of 3,000 volunteers for the expedition, but Clark could not find enough men willing to go. It was perhaps just as well, for while Congress had allocated the money, they did not in fact have it. Under the Articles of Confederation, the Congress could ask the states for funds, but had no power to actually collect them (Griffin, 2007; Ward, 1995).

While Clark desperately tried to convince his countrymen of the need for a renewed offensive in the West, the British were on the move. They sponsored a new series of raids into Kentucky, with the ultimate goal being the capture of Fort Nelson (modern Louisville). Another force of 950 men, Redcoats, Tory militia, and western Indians – including some Sioux – under Captain Emmanuel Hesse, moved through Wisconsin and down the Mississippi River, hoping to capture Spanish St. Louis. (In 1779, Spain signed an alliance with France against Britain, though they declined to make any official agreement with the U.S.)

Despite the promise of Hesse's attack on St. Louis – the administrative capital of Upper Louisiana, the Spanish commander there, Captain Fernando de Leyba and his 350 men, withstood the attack. In an example of who really controlled the West, Hesse's Indian allies feared a relief army under Clark, and so beat a hasty retreat, obliging Hesse to follow them. Clark sent a force of American, French and Spanish volunteers after them, chasing them as far as the Rock River, burning several Indian towns in Illinois (Ward, 1995).

In June of 1780, Captain Henry Bird, with 150 Redcoats and rangers, accompanied 800 Indians, mainly from Ohio, into Kentucky. Bird's troops carried some light artillery, which proved more than a match for any wooden palisade, and so this large war party had the potential to wipe out every American station in Kentucky. The British Indian Department's Major Alexander McKee, the son of a Shawnee woman, was nominally in charge of Bird's Indian allies. On June 9, the army reached the Ohio River. (Despite the disparity in numbers, Bird considered it his expedition.) Though Bird's primary goal was to attack Ft. Nelson, most of the Indians preferred to seek softer targets, taking revenge and plunder, rather than face George Rogers Clark and his men. Further, they saw Kentucky settlers as their primary adversaries.

Bird was forced, therefore, to attack settler stations along the Licking River. "Ruddle's Station was compelled to surrender, and Bird burned the fort." But against his orders, "the Indians slaughtered 200 of the station's 300 inhabitants – men, women, and children. Mrs. John Ruddle's infant was tossed into the fires, and when she leaped to save the baby she was tomahawked and also thrown into the flames." (Indian raiders often summarily killed captives, including infants, whom they felt would not survive the march to their destinations.) A few Americans escaped, spreading word of the massacre, while 50 were taken as prisoners to Detroit (Ward, 1995:177).

Bird then attacked Martin's Station, which surrendered "without firing a shot." Bird managed was to prevent another massacre, but he feared that he would not be able to do so in future attacks. He also recognized that the Americans and his superiors would surely hold him responsible if another massacre occurred. The last straw came when the warriors killed the station's livestock, which Bird had hoped to use for his army. With that pretext, he refused to attack any other settlements, and headed back to Detroit, with his cannon. The Ohio Indians had lost a golden opportunity in the war for Kentucky (Ward, 1995:177).

Shocked by the massacre at Ruddell's Station, Kentuckians sought vengeance across the Ohio. George Rogers Clark, now a general, with John Bowman and Benjamin Logan, took 970 men across the Ohio in August of 1780 on a "punitive expedition" against the Shawnees. They destroyed the village of Chillicothe and then marched on Piqua. The battle at Piqua would be the largest military encounter of the American Revolution in the West. Clark was met by 1,500 Indians, led by the venerable chief Black Hoof. After a sharp firefight outside the town, the Shawnees then retreated to their log-walled council house. When Clark's six-pound brass cannon began to splinter the log walls, the Shawnees escaped out the back (Ward, 1995:177).

Clark counted 14 dead Americans and 13 wounded, while his men took 73 scalps. Among the Shawnee casualties was the mortally wounded Joseph Rogers. Rogers, an adopted Shawnee captive, was Clark's cousin, and the men had a brief, awkward reunion as Rogers lay dying. Clark's men spent two days looting and burning the town and surrounding fields. Then, lacking provisions to go any further, they returned to Kentucky (Ward, 1995:177; White, 1991). It would not be the last time that an American army destroyed vast quantities of Indians' food, then had to march home hungry for lack of rations.

In 1781 Virginia, cash strapped and reeling from British raids, had to withdraw its men from the garrisons at Kaskaskia, Cahokia, Vincennes, and Fort Jefferson. Surrounded by numerous hostile Indians, these positions were in constant danger of being overrun. Also, it was difficult to resupply them, because the French and Spanish in the area usually refused to accept Virginia's increasingly worthless paper money. Finally, they were desperately short of men for defending their "western district" of Kentucky (Ward, 1995).

Further south, while Dragging Canoe's faction had never ceased fighting, most of the Cherokees were still trying to recover from the 1776 campaigns, and labored to remain neutral. But further encroachments, and a desire to maintain the British alliance, led some of the Overhill warriors to join with Dragging Canoe's men on raids in 1780. They drew a harsh response from Virginia and North Carolina. Governor Thomas Jefferson of Virginia sent John Sevier and Arthur Campbell to invade the Cherokee heartland. A combined Cherokee force lost a tough battle at Boyd's Creek in December of 1780. By the spring of 1781, American expeditions had destroyed more than thirty Cherokee towns, leading the Overhill leaders to once again sue for peace (Calloway, 1995).

But Dragging Canoe and the Chickamaugas continued to resist the invasion of Tennessee. Along the Cumberland River, at what is now Nashville, settlers led by James Robertson had built a fort they dubbed Fort Nashborough, named for the late General Francis Nash. A substantial post on bluffs overlooking the Cumberland, the fort enclosed two acres, had its own spring (a lack of water being a natural weak point for most forts), and even boasted a swivel gun, or small cannon. The fort was defended by the Washington District (North Carolina) militia. The size as well as the location led Dragging Canoe to wish its destruction. Too large to be taken by storm, the Chickamaugas would need a ruse to eliminate the post.

What came to be known as the Battle of the Bluff began late in the night of April 1, 1781, as Dragging Canoe's men took up positions outside Nashborough. Early in the morning on April 2, two warriors appeared outside the fort, and about two dozen foolhardy defenders rushed out on horseback to meet them. Against his better judgment, James Robertson accompanied them. Soon, as he had predicted, they found themselves surrounded by a few hundred warriors. As the party jumped off their horses to fight, the Chickamaugas sprung their ambush. What was worse, the men could also see more Indians attacking the fort. Desperately, the whites fought to get back to the gates, and much of the combat was at close range – one of Robertson's men primarily used his sword.

At this point, the wives of the defenders – who had wisely urged them not to leave the gates – bailed them out with a desperate, but successful, gambit. Led by Robertson's wife Charlotte, they grabbed rifles to lay down covering fire to the party trying to regain the fort, and then, they loosed the settlers' hounds upon the Chickamaugas. Though they would later recount that the dogs had been almost docile, even lazy, before, they became crazed on the attack, and their vicious counterattack stunned the Chickamaugas, allowing Robertson's party to get back to the gate. At least one of the dogs, it was recorded, had taken such a frenzy that he even attacked one of Robertson's party, and had to be killed. Between

Nashborough's women, their dogs, and the Chickamaugas breaking off their assault to recover the defenders' runaway horses, the attack failed. Still, the Chickamaugas had demonstrated just how vulnerable the outpost was, and the settlers would practically abandon it until 1785 (Blackmon, 2012; Putnam, 1971).

Violence Surges in the West

The last full year of the war was one of the bloodiest in the West, and the situation in the Ohio Valley grew truly horrific. The Delawares in western Pennsylvania had largely tried to remain neutral in the early years of the war, but the pressure for trade goods and indiscriminate killings by whites made it increasingly difficult. By the early 1780s, a number of them had openly sided with Britain. Wyandot and Shawnee war parties continued to strike at Kentucky, while Delawares hit the Pennsylvania frontier hard. In 1781, Colonel Daniel Brodhead led Continental troops to destroy the village of Coshocton (Ohio) in retaliation. But other Delawares, especially a group of Moravian (Protestant) converts living at the village of Gnadenhütten in eastern Ohio, kept the peace. These Delawares followed the Moravian missionary David Zeisberger, who preached pacifism and pietism. The village had few if any arms, and lived primarily by farming and trades, like carpentry. They were mildly prosperous, which may have been part of why they were targeted by Pennsylvania militia in March of 1782.

Colonel David Williamson and 300 Pennsylvania militia set out to punish the Delawares. At the village of Gnadenhütten, on the east bank of the Muskingum River, on March 8, 1782, they found some Moravian Delawares, most of whom were working in their fields. Clothing belonging to Mrs. Robert Wallace, who had been tortured and killed by Delaware raiders, was discovered in the area. Though the Moravian Delawares had relatives involved in the fighting, they themselves had taken no part. But Williamson's militia did not care. Williamson and his men rounded up the unarmed pacifists, bound them, and herded them into three buildings, one each for the men, women, and children. In very American fashion, Williamson put the captives' fate to a vote of his men, and all but 18 voted to kill them. Sitting on the floor with their ankles bound, the Christianized Indians sang hymns and prayed aloud as militiamen took turns bashing their brains in with a cooper's mallet. Ninety were so murdered – 29 men, 27 women, and 34 children. The militia then set fire to the buildings. Two Indian boys, stunned but not killed, managed to escape and spread word of the horror (Schmidt, 2014; Sadosky, 2001).

The militia then looted the town, and it took eighty packhorses to carry off the plunder. While some frontier residents expressed outrage at the mass robbery-homicide, a great many more approved, or at least declined to criticize it. None of the perpetrators was ever officially sanctioned, and American newspapers, always quick to exploit the misdeeds of the King's Indian allies, remained largely mute on the affair. The relatives of the slaughtered, however, did not rely on newspapers (Schmidt, 2014).

The massacre at Gnadenhütten infuriated the Ohio Indians, especially the Delawares. Raids into Kentucky increased. In response, an expedition of 400 volunteers, led by Col. William Crawford, a Continental officer and friend of George Washington, invaded Delaware territory. In June they fought a force of Delawares and Shawnees. Later reinforced by British rangers and more Shawnees, the Indians routed Crawford's volunteers, who fled. Crawford and a small party got lost, and were captured by the Delawares. Though he had not been present at Gnadenhütten, the Delawares reserved a special torture for Crawford.

Thirty-five warriors and 70 women and children took turns slowly burning and mutilating Crawford, whose agonizing death took about two hours. As they had previously, American propagandists managed to turn this awful event to some rhetorical advantage, focusing on a "British renegade," Simon Girty. Girty, actually an American, had been captured as a child and raised by the Senecas. Serving the U.S. as a scout out of Fort Pitt early in the war, he and several others, including Alexander McKee, deserted and threw in with the British Indian Department. American legend held that Girty, who was present at Colonel Crawford's execution, coldly refused Crawford's pleas for help, even his desperate request that Girty shoot him to end his misery. Girty later maintained, and Indian oral tradition supports, however, that he in fact pleaded for Crawford's life, and offered the Delawares his horse, money, and his rifle, to spare him. But such was the Delawares' anger that only the colonel's death would appease them. Crawford himself appealed to an old friend, a Delaware priest named Wangomend, but the furious Delawares refused to spare him. For outraged Americans, the tale would be spun as yet another example of British-Indian barbarity (White, 1991; Calloway, 1995).

Indian raids into Kentucky continued unabated. In August of 1782, a party of 500 Wyandots, Shawnees, Great Lakes Indians, and Canadian Rangers under Captain William Caldwell, plus Simon Girty and Alexander McKee, laid siege to Bryan's Station, and then moved west along the Licking River. Kentucky militia quickly rallied, and several militia officers, including Daniel Boone, took 182 men after the war party, rather than waiting for reinforcements. The Indian raiders were elated, rather than fearful, and set an ambush for them at the Blue Licks. On August 19, as the Kentuckians approached the Licking River, with bluffs on either side, Daniel Boone smelled a trap, and wisely called for a halt. As the militia officers weighed their options, one, Colonel Hugh McGary, denounced the others for their "cowardice" and led a headlong charge. The vengeful militia rushed forward with him into the trap. Seventy-seven Kentuckians were killed, including two officers – but not McGary – and Daniel Boone's son, Israel.

In response to the loss at Blue Licks, George Rogers Clark, took over 1,000 mounted Kentuckians into the Ohio country, on what would be the final major campaign of the Revolution. The Shawnees had fled before their arrival, so all Clark's men could do was raze a half-dozen Shawnee towns and their cornfields, sometimes disinterring burial plots to scalp the dead (Calloway, 1995; Ward, 1995).

Britain's Indian allies in the West were not just holding their own by 1782, but actually seemed to be winning. They would be shocked to learn how events east of the mountains, over which they had no control, could nevertheless affect them. On the ground, some British agents, like the fierce Georgian Thomas Brown, hoped to continue to work with Indian militants like Dragging Canoe. The Chickamauga chief attended a conference at St. Augustine, Florida, in early 1783. Meeting with a number of Northern pan-Indianists, they wanted to coordinate a unified Indian resistance to the Americans. But that summer, Brown and other Indian agents received official orders to stand down – the British government did not want to jeopardize an end to the North American war (Calloway, 1995; Schmidt, 2014).

Aside from humiliating (if not fatal) defeats like the battle of Yorktown (1781), Britain wanted to end the war before they lost even more valuable territory than the thirteen rebellious colonies. Both France and Spain sought to capture valuable sugar-growing islands in the Caribbean, and Spain had also taken crucial posts in Florida, like Pensacola. The latter had significant ramifications for Southern nations, as now Britain would be unable to supply them with goods, and they would be forced to negotiate with Spanish officials again (Duval, 2015).

As in previous conflicts, Americans and Europeans saw native allies as merely pieces on a chessboard, and it would seem, expendable pieces. British negotiators spent little time worrying about the plight of the Shawnees, or the Chickamaugas, or the Mohawks. The war was terribly expensive, and also the sixth costly, fatiguing conflict they had fought against either Spain or France (or sometimes both) in less than a century. They wanted to get out of the war before they lost still more territory. Indeed, when Spain and France had signed their alliance against Britain in 1779, Spain made it quite clear that they would not stop fighting until they had reclaimed the island of Gibraltar, the gateway to the Mediterranean, from Britain. Further, when Lord North's ministry, which had led the effort to suppress the rebellion, fell, their successors hoped to make nice with the U.S. as a potential counterweight to Spain in the Americas. For a time, Britain felt generosity towards the victorious rebels was the prudent gesture. Not only did they recognize American independence, but also ceded the King's claims to the land south of Canada, east of the Mississippi, and north of Florida, the latter of which would soon be formally Spanish again (Ward, 1995).

Shrewd native leaders became increasingly concerned in 1782 and into 1783. While they were at least holding their own in defending their lands, and in some cases perhaps gaining ground, British directives to stand down at what seemed the precipice of victory gave them rational concern. This might have been somewhat assuaged had any Indian leaders been a part of the peace process, but they were not. In the end, American negotiators double-crossed their French allies – the 1778 treaty had specifically barred either nation from making a separate peace agreement with Britain – and the British did the same with their native allies. Or as one Cherokee chief ruefully noted, "You have given away our lands at a rum drinking" (Calloway, 2007:169).

3 Confederations

Americans rejoiced upon learning of the Definitive Treaty of Peace, what would later be known as the Peace of Paris, in 1783. In addition to recognizing them as an independent nation, Britain had made a seemingly generous cession of territory. All the lands east of the Mississippi River (excepting Florida, which would soon be transferred back to Spain), and south of Canada, now, the treaty stated, belonged to the U.S. Thus, so many of Britain's most irksome acts, including the Proclamation of 1763, banning settlement west of the Appalachians, and the Quebec Act of 1774, which had extended the province of Quebec (and its newly tolerated Catholicism) to the Ohio River, were now null and void. Americans assumed they had carte blanche to lay claim to all the lands currently occupied by Indians east of the Mississippi, and proceeded to act accordingly. The reality, of course, proved far more complex.

As Colin Calloway has noted, the treaty of 1783 was the "peace that brought no peace." Perhaps because Indians had been excluded from the discussion, the treaty did not address backcountry feuds and vendettas between Indians and whites. (It also did little to settle disputes between backcountry whites, for that matter.) Issues of blood vengeance, horse thefts, kidnappings, and extensive property damage had been left unresolved. Little wonder, then, that the killing continued. Worse still for Indians, American soldiers and militia who had taken part in campaigns in native territory returned home with stories of the tremendous potential of Indian lands. At a time when more than ninety percent of Americans were farmers of one sort or another, the huge yields provided by Indian women's agriculture gave ample evidence of the land's utility, even as it was being put to the torch (Calloway, 1995:272).

While British negotiators had agreed to exceedingly generous terms with the U.S. in an ill-advised stab at normalizing relations with their American cousins, British agents and soldiers still in North America viewed the treaty with great alarm. They recognized immediately that the King's Indian children had been betrayed, and would be furious when they learned of the cession of their lands. The King's allies had emerged from the war itself largely unconquered, and further had in no way been consulted for, or included in, the peace negotiations. British troops feared that, upon learning of this betrayal, incensed warriors would fall upon their isolated, undermanned outposts and slaughter them, in a fearful sequel to Pontiac's War. Understandably, if not realistically, they tried to keep the terms from Indians. Meanwhile, American authorities went out of their way to gleefully broadcast them to Native Americans.

In order to contain Indians' fury, British soldiers and agents on the ground resorted to pragmatic self-preservation. As their former allies first seethed, then demanded aid in the form of weapons and supplies, British agents and forts handed them over. Despite the financial peril of the Treasury and a great desire to cut costs, they did not repeat Jeffery Amherst's mistake of penny-wise parsimony with Native Americans. No expenditure of gifts could cost as much as a disastrous war on the frontier. The Fort Stanwix Treaty line of 1768 was now touted as a protection for Ohio Indians' lands, north of the river at least. British officers and agents now felt that if they did not endorse pan-Indian efforts to protect native territory from the Americans, angry Indians would destroy them (Willig, 2008; Owens, 2015).

Nor would British troops abandon their western forts that now lay within the borders of the U.S. The official position was that they had no obligation to do so until the Americans financially compensated the Loyalists who had been ruined during the war – and it was increasingly obvious the Congress had little stomach, power, or cash for such a venture. Internal British documents make it quite clear that the primary reason, aside from a hope of maintaining the fur trade in the heart of America, was the fear that evacuating troops would fall to native vengeance. Americans, meanwhile, would spend the next two centuries assuming that British agents (or sometimes Spanish or even French ones) went out of their way to stir up Indian resistance to American expansion. They would not consider that their own actions largely fueled Indian anger. They could not comprehend that the King's aid to Indians arose from Indians' insistence, and not British perfidy (Willig, 2008).

In September 1783, Indian agent Alexander McKee addressed a council of Hurons, Shawnees, Delawares, Mingoes, as well as Cherokees and Creeks, at Lower Sandusky in Michigan. He offered that he could not "harbor an Idea that the United States will act so unjustly or Impolitically as to endeavor to deprive you of any part of your Country under the pretence of having conquered it." The King, he offered still valued his native children, but that they should accept their "losses with manly forgiving and forgetting" with an eye toward a hopeful and peaceful future. It is most unlikely that either McKee or translator Simon Girty actually believed those words. But for the moment, at least, they followed orders (Owens, 2015:88).

At the same time, both the states and the Congress made few attempts to calm Indians, regardless of their stance during the war. As the Oneidas and Tuscaroras would soon learn, neither the state of New York nor the Congress chose to remember their valuable sacrifices to the American war effort. Indeed, Americans adopted the *conquest* theory, which assumed that all Indians had been defeated during the war and therefore forfeited their lands, despite their having no representatives at the Paris negotiations. Officials from both Albany and Philadelphia insisted that the Iroquois – even their recent allies the Oneidas and Tuscaroras – sign over lands for no compensation. While the Treaty of Fort Stanwix of 1768 paid the Iroquois for land to which they had little claim, the Treaty of Fort Stanwix of 1784 took Ohio country lands from them for nothing. Once again, the Ohio Valley peoples who actually lived there were excluded.

The U.S. did invite Ohio Valley tribes to treaty councils at Fort McIntosh (PA), in 1785, and Fort Finney (OH), in 1786. As at Stanwix, the commissioners demanded large, uncompensated cessions of Indian land, this time from natives who actually lived in the region. The commissioners, including Revolutionary War hero George Rogers Clark of Virginia, and General Richard Butler of Pennsylvania – the latter had previously been known for his amicable relations with the Shawnees – bullied the Ohio tribes who attended, threatening to unleash the Army against their villages if they did not consent. While they did participate in some native ceremonies, the American commissioners saw little need to be diplomatic. Clark, who always maintained that Indians understood only force, at one point tossed a Shawnee peace belt of white wampum down and ground it under his heel – an extraordinarily indecorous act. While some chiefs did mark the treaties, many Ohio Indians, especially Shawnees, whose land had been primary targets of the cessions, considered them unjust and invalid. The Shawnees had largely boycotted the Fort McIntosh council, but were threatened with destruction if they did not attend at Fort Finney. They would spend much of the next decade making their displeasure known (Calloway, 1995).

Americans looked forward to the 1780s as an era of easy expansion west of the Appalachians, but native resistance, with arms from British and Spanish officials, would stiffen. Natives, Britons, and Spaniards would all seek to utilize pan-Indian alliances to slow, and hopefully stop, American encroachment. In time, increasing Indian unity would help demonstrate the need for American unity as well.

Patriotic Paternalism

Why did Americans pursue Indian lands so relentlessly? As is often the case, the answer takes several parts, interwoven and reinforcing each other. Like European invaders before them, Americans saw land acquisition as the most direct route to financial gain, *real estate*, as it were. Along with this, we can see a similar level of assumed *racial* superiority, and ethnocentrism – the assumption that one's culture is manifestly better than others. Indians could be rather ethnocentric themselves, and by the mid-eighteenth century their views of race were taking a parallel course to those of whites. But they did not have the population or manufacturing capacity, nor the hierarchical political structures, to implement them to the same degree. Americans had all of the motivations for taking Indian lands that Europeans did, and more.

To these motives Americans added what would later be called a sense of their own exceptionalism, the idea that the United States had been chosen by God to demonstrate the viability, even superiority, of a republic. America's victory over the British Empire in the Revolution had been so inconceivable, many Americans now believed, that only divine intervention could have led them to independence. As such, failure of the republic would constitute an insufferable insult to the Almighty. Therefore, the United States must prevail, and thrive. To do so required a continual expansion of territory, to employ and feed the fruitful multiplication of God's chosen nation. That these notions were self-serving and quite absurd received little attention. While the phrase "Manifest Destiny" would not be coined until 1845, white Americans had been practicing the concept from the beginning.

Even children of the Enlightenment, like Thomas Jefferson, pursued these goals for similar, if secular, reasons. The American aristocracy, run exclusively by white men, viewed the world through the lens of *paternalism*. The simplest definition of paternalism is "one group of adults treating another group of adults like children, allegedly for the latter's benefit." When it came to Indians, Africans, and women, American elites would dominate and manipulate them for their own gain, while maintaining that it was all for the best. Paternalism proved highly effective in masking perhaps the greatest motivator of them all; greed.

During the war, and for decades after, American propaganda conflated British soldiers and their Indian allies, branding both as "savages." Doing so had presented the dual benefits of painting America's enemies as less than truly human, and also justifying any potentially questionable acts Americans undertook to combat these foes. By seeing Indians as sub-humans, they could heap any negative imagery of North American life – and the acquisition of their growing empire – onto Indians, while keeping the wholesome and noble characteristics for themselves. As the stereotype of brutal, barbarous Indians became more uniform, it mattered little to Americans in the immediate postwar years just whom Indians had sided with during the war; their lands would now be taken (Silver, 2007).

American elites saw themselves as facing a conundrum by the late eighteenth century. They wanted Indians' lands, which would be sold to their countrymen, bringing in desperately needed cash to the Treasury of the indebted nation, while providing farmland for the working and middling classes. Simultaneously, for the nation's honor, they did not want to be seen as neo-Conquistadors. So, while they might bluff and try to bully Indians off their lands, they needed to see themselves as benefactors, bringing "civilization," as they defined it, to peoples who, they assumed, desperately needed and wanted it. While Jeffersonians would excel in this form of paternalism in the early nineteenth century, its roots lay in the immediate post-Revolutionary era.

In 1785, the Congress passed the Land Ordinance, an optimistic piece of legislation outlining how the land north of the Ohio River, presumably now controlled by the United States, would be surveyed and sold to the American public. Borrowing an idea from Thomas Jefferson, the territory would be marked off in a regular grid pattern of square-mile (640-acre) patches – which would allow for far more precise sales and ownership. This would prove a significant improvement over the old European system of surveying by "metes and bounds," marking off portions of land based not on mathematics, but by following natural features, like creeks, tree lines, and the like (Linklater, 2002). One can observe the effects of this even today when flying between the East Coast and the Midwest. From above, one sees the crazy quilt, seemingly random geographic features of the former, contrasted with the right angles of roads and sections of the latter. This even plays out in the plotting of city streets. While Midwestern and Western cities tend to be laid out in grids with right angles, a street map of Boston bears a striking resemblance to late-stage mitosis.

These more precise plots of land were to be auctioned off for a minimum of $1 per acre, at a minimum of one square-mile at a time. Initially, the buyer had to pay in cash – $640 minimum. This was deliberately pricey. Given the fertility of the soil and salubrious climate in the region, Congress feared that feckless whites would drift in and "live like Indians," by hunting. As the Congress hoped to discourage ne'er do wells who would not *improve* the land, that is, cut down trees, plow fields and build fences, they made it an expensive investment, which hopefully only the thrifty and hard-working would undertake (Onuf, 2019).

The law saw American settlement of the Ohio Country as a fait accompli. In 1787, in one of the last significant acts of the pre-Federal government, Congress passed the Northwest Ordinance. Also concerning the land northwest of the Ohio River, the Ordinance of 1787 provided a template for how that land would eventually become between 3 and 5 states that would join the Union as coequals, after passing through several stages as territories. That in and of itself was something of a radical act, as existing states of the world tended to colonize, rather than dilute their own power by allowing others to join their union. This ordinance also featured some very progressive measures, including support for public education, a ban on (or at least discouragement of) slavery,[1] and a pledge to show "the utmost good faith" toward the Indians of the region (www.ourdocuments.gov). Americans now formally recognized that Indians had rights to their lands, and deserved financial compensation for yielding them. Yet in the same sentence, Congress also reserved the right to authorize righteous wars against those same Indians, should the need arise. The *need* would arise when said Indians declined to sell their land (Onuf, 2019).

Though both remarkable pieces of legislation, the Land Ordinance and the Northwest Ordinance were in practice unenforceable under the old Congress. Examples of a great post-Revolutionary enthusiasm, at once myopic and grandiose, they would influence American negotiations with Indians in the Ohio Country for years. Even when the United States began to see the true situation more clearly, the clumsy steps toward empire in the early 1780s would continue to color the Ohio lands with blood. Without the power to tax, or an executive branch to lead, potential settlers in the Ohio Valley were largely on their own.

Congress could call upon the Secretary of War, Revolutionary War veteran and George Washington confidante Henry Knox, to direct Indian affairs. The fact that Indian affairs would be led by the War Department (for decades) speaks volumes. But with such a weak, impoverished government, Knox, who would later hold the same position in the Federal government, advised caution, and avoidance of war if at all possible. For reasons of honor as well as practicality, Knox did not wish to be seen as an heir to Cortez and Pizarro. It was just as well, given that the entire U.S. Army in the late 1780s numbered less than a thousand men, who rarely received pay or supplies on time (White, 1991; Ward, 1995).

On paper, all was settled and proceeding nicely. On the ground, chaos reigned. The Shawnees took great exception to the treaties of Fort McIntosh and Fort Finney. While older civil chiefs tended to urge caution and restraint, this cost them influence with younger warriors, who felt they had far more to lose by ceding hunting lands. Now encouraged by

---

1 Though Article VI stated, "There shall be neither slavery nor involuntary servitude in the said territory," all appointed governors in the region chose to interpret that as non-retroactive. The stated reason being that they did not want to offend the pre-existing settlers in the region, primarily French, by emancipating the slaves they were already holding. Later territorial governors, like Indiana Territory's William Henry Harrison, not only lobbied extensively to have Article VI repealed, but sought work arounds, like *indenture* laws that permitted the dubious practice of converting black slaves into "indentured servants," whose term of indenture in some cases ran for 90 years or more.

British Indian agents like Matthew Elliott and Alexander McKee, they sought to forcefully resist white encroachments. As raids on Kentucky settlements increased, so did calls for retaliation.

Rhetorically, the American government would insist on conducting diplomacy with Indians on the level of a tribe/nation. Doing so offered considerable advantages to the U.S., like simplicity/finality of agreements. It drastically oversimplified how native politics actually worked (and in many ways still works). Further, as Richard White demonstrated, in the wake of the American Revolution, little if anything got done on a *tribal* level. Towns and villages were increasingly the only political units that really mattered to Indians. The post-Revolutionary Shawnees provide a good example (White, 1991).

In October of 1786, the Shawnee town of Maquachack was laboring to convince their fellow Shawnees to cease attacking Americans. Prior to colonization, and into the eighteenth century, the Shawnees had been organized into five divisions, each of which was at least semiautonomous. The Chillicothe and Thawagila divisions had supplied principal civil chiefs for the nation. The Piquas maintained spiritual/religious rituals. The Makujay/Maquachacks were known for producing healers, and the Kispokos tended to supply the war chiefs, including the principal war chief for the nation. Puckesinwa, the father of Tecumseh who died at Point Pleasant, was a Kispoko. But the traditional roles for these divisions took a beating in the upheaval of the Revolution, and increasingly individual towns carried out their own policies (Edmunds, 1983).

In 1786, as the people of Maquachak counseled peace with the Americans, they themselves were attacked by almost 800 Kentuckians led by Benjamin Logan. These Shawnees flew an American flag over their town, and their elderly leader, Chief Moluntha, had long called for peace. He had signed the humiliating treaty of Fort Finney, and was holding his copy when the Kentuckians rode up to him. Among them was Hugh McGary, the man whose stupidity had led the Kentuckians into disaster at Blue Licks four years earlier (Calloway, 1995).

McGary asked the aged Moluntha if he had fought at Blue Licks. Apparently not understanding the question, Moluntha, who would already have been at least eighty years old in 1782, smiled and nodded yes. Though Logan had directed that any Shawnees who surrendered should be spared, McGary tomahawked the elderly unarmed prisoner to death. McGary was actually court martialed for the murder, but his only punishment was to be suspended from duty for a year (Calloway, 1995).

As with Cornstalk's murder, Moluntha's death sent a clear signal to the Shawnees and other Ohio Valley Indians –the Americans could not be trusted, and their treaties meant nothing. Similarly, between that realization, and a simple desire to avenge such a horrific crime, it spurred many Shawnees to redouble their resistance to white encroachment. They would have ample opportunity to do so. Between 1775 and 1790, tens of thousands of whites poured into southern Ohio, taking Shawnee farmland and killing much needed game animals (Schmidt, 2014).

White settlement in the Ohio Valley often took the form of quasi-military colonies, populated by former soldiers or militia from the Revolutionary War. Some, like Clark's Grant, in what would become southern Indiana, were grants of land given as payment for wartime services, in that case, veterans of George Rogers Clark's campaigns. But others were land speculation ventures, like the Ohio Land Company, founded by Continental Army officer Rufus Putnam and friends. Having old soldiers, who could presumably organize their own defense, lead colonization efforts, made some sense. The Ohio Company established Marietta in southeastern Ohio, the first real American settlement north of the river (Ward, 1995).

By the late 1780s and early 1790s, however, it became quite obvious that these settler colonies were tenuous at best, and would need considerable support from the national level if they were to survive. In 1787–1788, when the east coast merchants and planters who called themselves Federalists advocated adopting the Constitution and creating a stronger national government, which could raise taxes and an army, they found allies among the settlers of Kentucky and southern Ohio. While no fans of taxation, they desperately wanted a Federal army.

Creeks, Cherokees, and Southerners

To the south, the conflict between whites and the Creeks and Cherokees continued.

Between November 1785 and January 1786, American commissioners, including North Carolina's Benjamin Hawkins and South Carolina's Andrew Pickens, conducted treaties with the Choctaws, Cherokees, and Chickasaws. While these treaties ceded land to the U.S. – and did not pay the tribes for it – they also promised to keep the peace, prevent white settlers from trespassing in Indian territory, and to punish criminals while restraining violent personal retaliation. As became commonplace, Americans enforced the land cessions, but largely failed to deliver on their own obligations, much to the commissioners' chagrin. Worse still, the Creeks, the largest of the Southern nations, had not been a party to these councils. The skirmishes between them and whites in Georgia would continue well into the 1790s (Wright, 1986).

Andrew Pickens, a bona fide Revolutionary War hero of South Carolina, had distinguished himself as a fierce fighter against both Indians and Redcoats. The Cherokees dubbed him *Skiagusta*, or Warrior, after he had defeated them in brutal combat. Yet in April of 1784, even Pickens acknowledged that one of the primary causes of friction with the Indians was that "many disorderly persons goes up amongst the Indians [in this case the Cherokees] and Creates uneasiness amongst them." As British officials had before him, Pickens hoped the Congress would regulate the Indian trade, which would "graitly [sic] add to the security and safety of the Fronteers [sic] of this State." The next month he reiterated the problem of white encroachment, now noting that it "much Dissatisfied" the Creeks, Chickasaws, and Cherokees, who were frequently joined by emissaries from the Choctaws and the "Northward Indians" [in this case the Ohio tribes], offering "their assistance to Defend their just Rights." Pickens concluded that only by Congress' setting rigid boundaries and halting such unlawful incursions on Indian land, could they hope to "prevent Mischief." Congress did appoint an agent, but had little power to do much else, and the situation only worsened (Owens, 2015:90–91; Hatley, 1993).

The Creeks ended the Revolution with most of their lands intact, but the state of Georgia would soon demand the territory "between the Oconee and Ocmulgee rivers as war damages." (A large swath of central Georgia, the area now includes the city of Macon, and much of the Interstate 16 corridor. In the eighteenth century, it was a valuable Creek hunting ground.) A few Creek chiefs did agree to this at the Treaty of Augusta in November 1783, but other Creek leaders denounced the cession. While the Creeks did not have a principal chief – language and custom linked the Upper and Lower Creeks far more than any political affiliation – by the 1780s one Upper Creek, Alexander McGillivray, had become increasingly influential. As a counterweight, he and other Creek chiefs signed a treaty at Pensacola, Florida, in 1784, placing the Creeks under the protection of the Spanish (Calloway, 1995:284).

McGillivray, the son of a Scottish trader and white captive adopted by the Creeks, had an English-style education, but apparently mastered little of the Muskogee language, and less of the arts of war. However, in the eighteenth century, Creeks did not adhere to a Euro-American understanding of *race*. McGillivray's mother had been adopted into the powerful Wind Clan, and that helped give him considerable influence. The fact that he was also brilliant and an ambitious Creek nationalist, bent on Muskogee independence, led to his holding the position of "Beloved Man" – an appointee to lead negotiations – and his words carried considerable weight, even if they were often in English. Indeed, his fluency with the written word allowed him to communicate easily with American officials, but sometimes directly to the public through letters to various newspaper editors (Caughey, 1959). [**See Docs. 9–11**]

Figure 3.1 William Augustus Bowles (1763–1805). A Loyalist soldier from Maryland, Bowles married a Creek woman and later styled himself as "Director General" of the Creek Nation and attempted to organize pan-Indian resistance to American expansion.

McGillivray would not be the only man trying to bring about a Creek-centered pan-Indian resistance to the Americans. An American Tory from Maryland named William Augustus Bowles had served as a Redcoat officer during the Revolution. He married first a Cherokee woman, and later a Creek, and would eventually call himself "Director General of the Creek Nation," a title he had invented. He would ludicrously claim to hold sway over tens of thousands of (sometimes nonexistent) Indian warriors, Creeks, Cherokees, Chickasaws and Choctaws, for a time bamboozling even some highly placed British officials. Bowles and McGillivray, initially allies as Tories with strong ties to Indian Country, soon became rivals. Bowles proved equally adept at lying to British officials and alarming American ones with his stated efforts to establish a pan-Indian union to keep the American republic in check. But what would prove his downfall was his willingness to wantonly antagonize Spanish authorities in Florida (Owens, 2015; Wright, 1967).

As a Tory during the Revolution, Bowles had fought against Spanish efforts to take over the Gulf Coast. With the advent of peace, pragmatists like McGillivray made nice with their former antagonists. Bowles did not. When Spain realized they could not possibly supply all the Indian trade goods demanded in the American Southeast, they allowed a Scottish firm, Panton, Leslie, & Co., to meet that need. McGillivray managed to make himself a silent partner in the company, increasing his influence among the Creeks substantially. Bowles, meanwhile, tried to set up a competing interest, and touted his alleged authorization from the British government. For Spanish officials, though, the last straw was when he led a raid on the Panton, Leslie & Co. storehouse in Pensacola, Florida. They placed a substantial bounty on his head, and when some Creeks turned on him to collect it in 1792, he was whisked away to a Spanish prison overseas, and it was presumed he would die there (Owens, 2015; Din, 2012).

It proves a fair question as to who created the most headaches for the American government in this era: Indian warriors, or frontier whites, both of whom showed little interest in being governed by the Congress in Philadelphia. One of the most dangerous irritants came from rebellious North Carolinians, who protested their state's cession of western lands – what would become Tennessee – to the national government in 1784. These frontiersmen formed their own extra-legal republic, named Franklin, out of what would eventually be the twelve eastern counties of Tennessee. They elected John Sevier, a hero of the Battle of Kings Mountain (1780), wherein frontier militia had slaughtered their Tory counterparts, and leader of multiple punitive campaigns against the Cherokees, as their governor, and hoped to become a state of the Union (Barksdale, 2009).

The Franklinites immediately quarreled with the Cherokees, from whose hunting grounds (confirmed to the Cherokees by the 1785 Treaty of Hopewell) their state had been carved, and some called for the immediate slaughter of the Cherokees. Though the quasi-republic did negotiate treaties with some Cherokee leaders, the Lower Cherokees/Chickamaugas, and their militant chief Dragging Canoe, refused to recognize them. The Lower Cherokees and Sevier's people clashed violently and repeatedly.

Joseph Martin, the U.S. agent to the Cherokees, noted in September of 1785 that it had been his worst summer ever professionally. The Cherokees' blood boiled partly because of the encroachment of the Franklinites, but also because of the martial talks from Spanish authorities and Ohio Indians. Four Wyandot chiefs (from the upper Ohio Country) were acting as emissaries to the Chickamaugas, who needed little encouragement to resist invading settlers. Old Tassel, the respected Cherokee chief from the town of Chota, diplomatically asked the governors of North Carolina and Virginia for help as the rapidly encroaching Franklinites insisted they had purchased the land near the French Broad and Nolichucky Rivers (modern Knoxville). Franklin governor John Sevier conducted this "Treaty of Dumplin Creek," which most Cherokees rightly refused to acknowledge. "We hope our Elder Brother will not agree to it," Old Tassel begged, knowing that neither he nor the state authorities could restrain their angry young men in such times (Owens, 2015:91; Nichols, 2008).

As Franklinites flooded into the disputed territory, they killed more Cherokees. In the spring of 1786, warriors responded by raiding some of the farms in the Holston River Valley, taking 15 scalps. This led to more retaliatory campaigns, including 250 militia under Alexander Outlaw and (future U.S. senator) William Cocke. The invaders burned down the town of Coyatee, and extorted still more land cessions from Old Tassel and Hanging Maw (Nichols, 2008).

Though Sevier's campaigns against the Cherokees would later bring condemnation from government officials at the highest levels – George Washington in particular found Sevier to be an unholy hybrid of rube and thug – most of his white neighbors loved him for it. His reputation as an "Indian fighter" would be key to his political career. Franklinites also fought skirmishes with the legitimate government of North Carolina, who eventually imposed their will upon the breakaway state, but not before a desperate Sevier had sought Spanish aid in fighting off Chickamauga and Chickasaw attacks (Finger, 2001).

It would not be the last instance of "Spanish Intrigue" in the region, as western settlers in Kentucky, Tennessee, and elsewhere would repeatedly seek (at least) material aid from Spanish Florida to ward off Indian attacks. Indeed, Tennessee's Mero District took its name from a poorly spelled tribute to the Spanish governor of Florida, Esteban Miro. They did so because the national government, both before and after 1788, often seemed unequal to the task. Spanish policy, meanwhile, swung wildly in the 1780s and early 1790s, from arming native warriors and urging them to drive out American interlopers, to trying to urge caution and restraint, depending on which strategy seemed best to protect Spain's tenuous grasp over the American Southeast (Finger, 2001).

Elusive Peace on the Frontier

With the adoption of the Constitution in 1788, the new Federal government could begin the arduous task of bringing order and stability to the western territories. As with any start-up, there would be numerous problems along the way. President George Washington's administration faced tremendous difficulty in containing white settler aggressions and Indian reprisals. Or, as historian David Nichols notes, by the late 1780s, "gunfire had become the dominant form of communication in the region" (Nichols, 2008:76).

Not that it was the only form of communication. A surprising number of written – if not cordial – communiques did actually circulate between Indians and whites. In addition to McGillivray's official letters to government officers, he sometimes received written notes and threats from Georgians. [See Doc. 11] The escalating violence made it that much more difficult for peace-minded leaders, native and American, to contain the bloodshed. Though by now, statistically, settlers killed far more Indians than the reverse, American officials did not depend on Indian approval to keep their positions. Likewise, native chiefs could not simply ignore the anger of their people, particularly when it was a matter of blood vengeance.

The fact that neither frontier whites nor Indian warriors were particular about *who* paid the toll for a killing greatly exacerbated the situation. Both sides had long practiced a basic *tribalism* when it came to blood revenge, and as more natives adopted a parallel, racialized mindset to the struggle for land and resources, it became all the easier to simply strike out at a "white" or an "Indian," rather than a specific perpetrator. As time demonstrated that Federal authorities could not live up to their commitments to punish whites who murdered Indians, and were only somewhat better at compelling Indians to hand over the killers among their villages, it undermined the government's prestige among all. Though the Constitution gave the national government a monopoly on Indian affairs, it would take years – and countless deaths – before they could even begin to assert that prerogative (White, 1991). Villagers, Indian and white, continued to kill, kidnap, and seek revenge against each other. [See Doc. 12]

In late June of 1788, John Sevier led another Franklinite campaign against the Cherokees, again without any authority from the national government. While this raid did target the Chickamaugas, who were actively engaged in combat with Franklin, it drove some of them to shelter with the Overhill Cherokees, putting economic strain on them, and possibly swaying some of the Overhills to join the militants. Despite such travesties, reported Superintendent to the Creek Nation Richard Winn, more than thirty Cherokee towns still wished to be at peace with the U.S. But that could of course change in an instant.

A series of white murders of Cherokees, including leading Overhill advocates of peace like Old Tassel and Abraham, brought many more Cherokees into the war. [See Doc. 13] When the family of John Kirk, Jr., died in a Chickamauga raid led by a warrior known as Slim Tom, the people of Franklin launched a series of indiscriminate retaliatory attacks. The younger Kirk and a party entered the Overhill town of Settico under a flag of truce, and then murdered Old Tassel, Abraham, and several other elders in their townhouse. When Overhill warriors responded by killing a settler family, John Sevier and the appropriately named Alexander Outlaw also led attacks against Overhill towns. This further pushed peace advocates, like Overhill chief Little Turkey, to call for revenge. He reportedly endorsed and circulated a bloody-minded talk from the Ohio Confederacy, and called for them and the Chickamaugas to help strike back at the Americans. Cherokee war parties now sometimes numbered into the hundreds, and had both Chickamauga and Overhill members. As Tyler Boulware notes, "Fighting in the winter of 1788–89, in fact, proved to be the bloodiest and most unified engagements for the Cherokees of the entire war" (Boulware, 2011:165).

The tit for tat of blood revenge was employed by both settlers and Indians, though by the late eighteenth century the Indians were definitely losing larger and larger proportions of their already smaller populations. Yet Americans, using their near monopoly of print media, repeatedly painted themselves as the underdogs, and the unoffending victims of vicious warfare. It was estimated that between 1783 and 1790, 1,500 Kentuckians died at the hands of Indians, and perhaps 20,000 horses were stolen in the same time frame (Nichols, 2008). Those accounts may well have been accurate. They do not mention, however, that native losses in those years (not to mention the previous century and a half) dwarfed them considerably.

American commissioners, charged with negotiating peace with the Southern nations, found themselves in a difficult spot. While their loyalty clearly lay with the United States, they knew full well that their government was either not able or not willing to live up to its end of the bargain. Their correspondence with McGillivray, for example – the Beloved Man did not skip opportunities to point out Americans' wrongs to his people – became increasingly tense and defensive. In fairness, McGillivray's followers had not been idle, either. Creek warriors did a brisk business in stealing and selling settlers' horses – sometimes other settlers served as the buyers, and killings did continue.

In 1790, as the ugliness deepened across the Ohio Valley, the Chickamaugas raided the Tennessee settlements, and the Creeks continued to battle Georgia's expansionists. The Washington administration saw making peace with at least some of the Southern nations as imperative to avoiding a disastrous "general Indian war." The numerous Creeks, with the wily but pragmatic McGillivray, seemed a logical, even crucial, choice for negotiations. Secretary of War Knox estimated that the Creek Nation, composed of the Upper Creeks in sixty towns along the Alabama River, and forty towns of Lower Creeks along the Apalachicola River, combined, could field about 6,000 warriors. Even as the war accelerated north of the Ohio, taking the Creeks out of the pan-Indian equation would be a priority. That priority had its own difficulties. While each town had its respective chief, Knox noted that the Creeks were clearly under McGillivray's influence (Schmidt, 2014).

Knowing that McGillivray's Georgia Loyalist father had lost his entire estate to Patriots during the Revolution, Knox inferred correctly that Alexander harbored a serious grudge against Georgia, and not entirely without merit. In reviewing a series of treaties Georgia had conducted with the Creeks – one of the benefits of the Constitution was that it gave the Federal government a monopoly on Indian treaties, theoretically rationalizing the process – he noted that one such treaty had included representatives from only two of the one hundred Creek towns. Knox realized that Georgia had been behaving badly, and saw an opportunity for the Federal government to intervene for the greater good, in this case defined as keeping both costs and the chance of a great Indian war down (Caughey, 1959; Ethridge, 2003).

After an attempted treaty at Rock Landing in Georgia in the fall of 1789 failed miserably, Knox wisely decided that holding a conference with the Creeks anywhere near Georgia (or Georgians) would be disastrous. North Carolina's senator Benjamin Hawkins, probably the foremost expert on the Southern Indians in government, suggested having a private conference with the Creeks in New York City, then the seat of the Federal government. By inviting McGillivray and the Creeks to New York, the administration could not only control the setting and tone of the conference, but hopefully awe the Creeks with the majesty (such as it was) of the nation's capital (Nichols, 2008).

President Washington did not leap blindly into his meeting with the Creeks. At Knox's suggestion, he had sent three companies of soldiers from the Ohio, where they were much needed, to the Oconee River, where they might be deployed against the Creeks if necessary. Secretary Knox also began seriously considering recruiting native allies, especially the Chickasaws. Chief Piomingo's warriors had practically begged for some type of military alliance with the United States since the early 1780s, and the resumption of the Creek war against the fierce but heavily outnumbered Chickasaws in 1789 only deepened that need (Owens, 2015; Atkinson, 2004).

In New York, McGillivray spent considerable time with Henry Knox, and was almost constantly escorted by American officers in an attempt to keep him away from British or Spanish agents. McGillivray did manage to meet with foreign officers, and skillfully parlayed that into an increase in American generosity toward himself. McGillivray and the other Creeks did agree to cede lands that Georgia already occupied – for annual payments, or annuities, of course – but maintained sovereignty over any lands that were not already part of the United States. In effect, this put considerable weight upon the extent of "West Florida" – southern Mississippi and Alabama – the boundary of which Spain and the United States disputed (Caughey, 1959).

Georgia, meanwhile, came out feeling like a loser, having wanted further cessions of Creek hunting lands along the Altamaha River, and would protest the published version of the treaty. Additionally, McGillivray had managed to secure a number of private goodies for himself, including a secret provision that gave him a brigadier general's commission in the U.S. Army. Why would anyone want to be a "secret" general? The commission carried a $1200 annual salary, and in McGillivray's case, presumably entailed doing very little, other than occasionally corresponding with the Americans. If Georgians had known about that, they would have been apoplectic. Meanwhile, Spanish authorities railed against the treaty, and against McGillivray, but they also raised his (Spanish) salary from $600 to $2,000 annually, hoping to keep him in their interest (Caughey, 1959; Weber, 1992).

Probably without realizing it, the Washington administration borrowed heavily from the playbook of their British predecessors, like Lord Dunmore. That is, they tried to humor larger, more powerful Southern Indian nations, in this case the Creeks, while risking and even prosecuting war with the smaller Ohio Valley tribes. Given the administration's limited financial resources, the strategy had its advantages.

In July of 1790, Congress passed the Trade and Intercourse Act, which spelled out some of the particulars of the Federal government's monopoly on Indian affairs. Specifically, it required anyone who wished to trade with Indians in the bounds of the United States to receive a license from the government. In addition to trying to address the old problem of unscrupulous traders infuriating Indians – in practice the vetting of Indian traders would not be as rigorous as originally hoped – the law aimed to prevent foreign, especially British, traders from "influencing" Indians. This reflected the long-standing belief that natives resisted American encroachments only when led astray by foreign agents. The law also established a system of trading houses, or factories as they were then called, to be overseen by a government superintendent. Unlike Jeffery Amherst, Congress did not seek to deny trade goods, even weapons, to Indians, but wanted some control over the supply. It also tacitly acknowledged that providing goods to Indians was necessary for maintaining peace. It was understood that the trading houses would likely not be directly profitable, but were considered a worthwhile investment if they could help prevent costly wars with native peoples (Nichols, 2016; Prucha, 1962).

The law also promised that whites who committed crimes against Indians were to be taken and prosecuted the same as if the victims were white – a high-minded goal that would almost never be reached. It denied the legitimacy of Indian land sales to any individual or group not specifically authorized by the government – an attempt to avoid the confusion of groups like Richard Henderson's Transylvania Company from the late colonial period. As with the old Congress' Land Ordinance (1785) and Northwest Ordinance (1787), the Trade and Intercourse Act contained a number of rational, progressive ideals. Also like those laws, it proved largely, even comically, unenforceable at the time of its passage.

As the summer of 1790 drew to a close, both Knox and Washington could feel some much-needed relief and satisfaction in the realm of Indian affairs. The treaty with the Creeks had, they assumed, taken the most dangerous of all the Southern nations out of a possible pan-Indian confederation, and done so bloodlessly. As Washington wrote to his old comrade, the Marquis de Lafayette – known for his sincere friendship with his Indian allies during the Revolution – that as long as Washington had any connection with the federal government, "the *basis* of our proceedings with the Indian Nations has been, and shall be *justice*." The next five years would see Washington's government stretch the definition of that word to its breaking point (Owens, 2015:106).

4 Dueling Unions

"Between October 1790 and November 1791, the United States waged two major offensives against the Indian confederacy north of the Ohio River. The first, led by General Josiah Harmar, resulted in 183 Americans killed and Harmar's eventual acquittal in a court martial. *It was by far the more successful of the two campaigns.*" Though the Northwest Ordinance had pledged the United States to benevolent treatment of the Indians north of the Ohio, it also reserved the right for Congress to authorize "just wars" against them. When the Ohio country's natives declined to sell their land to the U.S., Congress deemed it just to chastise them militarily and force them to attend a treaty council. In order to avoid looking like sixteenth-century Conquistadors while taking away Indian lands, the Americans (paradoxically) needed to smite those peoples who dared resist them (Owens, 2015:107).

Harmar's Campaign

In October of 1790, an American army led by Revolutionary War veteran Josiah Harmar sought to bring the Northwest Confederacy of Indians to heel. Not quite thirty-seven, Harmar commanded U.S. troops at Fort McIntosh, and so seemed an obvious choice to lead the campaign. But he also had a reputation for drinking – even by lax eighteenth-century standards. Worse, while a combat veteran, he had little experience against Indians and held them in contempt as warriors. As ordered, Harmar marched 1,300 militia and 350 regular troops deep into the territory of the Twightwee, or Miami, Indians. The Miamis and the Eel River war chief Little Turtle had become prominent members of the Northwest Confederacy, and a "punitive" expedition against them was intended to bring the confederates to their senses. To avoid a second war breaking out, American officials sent word to the British in Detroit, specifically stating that the campaign was against hostile Indians, not British troops in the region. The British politely responded that they would be unconcerned in that event, and then promptly warned their Indian allies that an invasion was coming (Calloway, 2014).

A separate American force under Major John Hamtramck, with 300 regulars and 300 militia, also invaded Miami territory, this time from the west. Hamtramck's force came to an abandoned Piankeshaw (part of the Miami Confederacy) village, burnt it down, and then promptly headed back to their fort at Vincennes. Hamtramck would later have to explain himself. He pleaded that he lacked both supplies and reliable militia. Again, invading Americans burned up Indian fields, then complained that they lacked food. Hamtramck did not cover himself in glory, but perhaps his discretion proved the better part of valor (Calloway, 2014).

Harmar's expedition did destroy the impressive polyglot village of Kekionga (future Fort Wayne, Indiana) after noting how orderly and well-constructed it was. They further took note of the massive, well-groomed fields maintained by the local women, and then burned thousands of bushels of corn. But Harmar's force, especially the militia, made a poor showing against Little Turtle's well-led and experienced warriors. After stealing about 100 packhorses and cavalry mounts from the Army, the warriors withdrew to the woods, hoping Harmar would be foolish enough to chase them. He obliged, sending 300 Kentucky militia after the horses. When those militia killed one Indian, but withdrew after seeing dozens more, Harmar cursed them for cowards.

The next day, October 19, he sent 150 militia (who needed considerable prodding to move out) and 30 U.S. Regulars to find the enemy. When Little Turtle sprang his ambush, nearly all of the militia fled without firing, while the Regulars followed orders and stayed put, and were immediately cut off. Most of them died shortly after in close-quarter, bayonet vs. tomahawk fighting. Harmar sent another combined force of militia and Regulars back to Kekionga on the night of October 21, and on October 22, Little Turtle engineered a second, even deadlier ambush that Americans would remember as "Harmar's Defeat." According to some sources, Harmar's army was saved only by a lunar eclipse, which the Miamis and others regarded as an ill omen, and so declined to continue the fight (Sword, 1985).

In the span of three days, 183 Americans died. While initial reports called the expedition a success, Harmar was later court martialed (though acquitted), and the Washington administration realized that they had merely emboldened the Northwest Confederacy to continue resisting American encroachment (Sword, 1985). What they did not realize was that Harmar's expedition would prove to be their most successful effort against those confederates for nearly four years.

Harmar's invasion of Indian country exposed a number of flaws in the American strategy. Though the nation now had a potentially strong government under the Constitution, that strength had yet to translate to military power. Recruiting and funding for regular, professional soldiers remained woefully inadequate, forcing them to rely on frontier militia for much of their manpower. Such militia, mainly from Kentucky, could be fierce, courageous fighters when properly motivated and led, but, not unlike their native counterparts, they insisted on following only commanders they respected and trusted. Josiah Harmar did not inspire them. Indeed, many of his militia were substitutes, paid (poorly) to take the place of men who had been called. So, even for frontier militia, the campaign fielded essentially second-string fighters.

During the Revolution, the undisciplined militia frustrated George Washington to no end, but he had found ways to utilize their strengths – scouting, skirmishing – and minimize their weaknesses, especially their tendency to run away when pressed sharply. Harmar had no such rapport with his militia, and at Kekionga, the militia fled when Little Turtle sprung his trap, making it all the more deadly for the Regulars, who followed orders and stood their ground. Further, it proved terribly difficult to acquire the necessary food and supplies for the army in the West. October was rather late to initiate a campaign into Indian country, yet Harmar had little choice, because he lacked the necessary provisions before then (Sword, 1985).

It would take time to raise another army. In the meantime, many Kentuckians were spoiling for a fight. Washington ordered General Charles Scott, a Revolutionary War veteran who, unlike Harmar, enjoyed great respect in the West, to lead a raid against the "hostile" Indian villages along the Wabash River watershed in what would become southern Indiana. It was partly an opportunity to satiate Kentucky's bloodlust and desire for revenge, as white Kentuckians had been at war with Indians both north and south for nearly two decades. While hoping to score an easy, morale-building victory, the President had a more strategic goal in mind. As historian Susan Sleeper-Smith notes, Washington's orders to capture as many Indian women as possible had a twofold design: to force enemy Indians to a meaningful treaty council (that part failed), and also to strike at the enemy's logistical support (Sleeper-Smith, 2018).

While largely absent from official rhetoric of the era, military men understood that Indian women in the Ohio Valley were absurdly productive farmers, whose abundant produce allowed warriors to carry on extensive military actions. Scott's militia army encountered few warriors, but they did manage to kidnap scores of native women and hold them hostage until they were released with the 1792 Treaty of Vincennes. Historians have largely ignored the treaty, as it was rejected by the U.S. Senate, and never ratified (Sleeper-Smith, 2018).

The St. Clair Disaster

Perhaps incredibly, the government seemed to learn nothing from the Harmar campaign. Having seen one former Revolutionary officer end his career in embarrassing fashion, another, Arthur St. Clair, the appointed governor of the Northwest Territory, now got the job. Like Harmar, St. Clair was a patriot and Revolutionary veteran, though "war hero" would be a stretch. Once more, the Regular force proved far too small to march against the Confederacy, and would need significant augmentation by militia. Kentuckians took one look at St. Clair, another unimpressive, over-the-hill commander – on the campaign, St. Clair's gout often made it impossible for him to mount a horse – and liked him even less than they had Harmar. Supply and logistics problems also remained acute (Sword, 1985).

When St. Clair's much-delayed expedition finally headed north, it was quite late for proper campaigning. The men, especially the Kentucky volunteer militia, grumbled considerably, and the army grew more and more sullen with each day's march. Even within the officer corps, friction compromised military efficiency. St. Clair's second in command, Brigadier General Richard Butler of Pennsylvania, had been a popular Indian trader before the Revolution, and an unpopular Indian treaty commissioner after it. Butler and St. Clair were often at odds, and deliberately avoided direct communications after a time, something that could prove deadly in war. When a large chunk of St. Clair's militia deserted the army and headed back to Kentucky, the general was more concerned about them, rather than the Indians, attacking his supply column. He detached a portion of his most reliable Regular troops, the 1st Regiment, to intercept them, or at least meet and guard the wagons and fend off the Kentuckians. They managed to do neither. St. Clair would sorely miss those men.

Prior to St. Clair's heading west, President Washington, the Seven Years' War veteran of three campaigns against Fort Duquesne, gave him a clear, and prophetic, warning. "Beware of surprise, general. Trust not the Indian." In particular, Washington admonished St. Clair of the necessity of fortifying one's camp every night while in Indian country, as surprise assaults were a favorite (and proven) tactic of Indians. St. Clair may well have heard the warning, but there is no evidence that he heeded it (Sword, 1985:145).

On the night of November 3, 1791, the army came to a halt near modern Fort Recovery, Ohio. The location is still the birthplace of the mighty Wabash River, which divides southern Indiana from southern Illinois. St. Clair's demoralized army pitched their tents, and the general did order sentries placed on duty. But his men were tired, and he did not order them to construct breastworks, or simple abatis, or any real defensive measures. General Butler, meanwhile, received reports of Indian warriors skulking about the army, but did not feel this intelligence warranted ending his spat with St. Clair, and so the commanding general went to sleep in blissful ignorance.

By contrast, about 800 warriors quietly surrounded St. Clair's army in the predawn hours of November 4. (St. Clair would later insist, while admitting he had little evidence, that he was outnumbered in the fight.) The Confederacy's fighters were led by Blue Jacket, the principal war chief of the Shawnees, Buckongahelas, the grizzled Delaware warrior, and Little Turtle. The native chiefs freely discussed their plans, and their men held great confidence in, and respect for, their leaders – as they should have. Though actually outnumbered by several hundred men, the ensuing battle would unfold as a lopsided, turkey shoot affair, partly because of the respective morale of the combatants, and partly because of the simple but brilliant strategy employed by Blue Jacket and his allies (Calloway, 2014).

They realized that one of the few tactical advantages St. Clair would hold came from his artillery, as the natives had none of their own. To neutralize that potential game-changer, teams of Indian marksman were detailed to focus on the cannon – any man who approached the pieces should be immediately shot down. Indeed, in the ensuing carnage, the artillery proved quite useless. Other native warriors likely did not need instructions to shoot down the officers first. It had long been a North American practice – copied by Anglo-Americans – to shoot anyone who looked like an officer (usually mounted and wearing flashier uniforms) to maximize chaos in the enemy. Like many native war tactics, it was eminently practical and effective.

Shortly before dawn, as St. Clair and his men began to stir, shots and war whoops rang out. As planned, when St. Clair ordered his artillery into action, the sniper teams quickly shot them down. Most of the officers quickly received wounds as well – St. Clair, miraculously, would escape the battle untouched, though by all accounts he was mounted and courageous, if ineffectual, in leading his troops. Many of the remaining militia soon fled, their lack of faith in St. Clair seemingly confirmed. The Confederacy's warriors continued to pour bullets into the army, until they finally charged in with clubs, tomahawks, and knives. At this point, the battle became a wild, one-sided scrum, and soon the soldiers literally ran for their lives. St. Clair did try to rally them, but soon rode out as fast as his last surviving horse could manage.

The retreat was pell-mell and panicked – many men simply threw down their arms and accoutrements and sprinted away as fast as they could – leaving the others to their fate. The badly wounded fell to tomahawks and knives, the fortunate ones dying before being scalped. The retreating mass left not only their wounded comrades but around a hundred "camp followers," women (in some cases the wives of soldiers) who had accompanied the army, cooking meals and doing laundry, and in some cases doubling as prostitutes. Few, if any, were spared (Sword, 1985; Calloway, 2014).

While thrilled with their great victory, the Confederacy's warriors were also furious that another American army had dared to invade their lands, and they wanted to drive home the point with macabre symbolism, practiced upon the corpses of their enemies. The camp followers and wounded might be dispatched fairly quickly, but the warriors then used their bodies as message boards for future interlopers. Many of the dead would later be found not only scalped but otherwise mutilated, including having their genitalia cut off. Some warriors stuffed dirt into the mouths of corpses, a mocking reference to the American hunger for Indian lands. Indeed, when American troops arrived on the scene weeks later to recover and bury the remains – hence they named the post they built on the site Fort Recovery – they were appalled and haunted by the sight for the rest of their days (Sword, 1985; Calloway, 2014).

When the remnants of St. Clair's army finally stopped running, the accounting revealed how catastrophic the losses were. Officially, 630 men died that morning. (This would prove to be the single worst defeat a native force ever inflicted upon the U.S., dwarfing Custer's losses at Little Big Horn eighty-five years later.) That did not count the scores of women abandoned on the field. By comparison, the Indians lost perhaps 60 combined casualties, mostly wounded, a not inconsiderable number given that they probably numbered 800 or less in the fight. Still, the battle had been a rout (Calloway, 2014).

The American losses might well have been considerably higher, as armies are rarely more vulnerable than when fleeing panic-stricken down a forest trail. However, the sheer scope of the losses may have paradoxically helped the men. The scene at the Wabash was such a disaster – so much material plunder, so many scalps and potential prisoners to be had – that most of the Confederacy's warriors gave up the chase after a few miles, well before they needed to. They hurried back to the battle site, where swords, guns, uniforms, horses, and all manner of equipment lay for the taking. It proved an unprecedented haul for the Confederacy's fighters. Aside from the blood, the battle cost the impoverished republic considerable treasure. Counting up just the lost muskets, wagons, horses, basic equipment, and provisions, the Army estimated that the battle cost nearly $33,000 – about $840,000 in the early twenty-first century (Calloway, 2014).

Understandably, it took St. Clair several days to gather information and compose himself to make his report. He tried to put as positive a spin on it as possible, but the enormity of the loss made that a darkly humorous exercise. Though the general tried to shift blame, chiefly to the militia and some of the officers, he had been in command. Among the dead was General Butler, not a favorite of St. Clair, but well-liked by many in Congress and the Army, and the highest-ranking American officer to die in combat since the Revolution. Badly wounded during the attack, Butler was too portly for his aides – including one of his brothers – to carry to safety. Manfully, he had handed over his sword and personal effects, and demanded to be left behind with a loaded pistol.

He would soon fall under the tomahawk of some Shawnees, who may well have remembered his role in the humiliating treaty of Fort Finney (Sword, 1985).

When word finally reached George Washington of the unmitigated disaster on the Wabash, he reportedly flew into a rage. Though often remembered as serenely self-controlled, the flesh and blood Washington was known for his occasionally volcanic temper. The scope of the disaster, and his rather direct warning to St. Clair, washed over him. "Oh, he is worse than a murderer," the President exclaimed. "The curse of Heaven, the curse of the widows and orphans, is upon him!" Fortunately for St. Clair, Washington had composed himself by the time the general slinked back to Philadelphia. As was customary in the eighteenth century, the inquiry into the events – the first Congressional investigation in U.S. history – officially cleared the officers, including St. Clair, and blamed the disaster on the men, in this case, the militia. But St. Clair's army career ended on the worst of possible notes (Sword, 1985: 201).

Obviously, the Northwestern Confederacy felt elated and emboldened in the wake of their victory, as did like-minded militants in the South. When the Washington administration called once more for councils and land cessions, the confederates responded that the U.S. would be better off using any money for a future campaign to simply pay off Americans who wanted lands north of the Ohio (Calloway, 2016). British agents in Canada – both in the military and the Indian service – were perhaps as shocked as Washington by the event. Yet they suddenly (if briefly) became more enthusiastic about the Indians' chances for, at the least, postponing American territorial expansion west of the Appalachians.

Many Americans, particularly Jeffersonians, felt that continuing the war would not only be pointless but also dangerous to the republic, particularly the Treasury. Some openly wondered if another campaign would bankrupt the nation and end the great experiment. Some civilians, especially in the East, openly questioned the basic validity of the war north of the Ohio. [See Doc. 14] By 1792, the government was offering the Ohio Indians $50,000 outright if they would agree to the Fort Harmar cessions, as well as an annual payment (annuity) of $10,000 worth of trade goods, and $20,000 in cash to bribe prominent chiefs into acceptance. (While that seems an extraordinary outlay for the impoverished nation, it would prove to be about one tenth of the cost of the army that eventually defeated the Northwest Confederacy.) The Confederacy, still flush with success after two great victories, and understandably reluctant to give up the lands they felt the Great Spirit had given them, refused (Nichols, 2008).

Washington's cabinet, including not just Thomas Jefferson but also Hamilton and the other Federalists, felt that the war should be paused or even ended. For once, Washington overruled them. As he had during the Revolution, Washington understood better than most the symbolic importance of the U.S. Army. As difficult as it would be, the army must be re-quickened and rebuilt, and they must defeat the Northwestern Confederacy. Failing to do so would demonstrate a fatal weakness, not only to foreign adversaries, hoping to limit or snatch away American territory, but also to the American people themselves. Furthermore, the government's need for land sales revenue in the Northwest had not gone away (Owens, 2015).

Wayne Takes Command

In early 1792, the task seemed nearly insurmountable. Seeking a new commanding general for the army, two of the President's choices – Benjamin Lincoln and Daniel Morgan – either demurred or failed to secure congressional support. Finally, he settled on Pennsylvania's Anthony Wayne. In retrospect an excellent choice, at the time Wayne did not look particularly promising. Deeply in debt and hard-drinking, like St. Clair and Harmar, he was a Revolutionary veteran whose best days seemed behind him. But despite some health issues, including gout, Wayne had little in common with his two predecessors. He had been one of Washington's most talented and successful field officers in the Revolution – "Mad" Anthony was a nickname based on his willingness to fight – and was probably the most talented general still capable of taking the field.

Further, Wayne refused to be a fool. He insisted that he would take the assignment only if he were made the highest ranking officer in the Army, answering only to Washington and Secretary of War Knox. Wayne recognized that the political pressure to move without sufficient supplies and well-trained men had helped doom the previous expeditions. "Mad" Anthony would take the fight to the Confederacy, but only when he himself knew he could win (Gaff, 2004).

Initially, the government hoped Wayne would destroy the Confederacy in the summer of 1792, but supply and recruiting issues pushed that back to 1794. Meanwhile, the Northwest Confederacy's confidence at times approached arrogance. In 1792, when Washington insisted on sending two American envoys to treat with the Northwest Confederacy, the envoys did not first pass through British posts, like Detroit, which offended the confederates. They murdered the envoys and their servants, sending a definitive "no" to Washington's requests for a cease fire. Then, in August of 1793, a northwestern Ohio conference including delegates from the Shawnees, Delawares, Potawatomis, Miamis, Ottawas, Ojibways, and, perhaps most ominously, Creeks and Cherokees, sent word to the Americans. They acknowledged that many Americans were poor, and hoped to settle upon Indian lands. However, the victorious confederates cheekily noted, it would be far cheaper for the U.S. to take the money they would have to use for raising an army and for paying Indians annuities, and instead give that as relief to poor Americans. Washington does not seem to have seriously considered doing so (Willig, 2008; Calloway, 2016).

While the delays in recruiting and supply proved frustrating, General Wayne made excellent use of the time, training the army's new recruits thoroughly, in some cases literally whipping them into shape. They practiced marksmanship, and engaged in war games, with some soldiers dressed as Indians and "fighting" from behind rocks and trees, while others fired blanks at them and engaged in mock bayonet charges. By 1794, for the first time since the Revolution, the U.S. had several thousand well-trained professional soldiers under arms. Secretary Knox himself dubbed the reborn army the "Legion of the United States," a nod to the uber-disciplined and efficient Roman armies. Wayne also made use of volunteer soldiers, again largely from Kentucky, though this time out the Kentuckians had greater respect for the commander, and therefore a much-improved fighting spirit (Gaff, 2004; Sword, 1985).

Wayne also made shrewd use of military intelligence, utilizing a company of "spies" (today they would be called scouts) composed of white men who had been captured and adopted by Indians, and who dressed and fought in "Indian style." Their leader was Captain William Wells, originally from Kentucky, who had been taken and raised by the Miamis, and served under Little Turtle at the battles of Kekionga and the Wabash. Reportedly, Wells had led the marksmen teams that silenced St. Clair's artillery at the Battle of the Wabash (Calloway, 2014). He even married Little Turtle's daughter. Defecting back to Kentucky after the Treaty of Vincennes in 1792, Wells and his spies provided invaluable information to Wayne's army.

Multi-tribal coalitions were hard to maintain for any length of time, and by the early summer of 1794, cracks began to show in the Northwestern Confederacy. Outside of Fort Recovery in June, a planned assault on one of Wayne's supply pack trains initially went quite well. Warriors killed several of the soldiers guarding the line of horses and mules, capturing the valuable animals and supplies. But then, a number of the Indians made an ill-advised, impromptu assault on the fort itself. It went as poorly as an improvised attack on a well-defended post – in broad daylight, no less – as one would expect. The charge was led by some of the "Lakes Indians" (Potawatomis and Ottawas) who had but recently joined the Indian forces. Many grew angry at their casualties and argued that their allies had not done enough to support them once the charge was made. In native fashion, they made their displeasure known with their feet and set off for home (Sword, 1985; Gaff, 2004).

It was not the only blow suffered by pan-Indian unionists since the stunning victory against St. Clair's army. In 1793, the Creek headman Alexander McGillivray, never of robust health, died on his plantation. A shrewd advocate for Indian resistance to American territorial encroachment, even if his self-indulgent materialism had wounded his reputation among the Creeks, McGillivray would be difficult to replace (Caughey, 1959; Ethridge, 2003; Saunt, 1999). Dragging Canoe, the fierce Chickamauga leader, had died, apparently from a heart attack, in 1792. The Washington administration had spent the early 1790s, meanwhile, proactively seeking to limit the potential of Indian alliances across the Ohio.

Like British Indian Department officials before him, Henry Knox pursued a simple but effective means for thwarting pan-Indianism – he sought to employ warriors from Southern nations, like the Chickasaws and Choctaws, in combat against the Northwestern Confederacy. The cultural practice of blood revenge, the Americans knew, would make it especially difficult for them to ally with the Ohio nations once they had joined the fight. Chickasaws and Choctaws, meanwhile, proved eager to solidify their ties to the U.S. for their own reasons, including securing arms and ammunition to sustain them in ongoing conflicts with traditional enemies, like the Creeks. The Chickasaw chief Piomingo, or Mountain Leader, had personally led a detachment of Chickasaw scouts under General St. Clair, and they continued in this role for Anthony Wayne (Owens, 2015; Atkinson, 2004).

President Washington insisted that while preparing for a military showdown with the Northwest Confederacy, the nation must continue diplomatic efforts with them. He also pursued a more delicate approach with the far more numerous Southeastern tribes. Knowing that his government had its hands full dealing with a war north of the Ohio, Washington took great pains to avoid driving the Creeks and Cherokees further into the arms of their militant factions. [See Doc. 15] In so doing, he risked alienating Americans in the Southeast, who continually agitated for a more aggressive military campaign to subdue their Indian neighbors and force additional land cessions. Politicians never lost frontiersmen's support by calling for aggressive military action on their behalf. Sometimes Indians even defended themselves in print. [See Doc. 16]

Frontier militia once more flirted with disaster. In June of 1793, Captain John Beard and the Knox County (TN) militia rode out after some horse thieves, which they had every right to do. Though the culprits were almost certainly Chickamaugas and/or Creeks, Beard and his men attacked the village of Cherokee chief Hanging Maw, which they had no right to do. Both the elderly Hanging Maw – one of the Cherokee chiefs most vocally in favor of peace with the Americans, and his wife, were wounded in the attack. Several other Cherokees, including Nancy Ward's daughter (and agent Joseph Martin's wife), Betsy, died. While Federal officials blasted this vicious attack, Beard's neighbors not only declined to prosecute but also elected him to the territorial legislature the next year. This likely only encouraged other attacks on innocent Indians, usually Upper Cherokees, because they were closer. While such attacks were manifestly unjust, and potentially counterproductive and imperiling for the republic, they were also locally popular and politically expedient (Boulware, 2011; Finger, 2001). [See Doc. 17]

In August of 1793, Chickamauga and Creek warriors retaliated, flirting with an attack on Knoxville, Tennessee, and then waylaying two settler communities, known as Henry's Station and Cavett's Station. The latter attack left thirteen settlers dead, several after they had surrendered. John Sevier would lead the militia response, and this time at least his raid did target Chickamauga and Creek villages in Northern Georgia, rather than Overhill Cherokees. Major James Ore, meanwhile, burned the Chickamauga towns of Running Water and Nickajack (Finger, 2001).

Sevier's expedition in particular infuriated the Washington administration. Not only was it completely unauthorized, but it would eventually cost the U.S. government $29,000 in damages. Washington was so angry that the government refused for years to reimburse Sevier's men. It would take considerable agitation, including the memorials of a Tennessee congressman named Andrew Jackson, to secure the militia's money (Finger, 2001; Owens, 2015).

Fearing the risk to both the Treasury and the frontier if a pan-Indian war broke out, Congress's Committee on Indian Affairs released a report that, while insisting Indians would be held to their treaty obligations, was primarily aimed at keeping the militia in the Southwest Territory in check. They suggested that any militia officer who made an unauthorized attack on Indians would be court martialed by the Federal, not territorial, military, and if convicted of murdering an Indian, should suffer death. Secretary of War Knox built on the committee findings in his December 29, 1794, report to the president. Bluntly, he noted that the stakes could not be higher, and that lawless frontier whites truly threatened to bring on a war that might destroy the republic.

While fighting against tribes numbering perhaps three thousand north of the Ohio was bad enough, he asserted, "this evil would be greatly increased [if it involved] the Indian Warriors of the Four Nations [of the Southeast] not being much short of fourteen thousand." Furthermore, such a war might draw even more interference from the British and Spanish, he offered, "with whom the tribes North and South of the Ohio are connected." Predictably, Knox's sensible and just report met its fate. Endorsed by the president, the reports by Knox and the Committee were combined into a Senate bill, designed to "Prevent depredations on the Indians South of the river Ohio." It passed in the Senate, but failed in the House by seven votes (Owens, 2015:157).

If Washington could not stop Americans from killing friendly Indians in the South, then encouraging those friends to kill America's enemies would have to suffice. The administration built upon the foundation laid by the Chickasaws, led by chief Piomingo, and some Choctaws, who were once again serving alongside the army in the Ohio country. Southwest Territory governor William Blount directed that the Chickasaws and Choctaws should be encouraged to attack the Creeks. (Piomingo especially did not need to be convinced of the utility of attacking Chickamaugas and Creeks.) [See Doc. 18] The year 1794 would prove a highwater mark for pan-Indianists. Despite the deaths of Dragging Canoe (1792) and Alexander McGillivray (1793), and the capture and deportation of William Bowles by the Spanish (1792), it is possible that one more victory by the Northwest Confederacy over the Americans in Ohio might have convinced fence-sitting warriors in the South to take the pan-Indian plunge. This placed intense pressure on Anthony Wayne's new army.

By August of 1794, Wayne had spent two excruciating years struggling to recruit, train, and equip the Legion. Unlike his predecessors, Wayne fortified his camps every night when in Indian country, and his refusal to make crucial mistakes frustrated his native opponents. Despite his careful nature, they noted that Wayne's disciplined army marched farther in a day than Harmar's or St. Clair's, and still had time to take precautions before bedding down. Surprising him would be nearly impossible. But in mid-August, he seemed ready to move, and though their numbers had dwindled, the Confederacy's warriors welcomed the opportunity for a decisive contest. As per their custom, the warriors fasted to be purified spiritually before the anticipated battle. (Doing so would also have the benefit of limiting the chances of a deadly infection should one be wounded in the abdomen) (Sword, 1985).

But Wayne did not march the next day as expected. The warriors continued their fast, and after two days, many began to feel weak. On the third day, the warriors decided that about half would stay to watch the Legion, while the other half would return to their camps to eat before spelling their comrades. It was during this moment, on August 20, that Wayne finally moved out. No records exist to say this was a deliberate plan of Wayne's, and he might have simply been lucky. It is tantalizing to think, though, that the detail about Indians' desire to fast before battle had been relayed to him by William Wells or one of his spies. Regardless, when Wayne and the Legion sought battle on August 20, their 3,000-plus man force would meet only several hundred Northwestern warriors (Gaff, 2004; Sword, 1985).

Despite the hunger pangs and size of Wayne's army, the confederates initially held great optimism. They had well-earned confidence in their chiefs, many of whom stood with them, and the site of the impending battle, outside of modern Toledo, Ohio, seemed to favor the outnumbered warriors. Known as Fallen Timbers, as a cyclone had knocked down many trees at the site some years before, the natives assumed it would give them excellent cover from which to snipe at and ambush the Legion. When a detachment of mounted riflemen gave chase to some warriors hoping to lure them into such a trap, it looked like Wayne would become another failure. But Wayne's discipline had taken hold of the men in the previous two years, and he managed to counter with a fierce bayonet charge. The warriors found themselves at a significant disadvantage, and the trees and brush they hoped would conceal them now seemed to trap them. Before long, the fight turned into a rout, this time in the Americans' favor.

Given the disparity in numbers, the warriors acquitted themselves well. They inflicted more casualties than they took, but of their fifty or so dead, a large number were chiefs, which seemed a bad omen. Soon, as was customary, they fled the hopeless situation to avoid further losses. The firefight ended so quickly, Wayne did not have time to bring all of his men into action. The dispirited Indians, many of whom had not lost a pitched battle in years, ran for nearby Fort Miami, hoping for shelter, or even aid, from their British allies (Gaff, 2004; Sword, 1985).

Fort Miami demonstrated some realities of British-Indian relations in the early 1790s, though Americans did not fully understand them at the time. Not only did the fort sit squarely on what, according to the Treaty of Paris, was American soil, but it was not an old fort Britain had simply refused to evacuate. The post had been built only months earlier – Americans knew that much – and at the insistence of Britain's Indian allies – Americans did not fully grasp that fact (Sword, 1985).

Many native warriors believed Britain would render direct military aid to them. Surely the Redcoat soldiers would welcome them, and perhaps turn their cannon on the insolent Americans. Apparently British Indian agents had promised, or at least strongly hinted at this, for some time, and indeed a few British agents had fought as volunteers at Fallen Timbers. However, King George III, despite American propaganda, had no interest in another North American war, especially an "Indian" one. The King continued to see himself as a benevolent *father* to his native *children*, but did not see a military answer to their pleas. Furthermore, the geopolitical calculus had changed considerably when the French Revolution of 1789 led to an Anglo-French War in 1793. A North American war had gone from being an unattractive option in 1792 to an unthinkable one by 1794. Though Fort Miami maintained its Redcoat garrison, their commander, Major William Campbell, was under strict orders to avoid any incident that would bring a war with the U.S. (Indeed, three months later, the U.S. and Britain would sign Jay's Treaty, which would prevent a needless war for Britain, and a disastrous one for the U.S.)

The native survivors arrived at the gates of Fort Miami and were somewhat stunned that they were denied entry. They watched, from a short distance, in disbelief as the Legion approached the fort, and Wayne paraded within a "pistol shot's" distance – about 30–40 yards – of the gate, essentially daring the British to shoot. He then dashed off the first in a series of curt, delightfully passive aggressive notes to the fort's commander, demanding that he leave the territory of the United States immediately. To further drive his point home, Wayne's men calmly and thoroughly burned down the Indian cornfields surrounding the fort, knowing that it was far too advanced in the season for replanting, and took great delight in burning down a nearby British trading post. The fact that the Redcoats could only seethe impotently at this spoke volumes to their Indian allies (Sword, 1985:309; Gaff, 2004).

One would think that Wayne and the Americans felt almost instantaneous relief in the aftermath of Fallen Timbers, but in fact tensions remained high for months afterwards. While no more large battles took place, isolated killings of soldiers and settlers continued into early 1795. Wayne sent word to the Northwestern Confederacy that they must meet with him in May to discuss terms for peace at his new post, Fort Greenville (named for his late friend, General Nathanael Greene).

The Treaty of Greenville

Wayne held most of the cards at Greenville, but not all of them. The confederates had been shaken in the summer of 1794, but they still had numerous warriors who could potentially prolong the war, which had already cost a fortune in blood and treasure. Wayne had two tactical goals for the treaty: to convince his opponents that continued resistance was futile, and to demonstrate that the rational benevolence of the U.S. also rendered it unnecessary. Many of the Indian delegates moved at their own pace – the treaty council did not begin in earnest until June – and we should note that while Wayne's orders called for a large cession of land, including much of what would become Ohio, St. Clair had been directed to demand the entire territory north of the Ohio River.

To demonstrate the futility of continuing the war, Wayne had the terms of John Jay's November 1794 treaty with Britain read to the delegates, likely the first most of them had heard of the agreement. The passage wherein Britain agreed to abandon its posts in the Northwest, like Detroit and Miami, combined with the lack of military assistance after Fallen Timbers, sent a clear message: If the Northwest Confederacy continued fighting the U.S., it would do so without supplies or help from the King (Sword, 1985).

To soften the blow, and dissuade all but the most radical, Wayne also informed the delegates that while they would need to cede land to the U.S., they would in fact be compensated with annual payments – annuities – usually of trade goods or agricultural implements, as the tribes chose. Typically, smaller nations would receive $500 worth in their annuity, while larger ones would receive $1,000. In exchange for about three-fourths of what would become the state of Ohio – all but the northwest quarter – the tribes would receive peace and protection from the U.S., in addition to their annuities. Compared to previous treaties, it was not a terrible deal, and most of the delegations consented. Little Turtle, the Miami war captain, held out the longest against the cession. But after it became obvious he would have little help, and the Miamis were granted additional annuities, he too marked the treaty.

The 1795 Treaty of Greenville ended two decades of brutal warfare in the Ohio Valley, and that peace largely held until the outbreak of the War of 1812. It also established the important precedent that Indians had rights to their lands, and must be paid for their cessions, and in that respect must be seen as at least a modestly progressive innovation. Unlike some councils before and subsequent to Greenville, many of the signatories were actually respected tribal leaders who could plausibly claim to represent their people. But the treaty, which became something of a template for future U.S.-Indian treaties, set other, more troubling precedents as well. Bribes for Indian chiefs became standard practice. During the negotiations, Wayne found the fearsome Shawnee Blue Jacket to be considerably more amenable once the government offered to build him a house. As president, Thomas Jefferson would later refer to a similar payoff to Little Turtle as a "liberality" (Owens, 2007:100; Dowd, 1992).

Though the tribes welcomed the annuity payments, as historian Gregory Dowd notes, they provided the government an unprecedented "permanent lever" for interfering in tribal politics. Most native peoples judged a civil chief's greatness in part by the benefits/goods they could provide for their followers. Increasingly in the years after 1795, the federal government would favor chiefs (sometimes even creating new ones) by delivering a tribe's annuities directly to them for distribution. Invariably, chiefs disposed to sell lands to the U.S., or who were otherwise cooperative, became favored. Some American officials would later simply refuse to deliver a tribe's rightful annuity payment until they agreed to attend still more land cession councils. William Henry Harrison, a veteran of Fallen Timbers who later became governor of Indiana Territory, would do so frequently. Finally, Greenville established a precedent of "purchasing" land from tribes who did not occupy it. The Miamis, for example, lost little of their own territory in the treaty, while they were compensated for lands occupied by Shawnees and Delawares in Ohio. With no real friends in the government, most tribes felt powerless to resist such practices (Dowd, 1992:114).

The peace that came from Greenville proved deadly to unified Indian resistance. Within a year of the war's end north of the Ohio, large-scale combat in the South ended as well. The Cherokees reaffirmed peace with the United States in 1796. From 1776 to 1794, there had been at least twenty-three invasions of Cherokee country, destroying well over a hundred towns, some more than once (Boulware, 2011). Indeed, in future conflicts, Cherokees would go out of their way to demonstrate their friendship towards the U.S., despite unceasing pressure on their territory from squatters and government agents. Creek militants, meanwhile, found themselves increasingly isolated, and also made peace with the U.S. in 1796. They did, however, continue to seek trade with Spanish authorities. American slave owners in the Southeast still viewed Spanish Florida, long a haven for runaway slaves and Indians raiders, as a thorn in the nation's side. But the widespread killings that had so typified the region were replaced by occasional intercultural murders. Southern Indians, especially the Cherokees, closed the eighteenth century seeing accommodation of their intrusive white neighbors as preferable to violently resisting them.

Bowles Bows Out

Pan-Indianism did receive a brief boost in 1799, when newspapers began reporting that William Augustus Bowles, the Loyalist/huckster/pan-Indian organizer, had escaped from a Spanish prison and made his way back to Florida. American newspapers feared that the alleged British emissary would funnel material aid to Indians who might resist American expansion. In truth, the British government had always viewed Bowles with a mixture of bemusement and embarrassment, and he certainly had no authority from Whitehall. Nevertheless, newspaper editors (who, like the public, were practically addicted to conspiracy theories in this age) [See Doc. 19] breathlessly speculated that Bowles would join up with British forces from Canada, or perhaps invade French Louisiana, and link up with Indians to oppose the U.S. What Bowles actually did, however, brought concern (Din, 2012; Owens, 2015).

Returning to the Florida coast, Bowles contacted the faction of Creeks who still supported him, and sought to thwart the marking of the boundary line between the Cherokees and the U.S. that had been agreed to the previous year at the 1798 Treaty of Holston River. Perhaps this notion frightened Americans because they realized the cession was not especially just. Worse still, he encouraged Indian friends to raid Florida for slaves and livestock, which he would purchase from them (Din, 2012). To white Americans, then, Bowles was now the ultimate nightmare. He was a renegade Tory, who had "gone native," consorted with the British (or so they thought), promoted pan-Indian resistance, and stole, liberated, and recruited slaves to attack their former masters (Owens, 2015).

He not only pledged to purge the Muskogee Nation of American influence, peacefully if possible, but also threatened death by hanging to Americans who refused to quit Creek lands. He singled out Benjamin Hawkins, the U.S. agent to the Creeks in that threat. But mostly he stayed in the bounds of Florida. He had friends among the Seminoles, despite their naming him Oquelúsa Micco, that is, King of Liars. When he and his white, black, and red followers captured the Spanish Fort San Marcos de Apalache – modern St. Marks, FL – in May of 1800, it sealed his fate (Din, 2012).

Spanish officers threatened to destroy Seminole towns and crops, to kidnap their women and children, and to confiscate their cattle and slaves, if they harbored or aided Bowles. Only when they handed the Director General over in chains, and returned all prisoners and slaves to Spanish authorities, would there be peace. His raids continued into 1802, and American newspapermen found themselves in the odd position of rooting for Spain. The fact that he continued to liberate slaves and recruit them to his small army made him doubly frightening to them. (Recent slave rebellions, including Gabriel's Rebellion in Virginia and the massive and successful revolt in Haiti, had made white slave owners especially edgy on the issue of armed, freedom-seeking blacks (Taylor, 2013).

Spanish agents continued to whittle down Bowles' support network, offering amnesty to chiefs who agreed to stop helping him. By the spring of 1803, delegates from the Creeks, Chickasaws, Choctaws, and Cherokees strongly agreed that he had to go. Meanwhile, Spanish efforts (and a lack of actual support from Britain, whatever Americans might have thought) made it impossible for Bowles to supply his supporters the trade goods they needed, while his enemies wielded them effectively. In May of 1803, Bowles was captured by a party of métis Upper Creeks, some of them friends of his old nemesis Alexander McGillivray. Among them was a man named William Weatherford, whose later career in Creek leadership would not always please American officials. After one brief escape, Bowles was taken in irons to the Spanish at Mobile. Out of miracles, and perhaps the will to live, he died in a dungeon in Havana, Cuba, shortly before Christmas in 1805. Pan-Indianism had lost a quirky advocate, and Americans had lost a charismatic boogey man upon which to fix their fears (Din, 2012; Wright, 1967).

Several factors both within and without the United States had combined to doom pan-Indian resistance in the mid-1790s. Wayne's victory at Fallen Timbers had broken the Northwest Confederacy's momentum. Britain's refusal to join them in an outright war, demonstrated both after the battle and with Jay's Treaty, broke their spirits. At the Treaty of Greenville, they would mark a document ceding most of what became Ohio, and inaugurate a peace north of the Ohio River for the first time in two decades. To the south, Indian militants also fell victim to forces beyond their control. Spain misinterpreted Jay's Treaty, which had merely prevented war between Britain and the U.S., as a strong alliance. Not wanting to be left out in the North American cold, they signed the

Treaty of San Lorenzo (ratified 1796). That treaty considerably thawed Spanish-American relations, as Spain guaranteed American rights to navigation of the Mississippi River – so crucial for western farmers to get their goods to market. Spain also agreed to abandon its forts north of Florida. In addition, Spain's capitulation to Revolutionary France (1795) and declaration of war on Britain (1796) ended any hopes of a joint Anglo-Spanish war (with Indian allies) against the Americans, and decidedly shifted Spanish priorities back to limited defense (Weber, 1992; Owens, 2015).

At the same time, pan-Indian unity had always been a longshot proposition. While the eighteenth century saw native peoples increasingly receptive to the idea that they had been created separately from whites and blacks, few genuinely saw themselves as one people. "Indians," much like "Europeans" or "Africans," saw themselves primarily in village or tribal/national terms, and rarely saw common cause with others. Along with that, pan-Indianists asked people to simply forget rivalries with traditional enemies that, in some cases, they had warred against for centuries. Further, to have any cohesive leadership, pan-Indianism asked that people forego their decentralized forms of village governance, something most Indians rejected. Finally, established chiefs often felt they had little to gain and much to lose when pan-Indianists, often outsiders, called for them to relinquish their own influence for an elusive common good. After the Treaty of Greenville, the U.S. became increasingly effective at rewarding chiefs who carried out government policy, especially regarding land sales. Pan-Indianism slumbered at the turn of the nineteenth century. But it did not die (Dowd, 1992).

5 Jeffersonians and Indians

Thomas Jefferson had a penchant for simultaneously holding incompatible goals. His famously eloquent antislavery rhetoric stood in contrast to his refusal to free his own slaves. He railed against debt while his own finances often stood in disarray. (Those situations were not unrelated.) Contrasting with Alexander Hamilton's prophecy of an increasingly urban and industrial America, Jefferson's preferred paradoxical vision was what he called an "Empire of Liberty." Jefferson contended that, for American virtue to continue, minus the "corrupt" ways of old Europe, the nation must continually expand its territory, creating affordable land for free, independent – and therefore virtuous – yeomen (i.e., middle class) farmers. Tellingly, he usually referred to himself as a *farmer*, rather than the owner of a large plantation worked by slaves. When Jefferson squeaked into the presidency in 1801, he considered it a mandate to pursue the Empire of Liberty. He would purchase lands from Indians cheaply, and they would, he assured himself, be grateful for the opportunity to become civilized, by abandoning hunting and adopting Anglo-American style agriculture. He was so attached to the notion that, despite being a man of science, he willfully ignored mountains of data contradicting him (Tucker, 1990).

Jefferson's Indian Land Policy

Jefferson's fears of foreign intervention in the West spurred him to gobble up Indian lands. A longtime Francophile, Jefferson nevertheless took great alarm when rumors, which were indeed true, circulated that France's ruler Napoleon Bonaparte, had orchestrated a transfer of the massive Louisiana Territory from Spain back to France. Having Spanish neighbors just across the Mississippi was one thing – by 1800 they seemed to offer little threat to the U.S. But with the aggressive, militarily brilliant Napoleon next door, Jefferson practically panicked. Not only could Bonaparte block the westward expansion that Jefferson needed for the Empire of Liberty, but he might even send his forces into Louisiana, and then east, removing vast chunks of territory from the young U.S.

As Jefferson had already begun cutting the size of the Army and Navy – Jeffersonians considered them expensive and possibly oppressive – he had few short-term options. To block a Napoleonic occupation of Louisiana, he sought the help of the Royal Navy – an unthinkable act for him previously – and British government generally. He also dispatched diplomats to the French, hoping to purchase the city of New Orleans, gateway to the Mississippi River (Tucker, 1990).

In the meantime, to safeguard American territory, he sought to purchase Indian lands along major rivers, especially the Mississippi and Ohio, as quickly and cheaply as possible. Those lands would then be rapidly settled with (white) Americans, who would serve as a militia to block Napoleon's advances. To say it was a desperate stop-gap measure would be kind. To carry out this program, Jefferson would have to rely on his appointed territorial officials in the West, particularly William Henry Harrison, governor of the then vast Indiana Territory and chief Indian commissioner north of the Ohio. On February 27, 1803, Jefferson wrote directly to Harrison with his plans, and made a point of marking the letter as "private," as unlike most official communiques of the era, Jefferson did not want this letter published in the newspapers (Wallace, 1999). [See Doc. 20]

The president laid out his philosophy of Indian affairs, and his (very common) assumption that assimilating to Anglo-American ways was obviously to the benefit of Indians. Indeed, Washington and the Federalists had felt much the same. But Jefferson's plans were strikingly devious, and an example of paternalism run amok. He directed Harrison to see prominent Indian chiefs run into debt at U.S. trading houses, as this would make them more willing to sell their lands to pay their debts. Insisting that Indians lived by hunting rather than farming – and so ignoring the crucial role played by Indian women – Jefferson stated that by buying their "surplus" hunting lands, and selling them to Americans, the U.S. would actually be doing Indians a favor. By forcing them to adopt allegedly more efficient, Anglo-American style agriculture on their reduced landholdings, it would speed their "civilization." The fact that Indian women were already astoundingly productive – for most tribes they actually produced the majority of calories consumed – was not mentioned. Though maintaining that this was largely benevolent in intent, Jefferson also cautioned that, for the sake of the Indians, the plans should be kept secret from them.

Not long after receiving these instructions, Governor Harrison began holding land cession treaties with the region's Indians. He proved remarkably successful in buying up vast tracts of Indian land, rarely for more than three cents per acre. Given that in the 1780s the Congress had directed that the land in the Northwest be sold for a minimum of $1 per acre, Harrison made quite a bargain for the government. The fact that he did so through many shady tactics, in particular buying land from Indians who did not actually reside on the parcel in question, raised no eyebrows in Washington. In fairness, Jefferson's letter should be viewed in the context of his fears about Louisiana and Napoleon. Fortunately for the U.S., France sold not only New Orleans but the entire Louisiana Territory, doubling the nation's size. Americans officially took possession of Louisiana by the end of 1803, in theory ending the threat of Napoleon, and therefore the mad scramble for Indian lands and rapid settlement in the West. Yet Harrison's treaties, and the rather shameless tactics used to secure them, actually accelerated over the next two years (Owens, 2007).

Harrison had learned much watching Anthony Wayne's negotiations at Greenville. He had a sense of when to bully and when to bribe. He further refined the American tactic of simply ignoring, or not even inviting, natives who were disinclined to sell land or otherwise cooperate. By rewarding those who complied, sometimes creating "new" chiefs, and generally dividing natives against each other, he managed to buy millions of acres of land. In one example, the Kaskaskia Indians, who by Harrison's own admission numbered perhaps three dozen souls, signed away about three million acres of what would become southern Illinois. The treaty infuriated the more numerous Kickapoos, who actually occupied much of that land (Owens, 2007).

Indians did complain, to Harrison and others, about the cessions, but the region's natives were horribly divided and demoralized by the early nineteenth century. While mostly at peace with the U.S., they reeled from economic woes, like the collapse of the fur trade, largely brought on by the Napoleonic Wars in Europe, and exacerbated by Harrison's land purchases. Further, despite the efforts of the Jefferson administration, Harrison included, to staunch the flow of whiskey into Indian villages, both the supply and demand remained tremendous. The alcohol trade did massive damage to Indians' short-term and long-term health, as precious capital was bartered away for whiskey. Indians in the Ohio Valley were seeing their spiritual and material worlds collapse before their eyes, and the ensuing despair only encouraged alcohol abuse, worsening the cycle.

As had happened before in many societies, native and newcomer, a religious revival arose to try to restore spiritual order and power. A number of Ohio Valley natives spoke of religious visions that would rebalance the universe. The most influential was a Shawnee man, previously distinguished for his social and economic failures. Known to his people as Lalawethika, or "He makes a Loud Noise," he was a drunkard and poor provider, who slipped into an apparent coma in 1805. As his wife began making funeral arrangements, he stirred, announced he had visited the underworld, and that the Great Spirit had given him a new name, Tenskwatawa, or "He opens the Door." Tenskwatawa, whom Americans soon dubbed the "Shawnee Prophet," preached that Indians' happiness and prosperity would return once they ceased angering the Great Spirit, who disdained their reliance on white Americans' material culture. Initially, government officials, including Governor Harrison, welcomed the Shawnee's message, as he preached abstinence from alcohol. But as his teachings evolved, particularly his insistence that the Great Spirit opposed selling Indian land to the U.S., the Americans came to see the Prophet as a threat (Edmunds, 1983).

By 1806, Tenskwatawa led a literal witch-hunt among the Delawares, identifying evildoers among them, who the Delawares themselves promptly executed in gruesome fashion. The fact that the "witches," men and women, all had close ties to the Americans' assimilation and land sales programs, did not escape notice. Tenskwatawa tried to lead another witch-hunt among the Wyandots, but the influential old chief Tarhe, who had marked the Greenville Treaty, shut him down. Interestingly, the Prophet had few adherents among his own Shawnees, outside of his own close kin. But he did manage to attract followers from several Indian nations, including Delawares, Potawatomis, and Kickapoos. Like Neolin and other Indian religious visionaries before him, Tenskwatawa preached of the need for Indian unity and their common creation. He sought to bring, ideally, all Indians together under his leadership. He first established a village in western Ohio, but in 1808, at the behest of a Potawatomi chief known as Main Poc (Withered Hand), he established Prophetstown on the Tippecanoe River, a tributary of the Wabash in Indiana. The village was a few miles from what is now West Lafayette, Indiana (Edmunds, 1983; White, 1991; Dowd, 1992).

Tecumseh: The Greatest Pan-Indianist

One of those followers was his older brother, Tecumseh. Unlike Tenskwatawa, Tecumseh was well-regarded among his people as a warrior and a hunter. A veteran of many fights against white encroachment, including Fallen Timbers, Tecumseh had ample reason to oppose U.S. territorial expansion. Though many Americans, including scholars, would later view his role in his brother's movement as a simplistic dichotomy – the warrior co-opting the religious revival for his own ends – his most recent biographer argues Tecumseh likely believed in his brother's vision. Prior to 1809, he does not seem, based on American correspondence, to have been considered the movement's leader. When mentioned at all, he was usually referred to as "the prophet's brother" (Sugden, 1998:187).

As the Prophet's revival increasingly opposed American purchases of Indian lands, he insisted that because the Great Spirit gave the land to

Figure 5.1 Tecumseh (1768–1813). Shawnee chief and pan-Indianist, he and his brother the Shawnee Prophet opposed Indian land sales to the U.S. He died fighting against the U.S. in the War of 1812.

Indians collectively, none could sell it to the U.S. without unanimous approval. The fact that such approval would be impossible to secure was likely intentional. But tensions between Americans and natives on the frontier really accelerated in the wake of an incident that seemed to have little to do with the Prophet or William Henry Harrison.

In June of 1807, just outside of the Chesapeake Bay, the British warship H.M.S. *Leopard* hailed the American ship the *Chesapeake*, demanding a right to search for Royal Navy deserters. Desertion had long been a problem for the Royal Navy, as sailors – often impressed, that is, forced into service – knew they could enjoy better wages and easier discipline sailing on American commercial vessels. During wartime, shorthanded Royal Navy commanders frequently stopped merchant ships and plucked off sailors, sometimes justly, sometimes not. But when the *Leopard* hailed the *Chesapeake*, demanding it stop and submit to a search, they addressed a U.S. naval vessel, whose commander understandably refused. The *Leopard* fired a broadside into the helpless vessel – the U.S.S. *Chesapeake* was so new they had not actually installed its cannon – killing three sailors, and removing four more. The *Chesapeake-Leopard* Affair eventually led to an official British apology, but also sparked a great war scare in the U.S. and Canada (Owens, 2007).

As in the 1790s, British Canada remained desperately outmanned in the event of a war with the U.S., and so depended upon Indian allies to make up the difference. Americans had long assumed that British agents, rather than Americans' own provocative behavior, stirred Indian resistance to the U.S. Especially on the frontier, Americans assumed that British-armed and instigated Indians would fall upon their cabins and villages. Governor Harrison gave a saber-rattling speech to his legislature in response to *Chesapeake-Leopard*, being sure to note that "the tomahawk and scalping knife" – arms Indians often obtained from Canadian traders – served "British vengeance." As a family man living in a frontier village, Harrison may well have believed he faced an existential threat. He certainly knew, however, that positioning himself as a defender of Americans on the frontier was politically beneficial (Owens, 2007:138).

The war scare gripped the West for months, well into 1808. Unbeknownst to Americans, British agents did actually propose a defensive alliance with Tecumseh and the Prophet in the event of an American war. But in 1808, the Shawnee brothers hoped that their goal of a permanent Indian homeland could be reached without war. Perhaps as veterans of Fallen Timbers, they also doubted the sincerity of British offers of aid. Tecumseh rejected the proffered alliance (Sugden, 1998).

By 1809, Indian-white tensions on the frontier had dropped significantly. But that summer, Governor Harrison sought a new round of Indian land cessions in a series of treaties held at Fort Wayne, an Indiana post named for his old commander. Indiana's white residents were by no means crowded, or lacking good farmland, in 1809, but Harrison had growing political concerns. His popularity had waned noticeably since 1805. Many Indiana residents charged that he was aristocratic, even dictatorial, and they lambasted his efforts to see slavery legalized in Indiana. The territory had shrunk by more than half that year, as Illinois became its own territory. Harrison's push for more land purchases in 1809 likely reflected his realization that buying up Indian country had consistently been his most popular act as governor.

The Fort Wayne cessions displayed Harrison's treaty chicanery at its zenith. He pointedly avoided dealing with Indians who actually occupied much of the territory, like the Kickapoos, until others had already agreed to sell. Those who did were bullied, manipulated, or bribed into approving the sale. He did not "get the Indians drunk" to secure the cessions. Rather, he announced that no liquor would be served until the treaty's conclusion. Upon completion of the council, gallons of whiskey flowed from the commissary (Owens, 2007).

While few whites in Indiana complained of Harrison's act, they had neither needed nor sought additional territory at that moment. The purchases would bring settlers noticeably closer to Prophetstown, and marked a very aggressive move into Indian country, at a time when the Prophet and his followers desperately hoped to hold on to their territory. When, several months later, Tecumseh learned of the extent of the recent sale, he grew furious. In 1810, he reached out to British forces in Canada, hoping for a war to stop the further invasion of his homeland. This time, it would be the British who counseled restraint. Still fighting Napoleon, they hoped to avoid another needlessly distracting war in America (Sugden, 1998).

Knowing that a war without material aid from Canada would be futile, Tecumseh and the Prophet did what they could to strengthen their coalition, and to try to keep Harrison in check. Tecumseh met with the governor in Vincennes, Indiana's territorial capital, in August 1810, a council which infamously came close to a homicidal brawl. As Harrison spoke of the United States as a benevolent patriarch, and insisted that the government had always dealt fairly with native peoples, an indignant Tecumseh sprang up, and shouted (in Shawnee) that Harrison was a liar. [See Doc. 21] Some of the Americans, including the Territorial Secretary John Gibson, an old Indian trader, understood the chief's words, as well as his obviously agitated body language.

Though both sides had agreed to leave their muskets away from the council, the American officers carried sidearms, pistols, and/or swords, and Tecumseh and his men carried their tomahawks. As some of the Americans rushed to a woodpile to grab improvised cudgels for defense, Harrison and Tecumseh squared off, Tecumseh cocking his arm with his pipe tomahawk, while Harrison drew his dress sword and pointed it at the chief's chest. After a seeming eternity, Harrison calmly lowered his weapon, and Tecumseh followed suit. The governor declared the council adjourned until the next day, when cooler heads might prevail. They did meet again the following morning, but while they avoided theatrics, they accomplished nothing in negotiations. With Harrison bent on territorial expansion and Tecumseh equally adamant about holding on to Indian lands, and not allowing the Fort Wayne purchases to be surveyed for sale, little compromise could take place (Sugden, 1998).

The two men would meet again at Vincennes in the summer of 1811. Once more, little true negotiation took place. Tecumseh continued to deny the Americans' right to survey the Fort Wayne purchase, and Harrison continued to insist he would do so. Both sides seemed increasingly convinced that war would come. Before leaving, Tecumseh informed Harrison that he would not immediately return to Prophetstown, but would head south to proselytize for his brother among the populous

Southern nations. In what might be his only recorded prevarication, Tecumseh insisted that this trip was strictly a pacific, religious one. To his credit, Harrison instantly recognized that Tecumseh was obviously seeking to recruit allies to his anti-U.S. coalition. Tecumseh stated his hope that Harrison would instigate no trouble while he was away. Harrison bid the chief adieu, and almost immediately began planning an expedition to Prophetstown.

As Indiana's governor, Harrison served as the general of the militia, and he soon called up hundreds of them, and further accepted a detachment of U.S. Regulars under Captain John Boyd, as well as some volunteers from Kentucky. Perhaps for political reasons, he declined the offer of the Illinois militia to join him – he likely did not want them to share in what he anticipated would be a glorious victory. Leaving Vincennes in the early fall with 1,000 men, he marched up the Wabash River to a place the French had called Terre Haute (high ground) and built a small post there. The location was within the disputed, recently purchased lands, and some warriors, likely followers of the Prophet, shot and wounded an American soldier. This gave Harrison all the pretext he needed to continue his march (Owens, 2007; Sugden, 1998).

Harrison proved bent on invading Indian country, advancing well past even the Fort Wayne purchase, with the goal of dispersing the Prophet's followers on the Tippecanoe River. His right to do so remained in question, as President James Madison's orders had been left purposefully vague. Tensions with Britain, largely over the rights of American vessels to trade with Europe and also to avoid impressment of sailors, had risen again. Fearing that war might touch off so quickly that the several weeks' time lag in communications would leave the frontier vulnerable, the Madison administration had not wanted to tie the governor's hands in dealing with any "Indian problem." Consequently, Harrison would have enough leeway to start a fight if he chose (Sugden, 1998; Owens, 2007).

In fairness, while Harrison fully intended to break up the Prophetstown settlement, and knew it might well bring a fight, he thought that a preemptive strike would prevent a larger war. Many scholars dismiss his reasoning, though many whites on the frontier applauded it. Governor William Clark of Missouri, for one, thought it to be the prudent move, and the campaign would also be the beginning of Harrison's wild popularity among Kentuckians (Owens, 2007).

By November 6, 1811, Harrison's army had come within a few miles of Prophetstown. Though the Prophet knew he was approaching, the army's crossing to the east side of the Wabash several days earlier had caught him off guard. As Harrison's army camped on a plain of what is now Battleground, Indiana, the governor and the Prophet held a tense, unproductive council. Harrison demanded that the village disperse, which, given the lateness of the season, the Prophet understandably declined. The two men agreed they would talk again the next day, and both retired likely anticipating a fight. Harrison ordered his men to sleep in their uniforms with their weapons at the ready, but a shortage of axes kept him from fortifying his camp in any meaningful way. "Mad" Anthony would have been most disappointed.

Shortly before dawn on November 7, the five hundred warriors of Prophetstown advanced on the camp, but the surprise failed when a sentry fired at one of them. An intense firefight ensued, and the Americans took heavy casualties, including many officers. Harrison was not among them. Though a team of warriors had been assigned to eliminate him, he may have been spared when his conspicuous white horse bolted away, and his aide (riding a light gray mount) was shot in his stead. Already outnumbered, the warriors realized that daybreak had nullified their only advantage, and running low on ammunition, they withdrew, abandoning Prophetstown (Sugden, 1998).

Harrison's badly mauled army – they had more than 100 casualties – cautiously advanced into Prophetstown, finding a few British-made muskets, and then burned the village. They claimed victory, but some initial accounts referred to it as an American defeat. The deaths of so many officers, including Major Joseph Hamilton Daveiss, shocked the public. The U.S. Attorney for Kentucky, Daveiss had enthusiastically volunteered to join the expedition, but because he was a Federalist and Harrison a Jeffersonian, some cruelly claimed that Harrison had somehow sacrificed him. It would take the governor's political machine, and a Madison administration desperate to have good news from the frontier, to spin the Battle of Tippecanoe into an American triumph. Interestingly, in Harrison's subsequent political campaigns, this questionable "victory" would feature more prominently than his far more consequential triumphs in the War of 1812.

While Harrison had destroyed Prophetstown, and killed about fifty of Tenskwatawa's warriors, he failed to end the threat of war. Having cleaved a hornet's nest with his sword, he had simply angered the hornets and dispersed them throughout Indiana and Illinois. Numerous attacks on isolated settler cabins in those territories, likely by veterans of Tippecanoe seeking vengeance, would testify to that failure in the coming months. Though most Indiana residents approved of the campaign, it did little to put them at ease. [See Doc. 22] Rather than preventing the War of 1812, Harrison had arguably started it – for the frontier, anyway – in 1811 (Owens, 2007).

Meanwhile, Tecumseh had spent the waning months of 1811 trying to build the anti-U.S. coalition. Historians and biographers have clearly been enthralled by the chief's ambitious efforts, traveling enormous distances to add the populous Southern nations, like the Choctaws, Creeks, and Cherokees, to his cause. Yet the grand tour yielded little. Though some younger warriors heard Tecumseh's call, few actually joined him. Almost universally, the influential chiefs of the Chickasaws, Choctaws, and Cherokees rejected his message outright. They resented the efforts of a Shawnee – an outsider – trying to usurp the influence they had over their own countrymen. Many also owed much of that influence to their relationship with the American government. Still others likely recognized the American threat, but felt that militant resistance would be futile and deadly. The one significant, if unintentional, result of Tecumseh's tour was to spark a civil war among the Creeks (Sugden, 1998; Dowd, 1992).

Upon his return to Indiana in early 1812, Tecumseh and the Prophet began rebuilding their movement. Tenskwatawa's influence may have been dampened by Tippecanoe, as he had supposedly promised his magic would protect his warriors from harm. A state of war now existed between whites and natives in the Illinois Territory. Even if they did not directly follow the Prophet, Indians furious with the U.S., like the Kickapoos, and the Prairie Potawatomis led by the fierce warrior and prophet Main Poc, attacked isolated American settlements throughout Illinois (Sugden, 1998; Dowd, 1992).

Sparsely populated Illinois saw little combat between U.S. Regulars and British soldiers. Instead, it might be characterized as an "Indian war," primarily of raids on villages and isolated cabins and families. As with their Indiana neighbors, the Illinois conflict began well before 1812. In early June 1811, not far from the present town of Pocahontas, three Potawatomi warriors, surly from having failed to meet with any of their Osage enemies, instead fell upon the cabin of the Cox family, mortally wounding and scalping 20-year-old Elijah Cox and kidnapping his sister Rebecca (Ferguson, 2012).

At a conference in Peoria, Illinois, that August, the Potawatomi chief Gomo spoke of his desires for peace, but also felt compelled to recite a long list of grievances, particularly the Americans' failure to bring to justice whites who killed Indians. Indeed, most of the warriors at Prophetstown on the Tippecanoe would be Kickapoos, Ho Chunks, and Potawatomis from the prairies of Illinois. After the battle they returned home and called for greater resistance to the Americans. Within a few months, they began attacking isolated settlers throughout the territory. By the end of the year, the vast majority of Indian communities in Illinois had sent warriors out to fight the Americans. Only the Kaskaskias – numbering perhaps three dozen, and the much larger Sauk and Mesquakie had declined to enter the fight. The Sauks and Mesquakies were both split into anti-American and pro-peace camps, and the war-minded would not remain idle for long.

Eventually, anti-American Sauks leapt into the fight with gusto, even reportedly killing twelve Sauk women who had cohabitated with American men. But, as had repeatedly happened, whites attacked their Indian friends as often (or more so) than their enemies. The tiny Kaskaskia tribe had sent some warriors to help the Americans, yet white Illinoisans still sometimes roughed them up. Though the U.S.

government was bound by treaty to protect the Kaskaskias, they did not. Illinois' territorial governor Ninian Edwards became so exasperated that he banned the Kaskaskias from leaving their villages to hunt, hoping to spare them violence from his own citizens. Instead, the tribe began to starve, a condition made worse when the distracted U.S. government failed to deliver the tribe's rightful annuities (Ferguson, 2012). Like other governors before him, Edwards became so desperate that he eventually authorized a scalp bounty against "hostile" Indians.

Chief Gomo tried mightily to keep his Illinois River Potawatomis out of the conflict, a task made considerably more difficult when Illinois militia raided his village and did tremendous property damage to a people already racked by the disruption of the fur trade. A party of Potawatomis hunting for deer to feed the American garrison at Fort Clark (Peoria, IL) was ambushed by a party of Illinois Rangers, who apparently mistook them for enemies. The Rangers killed five in the party, including a woman and an adolescent boy, and wounded Gomo's own brother. Still, Gomo strove for peace. He notified the fort's commander that he could not stop a party of warriors, who would soon leave for the Wabash to take revenge on whites. They would not, however, attack the fort. The next morning, Gomo's people left several fresh deer carcasses at the gate of Fort Clark, signaling their continued friendship to the Americans (Ferguson, 2012).

A Civil War Among the Creeks

Scholars of the Red Stick movement (so called because they painted their clubs red, the traditional color for war) note that they defy easy categorization, but in broad strokes, many of the Upper Creeks disdained the growing influence of the U.S. in Creek life, and would be willing to fight to maintain their cultural independence. They especially resented Creeks of mixed parentage – *mestizos* – who had become increasingly acculturated and willingly did business with the Americans. (As if to demonstrate the complexity of the issue, however, two of the most prominent Red Stick leaders, Peter McQueen and William Weatherford, were themselves mestizos.) Having rallied to Tecumseh's call for militant resistance against American encroachment, Red Sticks soon came to blows with the National Creek Council, or White (the color of peace) Creeks, who largely held sway among the Lower Creek towns (Martin, 1991; Waselkov, 2006).

When a few Red Sticks followed Tecumseh back north, and later killed some Americans on the Duck River in western Tennessee in May of 1812, American officials demanded satisfaction from the Creek Nation. Accordingly, the murderers were themselves put to death by Creek kinsmen, but that did little to appease frontier whites, and it helped bring on open warfare between Red Sticks and National Council Creeks. The year 1812 saw considerable violence in Creek country, though after Duck River, it was confined to Muskogees. That did not stop Western whites, like Andrew Jackson, from calling for an invasion of Creek lands.

Jackson, a rising Tennessee politician, also served as the ranking general of the Tennessee state militia. Along with his governor, Willie Blount (pronounced Wy-lee Blunt), he had legitimate reasons to fear the Red Sticks. When Jackson later railed that the Red Sticks were a "matricidal band," he was not entirely inaccurate. Many Red Stick warriors saw white women as legitimate targets, as they would bear the next generation of white interlopers, and so they executed them in sometimes horrifying fashion. Like Blount, however, Jackson had been calling for an invasion of the Creek lands for at least a year. The fact that the Creeks occupied some exceptionally fertile, well-watered land ideal for cotton agriculture, had not escaped them. But prior to the summer of 1813, they failed to generate sufficient enthusiasm locally or in Washington for a preemptive invasion to swipe Creek lands (Saunt, 1999:268; Braund, 2012).

The U.S. officially declared war on Britain on June 18, 1812 – ostensibly because Britain refused to recognize American rights as a neutral to trade with Napoleonic France. Indeed, it would prove the most divisive, overtly partisan declaration of war in U.S. history, with Jeffersonian Republicans voting for the avoidable conflict, and nearly all Federalists voting against it. When word arrived, after President Madison signed the declaration into war, that the British had agreed to honor American maritime demands, the administration chose to continue (Cleves, 2009). As was often the case in American history, enthusiasm for the war far outpaced military preparedness, or even rational thinking, as Jefferson and Madison had cut the military budget significantly. Yet even American "War Hawks" – Republican Congressmen from the West and South who had clamored for the war, realized that there could be no direct attack on the British Isles, home to the world's greatest, if distracted, navy. Striking at British Canada would have to suffice.

Americans Take Aim at Canada

The wildly overoptimistic assumption was, in the words of the retired President Jefferson, that the conquest of Canada would be "a mere matter of marching" (Jefferson, 2008:293). Even if we grant him points for alliteration, it was an absurd statement. Though Americans enjoyed a significant manpower advantage along the Canadian border, in the first months of the war, the British-Indian alliance in the North held a decisive edge in skillful leadership. While many U.S. command decisions in the war would be driven by political calculations – fitting, given the political motives for the war itself – the British-Indian alliance had some excellent, proven leaders in the early days.

Tecumseh and his multi-tribal army linked up with General Isaac Brock outside Detroit in early 1812. The energetic and capable Brock and Tecumseh almost immediately recognized each other's talents and quickly forged a strong working relationship. Their first goal would be capturing the American fort at Detroit, which guarded the most obvious route for invasion between the American Northwest and Upper Canada. (*Upper Canada* is actually its southernmost land, as one sails *up* the St. Lawrence River to get there.) The American general at Detroit, William Hull, was in fact preparing to invade (Sugden, 1998).

The governor of Michigan Territory, Hull was a veteran of the American Revolution, and well past his limited prime as a field officer. He had already invaded Canada briefly, but faltered and returned. When he issued a proclamation threatening no quarter to any British soldier caught serving alongside a "savage" Indian warrior, Brock quickly deduced that the bombast sprang from a deep insecurity. Brock countered with his own proclamation, warning Hull that, if the Americans surrendered soon, the British could likely keep their vicious friends in check. If the siege went on for very long, however, the warriors would likely wreak brutal vengeance on the Americans, especially the women and children huddled in Detroit. At the same time, Brock's soldiers and Tecumseh's men continually paraded in sight of the fort, giving Hull a wildly exaggerated estimation of their actual numbers (Sugden, 1998; Owens, 2015).

Hull, a political appointee who had likely grown up with common American stories of Indians massacring their enemies, soon cracked under this psychological pressure. He had a well-built and armed fortress, and roughly equal manpower to Brock – about 2,500 men each, and therefore he actually held the tactical advantage. Yet he surrendered Detroit virtually without firing a shot, much to Brock's delight. The irony was that, unknown to Hull and most Americans at the time, Tecumseh was one of the few Indian leaders who viewed the lives of prisoners as sacrosanct, and was charismatic and bold enough to largely make that view stick. Though the vast majority of his followers might well have preferred to kill and scalp war captives, as had been the fashion for centuries, few if any had the stomach to directly challenge Tecumseh on the matter. At any rate, General Hull was eventually paroled back to the U.S., and the Army had him court martialed for cowardice, even sentencing him to death. He would be reprieved from the noose, but his public career would not (Sugden, 1998).

With command of Detroit, Tecumseh and his Redcoat allies could now carry out their planned invasion of Michigan and northwestern Ohio. The invasion was of course Tecumseh's primary objective, as he longed to wrest control of his beloved Ohio country from the U.S. Both he and Brock were quite perturbed when a temporary armistice was announced by the respective high commands, giving the Americans precious time to regroup. Worse still, Brock would head east to the Niagara frontier and die leading his troops at the Battle of Queenstown Heights in October of 1812. His successor, Colonel (later General) Henry Procter, possessed neither Brock's talents nor Tecumseh's trust (Sugden, 1998).

In January of 1813, Procter's men won a solid victory over the reckless American general James Winchester at Frenchtown, Michigan, along the River Raisin. However, the glow dimmed in the aftermath of the battle. When Procter evacuated the town, he left a number of Americans, too badly wounded to be moved, under the guard of some Indian allies. Tecumseh was not present at this engagement, and as the fearful Americans had warned Procter, a number of them were murdered in the aftermath by warriors seeking scalps and revenge. "Remember the Raisin" would serve as a battle cry for Americans in the West for the remainder of the war (Sugden, 1998).

In the spring of 1813, with considerable cajoling from Tecumseh, Procter invaded northwest Ohio, with the goal of capturing Fort Meigs, a stout new installation defended by Indiana's former governor, William Henry Harrison. General Harrison proved talented on defense, and his engineers made the fort largely immune to the bombardment of Procter's artillery, much to Tecumseh's annoyance. The attackers lacked the manpower to take the post by storm, though they did manage to crush a relief force of Kentuckians. Ordered by Harrison to move directly to the fort, the Kentuckians, shouting "Remember the Raisin!" – many of those killed had been from the Bluegrass state themselves – pursued Tecumseh's warriors right into a cleverly laid ambush. Procter, however, realized he had little chance of taking the post, and soon pulled back from his siege. Tecumseh seethed (Sugden, 1998; Edmunds, 1983).

The Shawnee's annoyance with Procter grew even before the British withdrawal from Ohio, then Michigan. After the successful ambush of the Kentuckians outside Fort Meigs, a number were taken prisoner and sent to be held at the ruins of Fort Miami. There, some Indian warriors who had not taken part in the battle, spoiling for war honors, menaced the prisoners. A British soldier valiantly tried to intervene, and was killed for his efforts. It appeared that the prisoners would all be slaughtered, when suddenly Tecumseh and the Indian Agent Matthew Elliott rode in. Tecumseh, as the grateful Kentuckians would later report, physically put himself between the killers and the remaining prisoners, daring the villains and cursing them for their cowardice in murdering the helpless. Such stories would later serve as the basis for Tecumseh's odd beatification in the minds of Americans, at least after his death (Sugden, 1998).

Procter again had failed to safeguard American prisoners. Probably, this offended Tecumseh's own sense of honor, but he likely also understood that such killings had negative consequences for his long-term struggle for Indian independence. He realized that Americans railed against such brutal acts – even when they did the same – and he hated to give them additional motivation to attack his people.

When events beyond Procter's control, especially the U.S. naval victory in the Battle of Lake Erie, compelled him to retreat, Tecumseh fumed. At one point, Tecumseh actually berated his counterpart publicly, comparing him to "a fat animal" that, when scared, runs away with its tail between its legs. However, to the chief's credit, once Procter pulled out a map and explained how the naval defeat meant his supply lines were fatally jeopardized, Tecumseh did consent to accompany the British retreat deeper into Canada. However, by October, he insisted that Procter make a stand (Sugden, 1998:359).

An advancing American army, led by Tecumseh's old nemesis General Harrison, nipped at Procter's heels. Worse yet, Tecumseh's scouts confirmed that Harrison's army included hundreds of mounted riflemen from Kentucky, led by the War Hawk congressman Richard Mentor Johnson. Tecumseh and his warriors saw the Kentuckians as a particular threat, as the Indians' wives and children were with the army. Tecumseh insisted that Procter make a stand to slow their advance, buying time for the warriors' families to escape from the knives and tomahawks of the vengeful Kentuckians. Procter finally agreed, choosing a field outside of Moraviantown, along a creek named after the famous Thames River in London.

On October 5, 1813, General Harrison sent the Kentucky horsemen in a headlong charge at the British lines. Exposed in a field – Procter had sent the entrenching tools to another location – most of the Redcoats fled immediately. Tecumseh and his warriors, holding a swampy wooded area on the flank, continued to fight desperately, knowing their families needed more time to escape. Throughout the battle, many Americans who knew Tecumseh recognized his booming voice, shouting encouragement (in Shawnee) to his men. Then the voice fell silent, and soon the fight ended as the warriors melted away. Colonel Johnson's men would insist that he had killed the chief, but it could not be confirmed, because Johnson did not know him by sight, and some of his men skinned a dead warrior found near the colonel, to make souvenir razor strops. This disgusted General Harrison, and infuriated him because he could not with certainty report the chief's death. The loss of Tecumseh did not end Indian resistance to the Americans in the North, but his leadership proved irreplaceable (Sugden, 1998; Owens, 2007).

Red Sticks and Old Hickory

In the South, the Red Sticks inspired by Tecumseh continued their war on the National Council Creeks, and some marched to Pensacola in Spanish Florida to demand arms from the governor there. Rightly intimidated, he provided them with ammunition, but no additional arms. As the Red Sticks headed home, they were ambushed by American militia at a place called Burnt Corn Creek. The Red Sticks rallied and drove the

Americans off easily. But the attack essentially accelerated their plans of eventually attacking the U.S. They now had to recognize that a state of war existed.

As frontier families – Americans and mestizos – throughout the southeast *forted up* in improvised defenses, the family and friends of John Mims, in what would become southwestern Alabama, did the same. They surrounded the Mims home with a wooden palisade, and about 300 Americans and mestizo Creeks, with some of their slaves, sheltered within. On August 30, 1813, despite being warned by some young slaves that hundreds of painted Indians lurked in the woods nearby, Fort Mims was caught largely unprepared. After a rather bloody (for both sides) battle, Red Stick warriors led by Peter McQueen and William Weatherford captured the post. About 250 Americans – who may have been secondary targets to the mestizo Creeks inside – died, in what the American press immediately dubbed the "Fort Mims Massacre." At long last, "Old Hickory" Jackson – the sobriquet referred to his perceived toughness – and Willie Blount had their pretext for a Tennessean invasion of Creek country (Martin, 1991; Waselkov, 2006).

Despite their later reputation, Jackson's army of militiamen did not initially impress. After almost a generation of frontier peace, the young men showed little aptitude for the rigors of a campaign, or even marksmanship. Jackson complained bitterly that a number turned out without functioning firearms, some without any at all. A lack of supplies, especially food, also bedeviled him. Much of his campaign consisted of burning down abandoned Red Stick villages. He was very fortunate to have the aid of hundreds of Indian allies. At least 500 Cherokee men volunteered. Despite American fears in 1812, the Cherokees, now surrounded on all sides by the U.S., wanted no part of the old British alliance. A number of National Council Creeks, eager to smite the Red Sticks, also joined. More prominent Cherokees and Creeks, often métis and assimilated, saw the Red Sticks as economically and socially backward, and a threat to their financial gain. The fact that the Red Sticks generally opposed owning slaves only intensified this notion. The key battle between Red Sticks and Jackson's army took place near a bend in the Tallapoosa River in what would become Alabama (Braund, 2012; Martin, 1991).

The Red Sticks had built a village in the river's bend – whites called the area Horseshoe Bend, while the Creeks called it *Tohopeka*. The river formed a peninsula, with the village at one end, and the Red Sticks built a stout log wall across the other, forming an impressive defensive site. About 1,000 Red Stick warriors, plus some of their kin, sheltered there in March of 1814. Jackson had two small fieldpieces, and began bombarding the log wall from a hill overlooking Tohopeka, with minimal effect. He had thought to send some of his Tennesseans, as well as his native allies, to the opposite side of the river to guard against a Red Stick escape. The general proved reluctant to order an assault until the log wall could be breached, which did not seem imminent.

One of the Cherokees, named Tuq-qua (the Whale), without orders, decided to swim the river and steal a Red Stick canoe – their only route for escape – and began ferrying his fellow warriors across. The Cherokees and Creeks, on their own initiative, set fire to the village and began an attack. When Jackson saw the smoke, he ordered a frontal assault on the surprised Red Sticks. The defenders fought fiercely, but aside from the deadly pincer movement, they found themselves outgunned. Despite American propaganda that the Red Sticks were in league with Britain, His Majesty had not yet made much effort to equip them. Indeed, only about one-fourth of the Red Sticks had a firearm, the rest relying on bows, tomahawks, and spears. Jackson's men, including a young Cherokee adoptee named Sam Houston, soon stormed over the wall, and a great slaughter ensued (Braund, 2012; Conley, 2007).

Cherokee allies had more than proven their value against the Red Sticks. In addition to the Whale's courage and initiative, a rising Cherokee named John Ross – who would later serve as the nation's first elected principal chief – had served as the Cherokee Regiment's adjutant. Even more directly, a Cherokee warrior named Junaluska saved Andrew Jackson's life by intercepting a Red Stick prisoner who had seized a knife and lunged at the general. Junaluska and Ross no doubt left the battlefield thinking that they were now blood brothers with Jackson, with an unbreakable bond forged in combat. Jackson had said as much to Junaluska. They would later be bitterly disappointed to learn that Jackson thought differently (Conley, 2007).

Jackson estimated that about 800 Red Stick warriors died that day. He reported that 557 had died on the ground at the Horseshoe – he knew this because his men cut the tips off of the dead men's noses and then counted them after the battle. They guessed that more than 200 additional Red Sticks died when, finding their escape canoes stolen or sabotaged, they had desperately tried to swim the Tallapoosa, to be shot down by John Coffee's Tennesseans and the Cherokee and Creek allies. It was said that the bend of the Tallapoosa turned red with blood for some time after the battle. Echoing the flaying of Tecumseh's corpse, some of Jackson's men skinned the dead warriors to make bridle reins for their horses. The carnage proved so great that even "Old Hickory" Jackson seemed a bit taken aback in his initial reports (Braund, 2012).

Horseshoe Bend made Jackson a national hero for the first time. It also impacted the Creek War, and the War of 1812 in the South, immensely. When British warships arrived on the Gulf Coast in the summer of 1814, finally (they thought) free of Napoleon and seeking to punish the U.S., they brought arms and military advisors for the great native army they assumed would help them wreak havoc in the Southeast. It took them

Figure 5.2 Andrew Jackson (1767–1845) and William Weatherford, a.k.a. Red Eagle (c.1781–1824). Jackson became a national hero by defeating the Red Stick Creeks at Horseshoe Bend and the British at New Orleans. As president, he led the charge for Indian Removal. Weatherford, a Red Stick chief, surrendered to Jackson after Horseshoe Bend, and so impressed the general with his courage that Jackson allowed him to leave.

some time to realize that the army they sought had largely been destroyed in the previous ten months. Most of the surviving Red Sticks had taken refuge with the Seminoles of Florida. The other nations of the Southeast, whom Britain hoped to recruit, had already joined the American war effort, or proclaimed a neutrality that, especially after Tohopeka, they had no interest in breaking (Owens, 2015; Owsley, 1981).

The other long-term ramification from Horseshoe Bend came in August of 1814, when Jackson dictated – there was not a whiff of *negotiation* – the Treaty of Fort Jackson. A bellicose Jackson bullied nine Creek chiefs – at most only one of them, William Weatherford, had been a Red Stick – to cede more than 20 million acres of their land to the U.S. Most of the land came from the Lower Creeks, who had aided the U.S., but Jackson's primary concern was that it abutted the border with Spanish Florida. He wanted that land for security as well as agriculture. Indeed, the treaty also banned Creeks from having any trade or other interactions with British or Spanish agents. The National Council and Lower Creeks protested the injustice, but to little avail. The cession was so outrageous that British officials tried to reassure the Creeks that it could not legally stand, especially after the peace treaty at Ghent, which would proclaim a return to *status quo antebellum* (Owsley, 1981; Martin, 1991).

The war in the South had not ended. Jackson would become an even greater national hero with his successful defense of New Orleans against a British invasion in January of 1815. Jackson's army there included a number of Choctaw Indians, as well as local pirates, free blacks, and some slaves. These would all be conveniently *whitewashed*, or wiped from the popular narrative, after the war's official end, as Americans wildly celebrated their supposed victory in the "Second War for Independence."

6   Indian Wars in the Age of Jackson

The Treaty of Ghent did end the fighting, but was more of an armistice than an actual treaty. It resolved exactly none of the declared causes of the war, and simply promised a return to *staus quo antebellum*, that is, the situation that had existed prior to June of 1812. That provision offered little comfort to the thousands who had died in the conflict, and when it came to Indian land claims, the U.S. showed little interest in honoring it. The Madison administration did seek to conclude formal peace treaties with their recent native enemies, and directed William Henry Harrison – who had retired in a huff after a dispute with the reviled Secretary of War, John Armstrong – to negotiate with them. Even Harrison, one of the great land grabbers in American history, realized that seeking additional lands at this moment would be disastrous, and Madison wisely allowed him to merely secure promises to bury the hatchet once more. Most of the Indians seemed quite ready to do so (Owens, 2007).

The Question of Florida

Along the Southern frontier, the proximity of (nominally) Spanish Florida, and the Seminoles, presented a far more complex problem. The Seminole Nation was a creation of the eighteenth century, an amalgam of refugees from northern Florida natives, like the Apalachees and Timucuas, as well as numerous Muskogees who had migrated south and east. Many of Florida's indigenous peoples evacuated with the Spanish to Cuba when Spain handed Florida over to Britain in 1763. This created a vacuum that Muskogee and other immigrants could fill. As a political unit, the Seminoles did not really exist prior to the American Revolution. British officials around this time began referring to Florida Indians as Seminoles, apparently a corruption of the Spanish word *cimarron*, meaning "wild" or "runaway." They were not technically independent of the Creek Confederacy prior to the Revolution. The distances involved, however, meant that in practice the Seminoles, not unlike American colonists, became accustomed to, and even fond of, local self-rule. The idea that the Seminoles were wild, troublesome, and incorrigible, did not end when Britain transferred Florida back to Spain in 1783 (Calloway, 1995:249).

During the last days of the Revolution, Florida's population swelled with a massive influx of thousands of British Loyalists, their black slaves, and native allies of the British. Since at least the 1730s, Florida had also been seen as a refuge for slaves who ran away from British colonies, and Spain periodically made formal offers of asylum to them. It further served as a natural refuge for Indians who might raid British, and later American, plantations in the Southeast. Though the Seminoles seem to have become increasingly open to European notions about the profitability of black slavery, in Florida generally and among the Seminoles especially, the line between slavery and freedom had some flexibility. Unlike in other colonies, both Spanish and British officials after the Revolution encouraged amiable relations between blacks and Seminoles as a defensive measure against Americans' territorial ambitions (Calloway, 1995).

Even after the Treaty of Ghent took effect in 1815, the remnants of the Red Sticks, their Seminole relatives, and hundreds of maroons – escaped former slaves – remained in a feisty mood. Partly, this was because the British military had left them both the means, and agents, to encourage continued resistance. At what was called Prospect Bluff, overlooking the Apalachicola River in the Florida panhandle, British engineers had constructed a well-designed fort, and they left it in the care of their native and maroon allies. They also left hundreds of small arms, ample artillery, and lots of ammunition for the use of their recent allies, many of whom they had trained in European military drill and tactics. During the war, British officers hoped to gather native allies and thousands of runaway slaves to smite the Americans in the Southeast. Some did so purely for military reasons, but others, like Edward Nicholls, were sincere, early abolitionists. Nicholls, a brevet (temporary/honorary) lieutenant colonel of the Royal Marines, had hoped to build a multiracial army in the Southeast that would not only punish the U.S., but strike a great blow against slavery (Millett, 2013). Had he not arrived several months after Jackson's crushing victory at Horseshoe Bend, he might have had a chance.

When that dream collapsed, and Nicholls was ordered to exit North America in 1815, he insisted on leaving his comrades with the means to defend themselves, and to serve as a beacon of freedom. Though Britain was officially at peace with the U.S., the defenders of the fort at Prospect Bluff (Americans called it, with equal parts scorn and terror, the "Negro Fort") flew the Union Jack above their walls. They served to encourage Indian raids on American plantations, as well as to inspire enslaved peoples for hundreds of miles to seek freedom. Andrew Jackson was not pleased.

The First Seminole War

Jackson, now the U.S. Army's commander in the Southeast, made reducing the fort at Prospect Bluff, and "pacification" of the Seminoles, his priorities. He was not alone in fearing the opportunity and example that the fort gave to Indians and would-be runaway slaves. By the dawn of the nineteenth century, as the cotton gin and plantation agriculture had breathed new life into slavery, white Americans, who had long feared both Indian attacks and slave rebellions, now became convinced that Indians and slaves would join forces. Any suggestion that they would make a common cause in defeating the republic sent imaginations running into near panic. Nor were American whites the only ones who saw Florida as a security risk (Millett, 2013; Owens, 2015).

Creek Indian leaders, like the métis chief William McIntosh, feared Prospect Bluff would encourage their own slaves to escape, or even attack. Further, they had long quarreled with the Red Sticks and Seminoles. Part of the reason that more acculturated Creeks, like McIntosh, as well as many prominent Cherokees, had fought against the Red Sticks was that they feared the militants threatened their new materialistic lifestyles, which very much included owning black slaves and plantations. McIntosh and other pro-U.S. Creeks backed the American incursions into Spanish Florida – which were quasi-legal at best – not only because they saw common cause with Jackson but also because the general promised that they might keep any maroons they captured for slaves. These incursions would later be called the First Seminole War (1816–1819).

Though named after the Seminoles, the war probably had at least as much to do with capturing or destroying maroons, as slave owners in the Southeast had Jackson's ear. In 1816, a U.S. Navy gunboat moved up the Apalachicola River, coordinating with American infantry under General Edmund P. Gaines, and Chief McIntosh's Creek warriors. A lucky shot from the gunboat detonated the fort's magazine, destroying the works in a spectacular explosion, killing most of the defenders. The leading chiefs at Prospect Bluff, one an Indian and one a maroon, were captured, wounded but alive. They were quickly scalped and executed by McIntosh's Creeks, however, who had become furious when they learned that the fort's defenders had burned a captured American sailor to death (Millett, 2013; Missall, 2004).

The destruction of Prospect Bluff greatly reduced the munitions available to the maroons and Seminoles, but not their incentive or will to raid American plantations. Spanish authorities, meanwhile, showed little interest or capability in stopping them. American civilians raided Seminole villages, killing and plundering – they were particularly keen on capturing slaves – and Seminoles responded in kind. By the time James Monroe became president in 1817, white Americans in the Southeast clamored for something to be done. Secretary of War John C. Calhoun pressed Jackson to end the raids and secure the border.

In 1818, Jackson himself led an army into the Florida panhandle. Though he had announced his intentions to the Spanish governor in Pensacola, the invasion itself was quite illegal. Jackson built Fort Gadsden on the ruins of Prospect Bluff – well within Spanish territory – and also captured Spain's fort at Pensacola, an aggression he claimed was justified because Spain supplied arms to Indians. His forces caught two Red Sticks, including the prophet Hillis Hadjo, also known as Josiah Francis, and summarily executed them in front of Hadjo's daughter, Millie Francis. Only a short time before, Millie had prevailed upon her father to spare the life of an American officer who had mistakenly stumbled into Seminole Territory (Missall, 2004).

The army also targeted maroon villages on the Suwanee River – subduing former slaves had been a primary objective for the invasion – and captured two British nationals, the trader Alexander Arbuthnot, and the former army officer (and Edward Nicholls protégé) Richard Armbrister. Both were swiftly tried by military tribunal for inciting the Seminoles – Armbrister probably had, Arbuthnot may well have been innocent – and sentenced to death. The fact that Jackson had no legal authority to invade foreign territory or arrest foreign nationals, much less execute them, mattered little. Armbrister died by firing squad, while Arbuthnot was lynched from the yardarm of one of his own ships. Unlike the execution of the two Red Sticks, Jackson's unauthorized killing of the two Britons became an international incident (Owsley, 1981; Millett, 2013).

Most of Monroe's cabinet, including Calhoun, distanced themselves from Jackson, save Secretary of State John Quincy Adams, son of the second president. Highly educated, aloof, and no friend to slavery, John Quincy seemed to have little in common with Jackson, whom he would continue to consider a volatile, violent bumpkin. But Adams, who had recently begun negotiations to acquire Florida, was also, like Jackson, a nationalist, and he knew that adding Florida to the Union would likely benefit the country as a whole. He recognized that Jackson's rampage, while totally illegal, had conclusively demonstrated Spain's lack of control in Florida, and knew it gave him considerable leverage. Indeed, in 1819 Spain ceded Florida to the U.S. in the Adams-Onís Treaty, and while the Americans did agree to cover $5 million of their own citizens' claims against the Spanish Crown, Spain received not a penny for Florida. For Jackson, he drew criticism in the Northeast for his actions, but Americans in the Southeast gloried in what they saw as his decisive actions on their behalf (Missall, 2004; Taylor, 2013).

Despite American hopes, the annexation of Florida did not end their fears of Seminole raids. Official correspondence and citizens' petitions from Florida Territory in the 1820s made frequent mention of the issue of runaway slaves and their being harbored by the Seminoles. Floridians tried various schemes, from unauthorized raids to purchasing them. Creek chief William McIntosh certainly saw both crisis and opportunity in Florida. In 1821, Seminole leaders complained bitterly that McIntosh and his Coweta warriors (at the behest of Andrew Jackson) had barged into their territory (again) and kidnapped many blacks and some Indians (Owens, 2015).

By the early 1820s, the government estimated that 22,000 Indians lived in Florida, and they held about 5,000 slaves. American slave owners had long complained that the Seminoles were lax slave masters. Their slaves, who often lived in separate villages, had remarkable autonomy compared to their U.S. counterparts. Their status was far closer to that of vassals who owed annual tribute to lords, rather than the gang-system laborers common on American plantations. American slave owners continued to insist that this set a terrible example for their own slaves.

Perhaps two-thirds of Florida's Indians were recently arrived refugees from the U.S., and the government argued they had little legitimate claim to Florida land. In 1823, the Treaty of Moultrie Creek sought to confine the Seminoles to a large reservation in central Florida. Not coincidentally, the reservation had no access to the sea, and would isolate them from the British or Spanish ships that still occasionally made landfall on the Florida coast to trade. Most Seminoles, understandably, showed little interest in moving to the reservation, but by 1826 had nevertheless done so. However, in what would become a pattern in the nineteenth century, when the government lagged in providing promised food, hungry Seminoles left the reservation to hunt, alarming white settlers, who called for their outright removal (Missall, 2004).

The election of Andrew Jackson as president in 1828 proved a great encouragement for such Americans. Indian policy, since the election of Thomas Jefferson, had combined all the avarice and presumption of Federalist Indian affairs, with a distinct lack of patience regarding land sales and "civilization" of Indians. That trend only accelerated under Jackson. His first State of the Union Address in 1829 called, among other things, for removing Indians from the American Southeast. While he admitted that some of the tribes in the Southeast had made progress toward "civilization," he could not abide their recent attempts to establish sovereign governments within the bounds of the U.S. His position largely ignored more than five decades of U.S.-Indian treaty language.

Jackson's argument, that Indians would inevitably become extinct if allowed to live near whites, was riddled with inconsistencies and half-truths. It is possible, however, that he believed it, despite all the evidence that the "Five Civilized Tribes"[1] were acclimating to their white neighbors remarkably well. The Cherokees, in particular, had developed a representative, republican government, with a written constitution – written in their own syllabary, thanks to the Cherokee Sequoyah. Though weak in logic, Jackson's call for Removal drew great support from white Southerners, eager to see the Cherokees, Creeks, and other Indians of the Southeast taken off their valuable agricultural lands, which could then be sold to white Americans (Howe, 2007).

Indians' removing from eastern America to lands west of the Mississippi, often to what would become Missouri or Arkansas, easily predated Jackson. Portions of the Shawnees had headed west to escape the carnage of the American Revolution in the 1770s. Portions of the Cherokees, cajoled by their agent, Return Meigs, Sr., had gone west prior to the War of 1812, with some government assistance. Some Creeks had also gone west. They had moved, more or less, voluntarily. But Jacksonian Democrats now professed that removing Indians from east of the Mississippi – and off of their terribly valuable cotton growing lands – was a crisis that must be tackled quickly.

With Jackson's prodding, Senate Democrats wrote the Removal Act of 1830 [see Doc. 23] which did prove controversial. Christian activists, especially in the Northeast, decried the manifest injustice of removing the tribes of the Southeast, where they had recently had success in converting thousands to Christianity. Southerners charged them with hypocrisy, noting the brutality of King Philip's War (1675–76) and other Indian conflicts in the seventeenth and eighteenth centuries that had largely removed Indians from the Northeast. Senator Edward Frelinghuysen of New Jersey, known as the "Christian Statesman," led opposition in the Senate, unleashing a 6-hour speech against the bill over three days in April. Nevertheless, it passed the Senate relatively easily, 28–19 (Lepore, 1998; Howe, 2007).

Removal faced a greater challenge in the House of Representatives, where even some Jacksonians, like Creek War veteran and Tennessee congressman David Crockett, blasted the bill. (Former congressman, Jackson protégé, and Cherokee adoptee Sam Houston, who had been badly wounded by the Red Sticks at Horseshoe Bend, also broke with the president on the issue.) The Removal bill actually failed two test votes in the House, before finally passing by a slim margin, 102–97, in late May. Two-thirds of Northern legislators voted had against it, while four-fifths of Southern ones voted for it. The Cherokees' elected Principal Chief, John Ross, who considered the president an old war buddy from

---

1 Scholars now tend to put that phrase, which referred to the Cherokees, Creeks, Choctaws, Chickasaws, and Seminoles, in quotes, owing to the inherent ethnocentric bias of its basic premise.

their service at Horseshoe Bend, wrote strenuous protests to Jackson, to no avail. Junaluska, who reasonably assumed Old Hickory owed him a favor, travelled to Washington, hoping for a personal audience with the President, but was turned away. Jackson, who had twisted numerous arms in the Congress to secure the bill's passage, eagerly signed it into law (Howe, 2007; Conley, 2007).

Among its many oversights, the Removal Act of 1830 allotted only $500,000 to purchase the lands of Indians living east of the Mississippi, and to relocate them to the Indian Territory west of the Mississippi River. (Note that the Removal Act did not specifically mention the Southeast, but merely Indians living within the bounds of the existing states.) Even assuming that every facet of the scheme went perfectly, it would prove a wildly optimistic, absurdly low number. Eventually the treaty annuities alone would run over $68 million. The figure, of course, did not include the military expenditures incurred in trying to effect Removal (Howe, 2007).

While President Jackson stated that the tribes must only be removed voluntarily, neither he nor any military or Federal officials actually took that seriously. Indeed, some nations made their reluctance to leave, if not eagerness for war, obvious. One of the first conflicts came not in the Southeast, but in western Illinois.

The Black Hawk War

The Sauk and Mesquakie (or Fox) nations had lived in the region of western Illinois and southern Wisconsin even after a series of treaties negotiated by Indiana Governor William Henry Harrison had purchased their lands in 1804. The Sauk and Mesquakie had done very well hunting in the region, often bringing in about $60,000 worth of furs per year. They of course rejoiced in a clause in the treaty stating that, while they had sold the land to the U.S., they could continue to hunt upon and use the land in perpetuity. (A similar clause in the treaty of Greenville had allowed for Indian hunting on the ceded lands until they were settled, but the 1804 treaty stated that "as long as the lands which are now ceded to the United States remain their property, the Indians belonging to the said tribes shall enjoy the privilege of living and hunting upon them") (Kappler, 1972:76; Wallace, 1999).

While a lawyerly reading might conclude that Harrison intended to say that, once sold to settlers, the lands no longer belonged to the U.S., the Sauks and Mesquakies were not lawyers. The chiefs who marked the treaty later claimed that they were misled – which seems accurate – and that they had been plied with alcohol to sign the document, which seems unlikely. Regardless, when the War of 1812 broke out, many Sauks and Mesquakies, including the war chief Black Hawk, sided with Tecumseh and the British. After the return of peace in 1815, a significant schism

Indian Wars in the Age of Jackson 107

Figure 6.1 Black Hawk (1767–1838). A Sauk War leader and disciple of Tecumseh in the War of 1812, Black Hawk hoped that his people could reoccupy their land in western Illinois. Instead, American forces crushed his band in the disastrous war that bore his name.

grew between Black Hawk's so-called British Band, and those who followed the holy man Keokuk, who increasingly advocated accommodating the Americans. By 1831, both groups had, at American insistence, crossed the Mississippi into what would become Iowa (Jung, 2007).

The British Band especially disliked the location. Not only did they have trouble farming – though rich, the soil was largely impenetrable without draft animals and heavy plows to cut the prairie grass roots – it also placed them nearer to longtime enemies, like the Sioux. In 1831, Black Hawk and his hungry followers crossed back over the Mississippi to their former village of Saukenauk, hoping to harvest the corn that they had planted before removing west. Though they made no martial displays, nearby whites, many of them illegal squatters, panicked. The Army, hoping to avoid an actual confrontation, made a show of force, sending in General Edmund P. Gaines, whose federal troops were augmented by Illinois mounted militia. The militia were hoping a fight would break out, and they sneered when Gaines agreed to supply the starving Indians with corn if they would recross the Mississippi, dubbing the agreement the "Corn Treaty" (Jung, 2007:65). [See Docs. 24 and 25]

As happened so often with accords between the government and Indians, Gaines did not deliver as much corn as promised, however, and in April of 1832, the British Band again returned to Saukenauk. The women in particular had been loath to abandon their well-groomed cornfields, and insisted on reoccupying the village, despite its having now been purchased by whites. Black Hawk, aided by a half-Ho-Chunk prophet named Wabokieshiek (whites called him the "Winnebago Prophet"), did not seek a fight. But Black Hawk did hope that other tribes in the region would join him. (He even sent emissaries as far away as Texas looking for allies.) He assumed the British would supply him from Canada with much needed supplies, and that, with numerous allies, he could intimidate the Americans into allowing his band to remain in Saukenauk. Black Hawk found, however, that few natives in the region had any interest in joining his movement. Nor did British officials in Canada, who replied to his request for arms and ammunition with a few twists of tobacco. By the time he realized his hopeless situation, the Americans were clamoring for war (Jung, 2007).

Like the Creeks during the War of 1812, the Sauks and Mesquakies had suffered a schism over how best to deal with the encroaching Americans. Like the Red Sticks, the British Band had chosen the path of resistance. But Black Hawk's followers faced even greater difficulties in gathering foreign aid and allies. A few Ho Chunks, Potawatomis, and Kickapoos joined him, but the vast majority of natives in the upper Mississippi Valley felt joining the British Band would prove futile. Some, including the Ottawa-born Potawatomi chief Shaubena – like Black Hawk a former lieutenant of Tecumseh – actively campaigned against their people's joining the British Band's struggle (Jung, 2007).

From the moment Black Hawk's people crossed the Mississippi into Illinois, a great many whites simply assumed that a fight was unavoidable. Indeed, many of the militia – who had grown up hearing romantic stories about the War of 1812, but were too young to have witnessed its ugliness – seem to have welcomed the opportunity for an "Indian war" that was stacked heavily in their favor. As with previous attempts at pan-Indian resistance, Black Hawk's band drew considerable attention from the media and the public (Owens, 2015).

With a warrior (who had been Tecumseh's ally) and a religious visionary, seeking a broad tribal alliance and British aid, American newspapermen and Indian agents quickly drew comparisons to the late Shawnee's movement. The government, therefore, responded with overwhelming force. The British Band did win some skirmishes and kill several settlers, but by the summer of 1832 a large force of Army Regulars and Illinois militia had chased Black Hawk's band into southern Wisconsin. In late June, at the Battle of Wisconsin Heights (near modern Sauk City, Wisconsin), the militia, 750-strong, caught the fleeing Indians. Black Hawk, who had fewer than 130 total Sauk and Kickapoo warriors, directed an impressive delaying action, which allowed the British Band's women and children to escape. Almost 70 warriors died, though, while the militia lost only one man (Jung, 2007).

Black Hawk later sent an embassy to the American camp, who stated that the British Band would now cross the Mississippi and cease fighting. Tragically, with no interpreter present, the Americans had no idea what he said, and so ignored him. By August 2nd, Black Hawk's followers numbered only about 500, and they were caught between the Bad Axe River and 400 Regulars, 900 militia, and a steamboat, the *Warrior*, which used its artillery to brutal effect. The ensuing battle left more than half of the British Band dead, including more than 100 who died trying to swim across the Mississippi. Black Hawk himself, now in his 60s, was taken captive. The misery did not end for what was left of his people. Once they crossed the Mississippi, they were attacked by the Sioux, and also by Menominee and Ho Chunk warriors, who had been encouraged by General Gaines to pursue them across the river. As a captive, Black Hawk would be taken on a tour of the great cities of the East Coast, both to impress upon him the folly of fighting the United States, and to serve the endless desire of Easterners to see an Indian (Jung, 2007).

The Second Seminole War

Other groups would have more success with military resistance than Black Hawk's band. In 1832, the Treaty of Payne's landing called for the removal of the Seminoles to lands west of the Mississippi, in what would later become Oklahoma. Several Seminole chiefs marked the treaty, and in late 1832 toured the "new" land – part of the existing Creek reservation there – and initially approved of the removal. However, many recanted in early 1833, claiming that they had been misled by the government. While some Seminoles consented to leave, and headed west in 1834, others resisted. When U.S. Agent Wiley Thompson banned sales of arms and ammunition to the Seminoles, they reacted not unlike Indians in the 1760s had viewed Jeffery Amherst's order.

Anti-removal Seminoles coalesced around several warriors, including a métis chief named Billy Powell, better known as Osceola. (Americans obsessed over the charismatic Osceola, downplaying the important role played by other Seminole leaders.) Osceola's opposition to removal had been clear since the Treaty of Payne's Landing when, rather than sign it, he stabbed it with his knife. Seminoles and whites engaged in isolated skirmishes in 1835. In November, a Seminole chief named Charley

Figure 6.2 Osceola (1804–1838). Seminole chief. Osceola, also known as Billy Powell, violently opposed Seminole removal from Florida, and fought the U.S. Army to a draw until captured under a flag of truce. Ill with malaria, he died in a military prison.

Emathala sold his cattle prior to removing west. Osceola, viewing him as a traitor, waylaid him, and tossed the cattle money contemptuously across the chief's corpse (Missall, 2004). [See Doc. 26]

Unlike the relatively weak government confronted by Alexander McGillivray, Blue Jacket, and Dragging Canoe, Osceola and the Seminoles squared off against an established nation that had grown up considerably in the intervening decades. With American industry booming, and a rapidly growing population, the American citizenry expected, and demanded, that the government settle the Seminole situation quickly, before things got out of hand. Though the actual threat of a pan-Indian coalition with foreign aid and black allies taking the offensive in the American Southeast was slim at best by the 1830s, several factors combined to make that chance seem plausible. Prior to the nineteenth century, and the rise of the Cotton Kingdom in the South, white Americans had dreaded both slave rebellions and Indian wars, but as separate events. In the nineteenth century, reflecting their own views of race/white supremacy, they came to fear that the two calamities would be combined to wipe them out (Owens, 2015).

After decades of rumors and the occasional thwarted plot, Southerners had confronted a true large-scale slave revolt in 1831. Nat Turner's 1831 uprising in Virginia killed about 60 whites, including women and children, before it was put down. (White militia killed scores of innocent slaves in their frenzied response to the rebellion.) The psychological impact extended far beyond Virginia's borders. Turner's revolt was seen in the context of repeated threats of British-backed slave insurrections – threats that had arisen in every major conflict from the Revolution – and slaves had repeatedly stated that they anticipated British aid when in rebellion (Taylor, 2013). This context made the Second Seminole War especially vexing for American whites.

The first major blow came in December of 1835, when about 180 Seminole warriors ambushed 110 soldiers under Major Francis L. Dade outside of modern Bushnell, Florida. The Seminoles took advantage of the heavy hammock for cover, and after shadowing Dade for days – they were supposed to wait for Osceola's arrival – they finally made their attack on 28 December. In what became known as Dade's Massacre, they wiped out the major's command. Dade himself died by the first shot, fired by Chief Micanopy, as a signal to his warriors. Only two of Dade's men returned to Fort Brooke alive. The Seminoles, meanwhile, suffered fewer than ten casualties. Osceola had not been present, as he was occupied at Fort King, near modern Ocala, Florida. There he succeeded in killing the Georgia Congressman-turned-Indian Agent Wiley Thompson, who had been appointed to direct Seminole Removal, and thus became a target. He died on the same day as the Dade Massacre (Missall, 2004).

Open warfare between Seminoles, settlers, and troops expanded in 1836. An early casualty for the Army was Captain David Moniac, a Creek, and the first American Indian to graduate from West Point Military Academy. He commanded a contingent of Creek volunteer cavalry – almost eight hundred Creeks aided the U.S. against the Seminoles – and died at the Battle of Wahoo Swamp. The Army had likely reveled in having Moniac on their side, as a related conflict had also broken out with his people in 1836. Like the First Creek War, this conflict also began as an internal conflict among the Creek Nation, with some

Lower Creeks resisting removal, while Upper Creeks mainly complied, and sometimes helped the Americans subdue the roughly 3,000 rebels. Primarily in Alabama, the Second Creek War was only put down when the Army sent General Winfield Scott – a hero of the War of 1812 and future star of the Mexican War – to end the resistance there. Even then, the conflict flared up periodically well into the 1840s (Ellisor, 2010; Missall, 2004; Haveman, 2016).

As the conflict with the Seminoles intensified, horrified Floridians passed resolutions calling for Federal troops to protect them from a potential rebellion of their slaves. General Thomas Jesup wrote his superiors explicitly that "this is a negro, not an Indian, war," and made dire predictions of impending slave uprisings if the war did not end quickly (Belko, 2011:193). In perhaps the most extreme reaction, the military storekeeper in the Federal arsenal in Charleston, South Carolina – quite a distance from Florida – confided his worst-case scenario plan to his commanding officer. Noting the outbreak of the Second Creek War (1836) in Alabama, and that the Second Seminole War was already raging, he also reflected that there were 20,000 male slaves (potential rebels) within a day's march of the arsenal. If those slaves took the example of the Creeks and Seminoles, he offered, and no reinforcements were sent to Charleston, he would simply blow himself up with the powder magazine to prevent the rebels from taking the arsenal (Owens, 2015). Fortunately for the eardrums of Charlestonians, the storekeeper's resolve was never tested.

By the spring of 1837, Brigadier General Jesup, directed to end the Second Seminole War, had some success, leading a war of attrition. By using the tried and true strategy of attacking villages and farming centers, Jesup slowly reduced the Seminoles' capacity and will to resist. The Army killed hundreds of Seminoles, including noncombatants, and captured hundreds as well. Those who were captured reluctantly agreed to Removal. But when Osceola led a raid that freed about 700 of them, the war began again in earnest. From the Army's perspective, this *treachery* obviated any obligation to deal honorably with the Seminoles henceforth.

Osceola, apparently ill with malaria, and several other Seminole chiefs were captured under a flag of truce near Fort Peyton in October, 1837. Though the others, including Coacoochee – Wild Cat – managed a spectacular escape through a tiny window high on the wall in their cell at Fort Marion (St. Augustine, Florida), Osceola was far too ill to join them. After the escape, the army transferred Osceola to Fort Moultrie, South Carolina, where he died a prisoner in 1838. Yet the war continued (Missall, 2004).

No sane military professional welcomes chasing guerrilla fighters through semitropical vegetation. The thick hammock of the Florida Everglades made an ideal ground for Seminoles to wage their war of attrition and ambush. A good example of how miserable a time the Army had chasing after the Seminoles, and the latter's brilliant use of terrain, came at the Battle of Lake Okeechobee, the largest engagement of the war. On Christmas Day, 1837, Colonel Zachary Taylor, a career Army officer (and future president), led 800 Regulars and Missouri Volunteers in pursuit of perhaps 400 Seminole warriors, led by Coacoochee, Alligator, and Sam Jones.

The Seminoles, hoping to buy time for their wives and children to escape, wisely took up a position that forced Taylor's men to wade through waist-high water and sawgrass toward their unseen enemy. In Coacoochee's first action since escaping from St. Augustine, the Seminoles inflicted heavy casualties on the American troops. Seminole riflemen focused on the officers, and by the end of the day, they had killed more than two dozen soldiers and wounded well over a hundred. Having inflicted worse than literal decimation on the Americans, and having bought ample time for their families to escape, the Seminoles withdrew. Americans, longing for any good news, touted the battle as a victory, and Taylor was hailed as a hero and promoted to brigadier general. But the Americans were no closer to winning the war (Missall, 2004).

After almost two years in Florida, the Army granted General Jesup's request to return to his previous job as Quartermaster General. Zachary Taylor, the "hero" of Lake Okeechobee, replaced him. Taylor had a little over 2,000 men – not enough to control all of Florida – and therefore concentrated on holding the northern portions, hoping settlers would return to their farms. He built numerous posts, and his men cut hundreds of miles of roads to connect them. By 1839, Taylor had managed to remove most of the Seminoles in northern Florida. However, the American public had grown weary of the great expense of the war, as well as lurid stories of not only Seminole attacks, but the breakdown in the Army's morale. Almost half of the officers in the Regular Army resigned during the conflict. Indeed, some officers committed suicide – one drove his own sword through his eye rather than continue – and at least one of the Creek warriors sent to Florida as a U.S. auxiliary hanged himself during the campaign (Missall, 2004; Haveman, 2016).

By 1840, the Army had grown so frustrated that they resorted to a tactic utilized by the Conquistadors and proposed by Henry Bouquet in 1763 – they used dogs to track the Seminoles. Editorialists had been suggesting such a move since at least 1836. [See Doc. 27] Public outcry over this seemingly last-ditch gesture reflected not only growing sympathy for native peoples east of the Mississippi, but also a general frustration with continuing a conflict that produced little in the way of glory or results. In response, the Secretary of War ordered that the dogs were to be muzzled and leashed. It was a sound public relations move.

The "Cuba bloodhound" had originally been bred to track and dispatch runaway slaves, and had a vicious reputation. In reality, bloodhounds depend on their noses, and they proved ineffective when their quarry moved through water, so the Seminoles easily lost them in the swamps (Missall, 2004).

Sporadic fighting continued until 1842, when the government agreed that the remaining Seminoles, perhaps 300, one-third of them being warriors, could stay in a large reservation in southwest Florida, primarily in the swampy Everglades. While still denied any direct access to the sea, most Seminoles were themselves exhausted by the years of fighting and the destruction of their resources. For the Army, and the American public, the war could not end too soon.

The war cost the lives of at least 1,500 American servicemen, mostly from the Army, though Navy and Marine forces also fought. The vast majority died from diseases, like yellow fever and malaria. It is estimated the conflict cost well into eight figures – $40 million being an educated guess. Perhaps a few hundred Seminoles died in combat, but likely far more, especially women and children, died from hunger as the Americans systematically destroyed their food sources (Missall, 2004). Since the 1780s, the Army had slowly but surely learned that waging war on Indian resources (and noncombatants) was far more effective than trying to catch their warriors in large battles. Those tactics would be further refined and utilized in the wars against the Plains Indians in the 1870s.

Though the vast majority of the Cherokee Nation, including their elected principal chief John Ross, staunchly opposed Removal, a group of influential métis led by John Ridge agreed to sign a removal treaty at New Echota in 1835. Known as the "Ridge Party," or the "Treaty Party," they knew when they signed the treaty that selling Cherokee land without their government's permission was a capital offense. Likely they felt that they might be forgiven once the rest of their nation realized the futility of resisting the U.S. They proved incorrect. Chief John Ross, Junaluska, and other Cherokee veterans of the war against the Red Sticks found President Andrew Jackson unsympathetic to their pleas to retain their homelands (Perdue, 2007; Howe, 2007).

The Cherokees, herded west at bayonet point during the presidency of Jackson's hand-picked successor, Martin Van Buren, named their journey the Trail of Tears. Ross' wife and son were among the 4,000 Cherokees who died en route, as the removal put a premium on speed and thrift, and minimal attention to life. The Choctaws and other southeastern nations lost fewer people than the Cherokees, but suffered deplorably nonetheless. A portion of the Cherokees ran to the mountains of North Carolina, and their descendants remain there today. Like smaller numbers of Seminoles and Creeks, the federal government found it easier to ignore than remove them. Often, they would simply be deliberately omitted from narrative accounts (Perdue, 2007; Buss, 2013).

North of the Ohio River, smaller, less publicized removals took place. The Potawatomis, for example, still refer to their march as the "Potawatomi Trail of Death." Yet as with some of the nations to the south, removal was never complete, and the states of Michigan and Wisconsin have native reservations to this day. While many of the Miamis were forced out of Indiana, and became the federally recognized Miami Tribe of Oklahoma, some of their relatives took advantage of private land grants and their descendants maintain holdings even now in the Hoosier state, though they lack Federal recognition. Much like native peoples in New England, they did not disappear, but did spend many years perfecting the art of blending in with their newcomer neighbors. American Indian history remains, perhaps above all else, a story of resilience (Bowes, 2016; Rafert, 1999).

Conclusion: Making Sense of History

By 1842, the U.S. had largely abandoned warfare to dispossess Native Americans east of the Mississippi, finding the legal process both more palatable and cost-effective. Yet almost inconceivably, a third Seminole War broke out in late 1855, allegedly because some Army troopers cut down some banana trees belonging to the Seminole chief Billy Bowlegs, a veteran of the Second Seminole War. The war (1855–1858) proved a last gasp for such violence in the East (Missall, 2004).

By the beginning of the Civil War, many of the nations removed from the Southeast into future Oklahoma faced a difficult choice – to side with the Federal Government, which had seen to their forced migration, or to ally with the slaveholding Southern Republic, largely populated with men who had insisted upon their removal in the first place. Many sided with the Confederacy, seeing it as the best chance to maintain their independence, and also their slaves, but the conflict further weakened unity in Indian country. The war's end in 1865 would free up the military and industry of the United States to subdue the other free peoples of the West. Ironically, unprecedented pan-Indian identity would only be achieved, peacefully, in the latter half of the twentieth century, which saw parallel civil rights movements for African Americans, women, Latinos, and the LGBTQ community.

Indian Wars in Memory

Eighty-five years after the Northwestern Confederacy crushed Arthur St. Clair's army on the Wabash, Lakota and Cheyenne warriors wiped out George Custer's detachment of the Seventh Cavalry at Little Big Horn. That disaster cost the U.S. less than half the men lost by St. Clair, yet Custer would become a household name and, for a long time, a martyr. Few Americans have ever heard of St. Clair, or Blue Jacket. Custer's legend was partly the result of his widow's relentless campaign to have her husband remembered as something other than a colossal, murderous fool, but it also demonstrated how much the U.S. had grown in those intervening decades. Telegraphs, railroads, and newspapers meant that word of Little Big Horn spread rapidly across a very large nation. While Anglo-American conquest of the eastern half of North America spanned over two hundred years, the United States crushed the Indians of the far West in a little over four decades (Mueller, 2013).

One of the most effective tactics the Army employed against Indians in the West was to place relentless pressure on the entire population, not just warriors, and to deliberately target food sources. Though often regarded as an innovation in that war, the defeat of native warriors through destroying their food had been a common tactic since at least the eighteenth century.

The conquest proved more than physical. In addition to pushing native peoples off their own lands and forcing them onto reservations, the U.S. used the printed word and storytelling to mold Indians to fit a triumphal narrative. Americans often reduced Indians to one-dimensional foils for American heroics – most nations do such things in forging their own creation stories. Perhaps more perversely, some Indians would be pressed into service as American icons. Americans cheered news of the death of Tecumseh, yet within months he would be celebrated as a true "noble savage," admirable for his courage, his vision, and his humanity toward prisoners and noncombatants. For America to be great, it needed formidable – but doomed – foes. In death, Tecumseh became, for Americans, an ideal Indian (Owens, 2015; Sugden, 1998; Sayre, 2005).

"Heroes" Need "Villains"

Colin Calloway's recent book, *The Indian World of George Washington*, argues that, in many ways, the first president's public career and personal fortune were largely based in his relationships, good and bad, with Indian peoples (Calloway, 2018). The same can easily be said for the United States. In so many ways, the conquest of native peoples *made* America. The fight to take Indian lands provided (eventually) not just tremendous wealth to the growing population of the U.S., and the resources that fed continued expansion across North America. It also proved a forge for (white) American identity. Chroniclers from George Bancroft to Francis Parkman, to Teddy Roosevelt and Frederick Jackson Turner, could turn the story of the armed suppression of Indian peoples into a triumphal narrative for the United States. This narrative saw Indians as worthy, but ultimately doomed, foes to Americans – challenging enough to strengthen American resolve, but not so strong as to defeat it. Great victories require great enemies. Most native warriors would have agreed with that part, at least.

As John Sugden observed, the War of 1812 created American heroes who would dominate the next several decades of American politics

(Sugden, 1998). Andrew Jackson remains the most obvious. His tremendous popularity with the American public, built largely on crushing Red Sticks and Redcoats during the war, never really flagged in the next thirty years. William Henry Harrison parlayed his fame from Tippecanoe and the Thames into a series of high-profile government jobs, including (briefly) the presidency. Richard Mentor Johnson, Harrison's ally in the war and rival in the years after, became vice-president in 1837, largely on the strength of his status as a wounded war hero. "Rumpsey-dumpsey, Rumpsey-dumpsey, Col. Johnson killed Tecumsey," sounds insipid and bloodthirsty today, but many Americans in the Early Republic found it appealing. Many more used the war as a springboard for their future careers, including noncombatants like Henry Clay and John C. Calhoun (Owens, 2007: 246).

As time wore on, American accounts of their "Indian Wars" became not only two dimensional, but increasingly sanitized, in part because they were so important to the United States' creation myth. While the value of the North American lands and resources the U.S. came to possess was obvious, the often-ugly fashion in which that possession came about proved too much for schoolchildren, or at least their parents. How could one inculcate the values of freedom, patriotism, and high-mindedness through accurate descriptions of violent conquest? Understandably, if not admirably, white Americans in the nineteenth and early twentieth centuries simply did not try.

Professors and Producers

Scholarship, and public opinion, shifted significantly in the decades after World War II, and especially with the Civil Rights movement of the 1950s–1970s. As African Americans demanded their basic citizenship and freedoms, so did others, including American Indians. By the 1970s, it became increasingly common for media imagery, particularly movies and books, to offer a more sympathetic, even heroic interpretation of Indians. The 1970 film *Little Big Man*, featuring Dustin Hoffman as a fictional white adoptee of the Cheyennes who witnessed the Battle of Little Big Horn, was perhaps the first widespread depiction of George A. Custer as a bloodthirsty lunatic, rather than a sacrificial hero. On the academic front, Dee Brown, a University of Illinois professor of Library Science, published *Bury My Heart at Wounded Knee: An Indian Account of the American West* (New York: Holt & Rinehart, 1971). Increased attention to the native peoples east of the Mississippi River would come largely in the following decades.

With greater political attention – and clout – minorities forced educators and academics to begin reversing the whitewashing of the nineteenth century. African American Studies, American Indian Studies, and Women's Studies programs opened up long-ignored peoples to scholarly inquiry, a trend which continues to benefit us today. We have (hopefully) reached a point where we recognize that honestly and accurately addressing our past ultimately strengthens, rather than divides, us. As scholars, our never-ending task remains to try to set the record straight.

Part II
Documents

Documents

Document 1
Agent George Croghan at Fort Pitt to Sir William Johnson, 31 March 1762. *The Papers of Sir William Johnson,* James Sullivan and Alexander C. Flick, eds. 13 Volumes. (New York: State University of New York, 1921–1951). 3:662–663 [spelling modernized for clarity].

   ... The Expence of Indian affairs since November last has been but Trifling as ye Winter has been so Severe here that very few Indians has come this Way, Except some parties of Senecas going to War against ye Cherokees who all behave very Ill when Refused ammunition[,] vermilion {red paint for war} knives & such things But as ye General {Amherst} is averse to giving them Such Necessaries Neither ye Commanding officer, Nor My Self Can Take upon us to give them any thing, though Col. Bouquet is of opinion they should be Supplied & I believe has wrote the General thereon.
   The Senecas are a very bad people proud & Mischievous and Look on themselves as ye absolute Lords of ye Soil and has been two Much Indulged by ye provinces of New York & Pennsylvania formerly & Now say that ye English is Setting up ye Western Nations against them so that unless you can Settle them at ye Ensuing Conference which you intended to hold at Fort Johnson & oblige some of their Chiefs whom you can Depend on to Come to Ohio & Chastise ye Rabble of that Nation hear I am of opinion they will make some Disturbance though all the other Nations this Way behave Extremely Well at present But the Senecas seem Ripe for some Mischief, and there Nott being Allowed ammunition & Necessaries as they pass an[d] Repass here to War Make them very uneasy, But if any accident should happen from that ye General Must Take ye Consequences, for my part I have Done Everything in my power to promote ye good of his Majesty's Indian Interest Since I have been in ye Service & with as Much Frugality as the nature of ye service would admit But ye future will Never putt ye Crown to Sixpence Expence what will happen without a Written order...

Document 2
Sir William Johnson at Johnson Hall, 18 March 1763, to General Jeffery Amherst.
Papers of SWJ, 10: 623. [Spelling as in original]

{On 15 March, 1763, Johnson held a conference to settle the issue of some whites murdered by Iroquois men}
...when all the Chiefs of Onondaga, Severall Senecas, Oneidas, & Mohawks amounting in the whole to 60 Men Arrived here, and yesterday had a conference with me.
At the opening the same, the Speaker of Onondaga, Acquainted me with the Steps they had taken in consequence of meeting at their Castle [palisaded village]... I then acquainted them with some Intelligence I received the other Day from Mr. Croghan, concerning the Examination of a Shawaneese Chief lately taken, who acknowledged that a War Belt was sent last Spring thro[ugh] their Towns to the Seneca's Country from the Cherokees, & the French at the Illinois, but that the same was not unanimously accepted of. Altho[ugh] all the Indian Nations were as he said become very jealous of the English, who had erected so many Posts [forts] in their Country, but were not so generous to them as the French, and particularly gave them no Ammunition, which was the chief cause of their Jealousy & Discontent. – the Senecas on hearing this, declared they were not acquainted with the Belt...

Document 3
Speech of Pontiac, Ottawa chief, 27 April 1763, near Detroit. Relaying the vision of a Delaware Indian, most likely Neolin.
From Francis Parkman, Jr., *History of the Conspiracy of Pontiac, and the War of the North American Tribes Against the English Colonies After the Conquest of Canada*. Boston, MA: Little, Brown, & Co., 1851, 182–183. [Note that, for the speeches of non-literate Indians, we are at the mercy of the translators, whose skills and loyalties could vary considerably.]

Having been led by a woman dressed in white to a beautiful plain with three great villages, he found himself before the Great Spirit. The Great Spirit bade him to be seated, and thus addressed him: –
I am the Maker of heaven and earth, the trees, lakes, rivers, and all things else. I am the Maker of mankind; and because I love you, you must do my will. The land on which you live I have made for you, and not for others. Why do you suffer the white men to dwell among you? My children, you have forgotten the customs and traditions of your forefathers. Why do you not clothe yourselves in skins, as they did, and use the bows and arrows, and the stone-pointed lances, which they used? You have bought guns, knives, kettles, and

blankets from the white men, until you can no longer do without them; and what is worse, you have drunk the poison fire-water, which turns you into fools. Fling all these things away; live as your wise forefathers lived before you. And as for these English, – these dogs dressed in red, who have come to rob you of your hunting-grounds, and drive away the game, – you must lift the hatchet against them. Wipe them from the face of the earth, and then you will win my favor back again, and once more be happy and prosperous. The children of your great father, the King of France, are not like the English. Never forget that they are your brethren. They are very dear to me, for they love the red men, and understand the true mode of worshipping me.

Document 4
Proclamation of Josiah Martin, Capt. General and Governor.
Cape Fear Mercury, NC., 18 May 1774.

Whereas it has been represented to me by John Stewart, Esq., His Majesty's Superintendent of Indian Affairs, that sundry Persons, supposed to be Emigrants from this Province, had settled on the Cherokee Lands, in Violation of the most solemn Treaties, which had given just Umbrage to the said Indians, and may be attended with the most fatal Consequences: I have therefore thought fit, by and with the Advise and Consent of his Majesty's Council, to issue this proclamation, hereby strictly enjoining and requiring the said Settlers immediately to retire from the Indian Territories, otherwise they are to expect no Protection from his Majesty's Government. 25th Day of April 1774.

Document 5
From Williamsburg, VA.
In Dixon & Hunter's *Virgina Gazette,* 17 August 1776.

The number of Indians concerned in the different ravages lately committed in Fincastle amount to 6 or 700, some say 800; and yet, sudden as their attack was, they murdered in all their butchering parties but 18 persons, and wounded 6, whilst our men killed in the skirmishes with them 26 on the spot (as many were carried off dead) took one prisoner, and wounded at least as many as were killed. As the Cherokees have been so completely checked in their career, and we understand from fort Pitt that the northern Indians are not disposed to attack us in that quarter, and have only engaged not to suffer us to march through their country against Detroit, we may hope that there is not much to be dreaded from the terrible combination of Indians we have been threatened with by our enemies.

126 Documents

Document 6
Written from Augusta, GA, on 21 August 1776.
In Dixon & Hunter's *Virginia Gazette,* 14 September 1776.

In late July

> a party of 240 men, under the command of Major Jack, set out from Fort James on the ceded lands, about sixty miles to the westward of Augusta, for Toogelo and Estatoe, the two nearest Cherokee towns. After three days march, they arrived that these places, where they killed about thirteen Indians, and burned both towns. They likewise took one Holmes prisoner, who had been in Cameron's camp that very morning. After having effected this, the party returned home, and Major Jack arrived at Augusta on the 10th of this month. The same advices add, that, in all appearance, the Cherokees will not receive any aid from the Creeks, but be left alone to extricate themselves out of a quarrel they so rashly and needlessly involved themselves in..... A skirmish lately happened between a party of them [British soldiers in East Florida] and some Georgia rangers, in which each lost two men: Some Creek Indians were with them, but on being called to by a Half-breed in our party, surrendered themselves. They were well treated, and have since been sent to their own nation in quite a different humour.

Document 7
From Williamsburg, VA.
In Dixon & Hunter's *Virginia Gazette,* 30 May 1777.

> Upwards of forty gentlemen and ladies of the Cherokee nation are now here on a negotiation of peace, which it is hoped will be lasting, and to request a boundary line may be drawn to prevent encroachments on their lands. They have had an audience, and it is expected a compact will be settled with them in a few days. Among them are Oconostoto, the Little Carpenter, the Pigeon, and other headmen and warriors. After the Talk was concluded, they favoured the public with a dance on the green in front of the palace, where a considerable number of spectators, both male and female, were agreeably entertained.

Document 8
Extract of a letter from Silver Bluff, 28 October 1779.
In Dixon & Hunter's *Virginia Gazette,* 25 December 1779.

> By the unwearied endeavours of Mr. Galphin the Indians are peaceable; a party of the headmen of the lower Creeks who over awed the rest, are now at Mr. Galphin's cow-pen on Ogeechie, and will be here in a few days. The Spaniards lately came from Cuba to St. Mark's,

near the Apalachee old fields, conferred with the Creeks, and sent to each town of the nation, Spanish pipes and tobacco, and five kegs of rum, as tokens of friendship; at the same time charging them always to hold the Americans firmly by the hand, as they, the French and we are united in a triple band of friendship, and would jointly revenge any injury that might be offered to either of the parties.

Document 9
Headline Savannah, GA, 25 April 1782.
From *The Royal South Carolina Gazette,* Charleston, SC, printed by Loyalist James Robertson.

On the 7th of this month ten Creek Indians, having crossed the Altamaha on their return to the Nation, fell in with a party of seventeen rebels, under the command of a continental Major Moore, at Reid's Bluff. Moore came up to them at a log house with his men dressed in red, told them he was a British officer, shook them by the hand, and said he was glad to see them. Supposing that the Indians were now in his power, this perfidious, treacherous, rebel villain, ordered his men to fire upon them, by which one was killed, and four were wounded. Roused by a sense of their danger, the Indians returned the fire, killed Moore, a Captain Smith, and two others, and, by an almost incredible exertion, routed the whole party, and drove them into the river, from which it is believed few, if any, have escaped.

On the 11th instant 65 mounted Rebels, under the command of Paddy Carr and one Robert Sallet, crossed the Altamaha, and marched to New Hope plantation, to intercept some boats under the charge of Capt. Cameron of the King's Rangers. The rebels having inhumanly butchered in cold blood one Hoover, a Loyal Refugee, at the house, took post near the plantation. Capt. Cameron having received information of the enemy's intention, and perceiving them formed, landed with 8 of the Rangers and about 30 of the Cherokee and Creek Indians; being joined by 8 Choctaws on his march, he immediately attacked, routed, and pursued the rebels two miles. The enemy lost many horses, and by their own accounts 14 men; of the soldiers and Indians not a man was either killed or wounded.

Document 10
A. McGillivray at Little Tallassee, 15 September 1788, to Richard Winn, Andrew Pickens, and George Mathews, Commissioners for treating with the Southern Nations of Indians.
American State Papers, Indian Affairs [hereafter ASPIA], vol. I. (Washington, D.C.: Gales & Seaton, 1834), 30.

Gentlemen:

... We expected that, upon Mr. Whitfield's return, a truce of arms would have been directly proclaimed in Georgia, and can't account for the delay of that measure; and in fact, there has been no observance of it on their part, from June till now. They have been driving and plundering our hunting camps of horses and skins &c. and it is only lately, that a Coweta Indian brought me a paper, which he found fastened to a tree near to Flint river, which, upon a close examination, I find to be a threatening letter directed to me. It is wrote on the back of an advertisement, with gunpowder; a part of it rubbed as it dryed, and with the carriage. The writing says something of the war, and your savage subjects, and an establishment of peace you must 'not expect, until all our damages are made good at the treaty, and satisfaction we will have for our grievances,' from all which, I foresee great difficulty in the attempt to preserve strict suspension of hostility. I can only assure you, that we shall regulate ourselves by the conduct of the Georgians, and act according to circumstances. The writing I mention, is signed Jam. Alexander, 5th August, 1788. The Cherokees are daily coming in to me, complaining of acts of hostility committed in the most barbarous manner by the Americans, and numbers are taking refuge within our territory, who are permitted to settle and build villages under our protection. Such acts of violence, committed at the time that the Congress, through you, is holding out to the whole nations and tribes, professions of the most friendly nature, makes it appear to all, that such professions are only deceitful snares to lull them into a security, whereby the Americans may the more easily destroy them.

Be not offended, gentlemen, at the remark; 'tis true that it is universal through the Indians.

I am, with great respect, gentlemen, your humble servant,

ALEX. M'GILLIVRAY.

Document 11

Commissioners Richard Winn, Andrew Pickens, and George Mathews, to Alexander McGillivray, Esq. and the head men and warriors of the Creek nation. Hopewell on Keowee, 28 November 1788.
ASPIA I:30.

Sir:

Your letter of the 12th August and 15th September are now before us. With regard to the former, wherein you mention *nothing has been done, and all is yet to do,* give us leave to tell you, that every thing in our power has been done, in order to bring forward a treaty, and, under the authority of Congress, to give full and ample redress in what concerns your territory. At the same time we must observe, that that honorable body will not lose sight of doing equal justice to the State of Georgia, whose claim to what you call the disputed lands, is confirmed by three different treaties, assigned by your head-men and warriors. Therefore, we earnestly recommend you and the chiefs to seriously to consider, under these circumstances, how impossible it is for us to comply with your requisition [i.e., request], relative to removing the people from the Oconee lands; this can only be the business of the treaty, after a full investigation of the right of claim.

In answer to your last, where you so pointedly attack that body under whom we have the honor to act, we cannot be silent, least it should be tortured into a conviction of guilt. Narrow and illiberal indeed must be that mind, that could for a moment suppose, that Congress, after withstanding one of the greatest Powers of Europe, with her allies, together with almost the whole of the Indian tribes combined, should at this day have recourse to base artifice, in order to accomplish the ruin of a few Indian tribes, while she is enjoying the blessings of peace at home, and an honorable name among nations of the world.

.... {They note the governor of Georgia has already proclaimed a truce.}

If we take a view of the conduct of the Indians on your part, we have more right to complain: we daily hear of the most cruel depredations, committed by the Creeks on the Georgians; the man you allude to (Alexander) we are credibly informed, was in pursuit of a party of Creeks that had stole twelve horses from Green county, and notwithstanding we have had every assurance given us, that hostilities should cease. The Governor of Georgia has lately handed us a list of the different counties that have recently suffered, to wit:

Liberty County, between 25 and 30 negroes, and several large stocks of cattle.
Effingham, one man killed.
Wilkes, from 6 to 10 horses plundered.
Greene, from 21 to 27 horses do. [Ditto, meaning the same.]
Washington, 6 horses do.
Franklin, from 16 to 20 horses do. One man wounded.

We must add to the above list, a pair of fine dun geldings, taken from General [Joseph] Martin, about a mile from his plantation, by some Coweta Indians, while he was acting under Congress as agent for the Cherokees and Chickasaws.

The Seminolean Indians are likewise doing a deal of mischief; we know not whether they belong to any part of the Creeks, but wish to be informed. From these violations committed, what can the Union expect, unless a stricter compliance on your part is observed in putting a stop to hostilities? We are well assured, Congress will not look on in silence, and see any part of the Union robbed of its citizens. Enclosed you will find a late resolve of Congress, and a proclamation relative to the Cherokees.

It is our sincere wish that you will meet us the eighth day of June next, at the place appointed before; but should this appear to you at too distant a period, a month sooner will be no object with us in holding a treaty. In the interim, we fully assure you nothing shall be wanting on our parts, in the observance of a strict suspension of arms, on a presumption that you will act in like manner. We request that you will consult the head men and warriors, on this occasion, and send us a pointed and decisive answer, signed jointly as soon as possible.

We are, sir, with due respect, your obedient servants,

RICHARD WINN
ANDREW PICKENS
GEORGE MATHEWS

Document 12
Kentucky Gazette, 12 April 1788, Lexington, KY, printed by John Bradford.

12 April 1788. A CERTAIN William Oats, who was an Indian trader some years ago in the State of Georgia, bought a white girl from one of the Chickamawga Indian squaws;[1] the child was about nine months old when he purchased it, the Indians informed the said Oats, that the child was taken on the Kentucky road, at which time there was one or two white people killed, but not the mother of the child, and that it belonged to people of the name of Stand – the child has some particular marks by which the mother (if living) may know it Mr. Oats now lives on the Pee Dee river, near Grooms ferry, has lived with the child baptized by the name of Nelly Oats, he has no child and is determined not to part with it, but is desirous her parents may know where she is. For farther particulars, apply to John M. Nabb living on big pigeon in (what is called) Franklin State.

Document 13
General Joseph Martin, agent to Cherokees, to Sec. War Knox, from Fort Patrick Henry, Sullivan County, North Carolina, 2 February 1789. *ASPIA* I:48.

---

1   Scholars no longer use that term, a corruption of the Iroquoian word for a *vagina*, in the place of 'woman.' The term was frequently used in the eighteenth and nineteenth centuries.

Sir:

I have certain accounts that some designing men on the Indian lands have assembled themselves to the number of fifteen, and call themselves a convention of the people, and have entered into several resolves, which they say they will lay before Congress; one of which is, to raise men by subscription to defend themselves, as the Legislature of North Carolina refuses to protect them on the Indian lands, but, on the contrary, have directed and ordered those people off the Indian lands. A certain Alexander Outlaw by name, I am informed, is to wait upon Congress on behalf of this new plan. I think it my duty to say the truth of him: Shortly after the murder of the Corn-tassel and two other chiefs, this said Outlaw collected a party of men and went into an Indian town called Citico [Settico], where he found a few helpless women and children, which he inhumanly murdered, exposing their private parts in the most shameful manner, leaving a young child, with both its arms broke, alive, at the breast of its dead mother. These are facts well known and cannot be denied in this country. Mr. Outlaw has done every thing in his power to drive the Indians to desperation, although I find some complaint by the said Outlaw against me, for carrying on an expedition against the Cherokee Indians without orders from Government. I have once stated that matter to you, but, least that may not come to hand, I beg leave to state the facts to you. In the month of May last, a boat, richly laden, was going down Tennessee [River] to Cumberland [River], the crew were decoyed by the Chicamoga [Chickamauga] Indians and Creeks together, all of which crew were killed and taken prisoners; after which doings, the Corn-tassel informed me of the cruel murder they had committed, also the repeated murders and robberies they were constantly omitting on the frontiers of Cumberland and Kentucky, also on the Kentucky road, in company with the Creeks. There was not the least hopes of reclaiming them as long as they lived so far detached from their nations. That the Corn-tassel had talked to them until he found it was of no use; that he, with the other chiefs, advised and thought it best to go against them and burn their towns, by which means they would return to their allegiance; that then they would have it in their power to govern them. This the Indian chiefs urged in the strongest terms, which account I laid before the Executive of North Carolina, who advised that peace should be offered them, and, if refused by the Indians, that then the principal officers of Washington district should pursue such measures as to them should appear most likely to put a stop to those merciless Indians on the frontiers and roads. It was unanimously agreed to march against Chicamoga, but by no means to give offence to the Cherokees, which has been a means of uniting the Chickamoga Indians to the other Indians. It will now be our own faults[sic] if we do not make all that race of Indians our friends.

So great the thirst for Indian lands prevails, that every method will be taken by a party of people to prevent a treaty with the Indians. They are now laboring to draw some of the Indians to a treaty, as they may purchase their country: this party say, if they can purchase of the Indians, they will have it without the consent of any other power; that the Indians have an undoubted right to it, and not Congress; that if they could only prevail on a few of the lower class to come into their scheme, they would get conveyances made and contend for the right. This I have heard from them.... I have the honor, with much respect, to be, your most humble and obedient servant,

JOS. MARTIN.

Document 14
"For the Indian Department"
"Anti-Pizaro" [sic], *Boston Gazette,* 2 January 1762. [Spelling as in original.]

>Shall COLUMBIA
>To NAYURES sons with tyrant rage deny
>The woody mountain, and the covering sky!
>Ah no! – Tho' late, the treach'rous with disclaim,
>Awake to justice, and arise to shame;
>No more with the blood the weeping soil deface
>But spare the patient, suffering warlike race.

The injustice and cruelty of the Indian war seems to be so generally admitted. – Is it not enough to secure the settlements which we have already made by drawing a *cordon* of forts around them, and leaving the natives quietly to possess their lands beyond them? Are we not already in possession of more lands than can be settled for a century at least? Have we not already driven the Indians from the Atlantic to the borders of Lake Michigan, and can we not be content to let them remain there in peace? What better right have we to march through the centre of their country, than Great-Britain would have to march a body of troops through the center of the United States? The lands do not belong to us, until we have bo't them of the Indians, the rightful possessors. By the treaty with Great-Britain, the right of *preemption* [i.e., the right to buy the land] only was ceded to the United States – they could cede nothing more, for they had never extinguished the Indian title – Wherefore then should we drive them to the Western Ocean, or extirpate their race?.... What can be the policy of prosecuting this cruel war? Is it to conquer more lands, or to serve as a pretence for augmenting the standing army? Is it to punish the Indians for retaliating the murders of our settlers, or to promote the interest of jobbers and speculators in western lands? Cannot our frontiers be secured by a chain of forts? And is it not certain that our frontier people are the agressors [sic], and that they drive the Indians to commit depredations upon them? Are they ashamed to tell you, *'that they think no more of killing an Indian than of a Deer?'* The ordinary process is thus – Encroachments are made upon the Indian territory – their Hunters are killed, or made drunk and robbed of their furs – the Indians make reprizals [sic]– the traders and settlers retaliate – murders are committed – a Hue and Cry is set up against the Indians – unlicensed parties go out against them – some of them get scalped – the Continent rings from one end to the other, of Indian cruelties, barbarities, murders and depredations – but not a word of the cruelties and injustice of the white Indians – The reason is plain – all the people from whom intelligence can be had in that country, are interested in the destruction of the natives – the hue and cry at length reaches the ears of government – influential men are interested in the Western lands – the importance of some depends on a military force – some think a standing army the best security for the punctual payment of Interest on six per cent stock – others that it is a convenient and necessary *engine* of government – all join in the hue and cry against the Indians, and government is precipitated into a fruitless war to gratify the interest and ambition of a few.

ANTI-PIZARO [sic]

Document 15
Sec. of War Knox to Gov. William Blount, Southwest Territory, 31 January 1792.
ASPIA I:245.

Statement of the measures which have been taken to conciliate and quiet the Southern Indians.

Sir: I have the honor to acknowledge the receipt of your letter of the 25th of December, by Mr. Allison, and enclose a duplicate of mine to you, of the 10th December last. The militia must not be called out, excepting in cases of real danger. I am confident, that this power will be used by you with a just regard to the interest of the United States.

It is important that the line should be run; but, perhaps, as there may be some misconception on that head, although I know of none, yet, as we may want the assistance of the Cherokees in our military operations, perhaps there may be a greater degree of delicacy in having the line ascertained previously than subsequent to the campaign.

I am impressed with the importance of having some of all the Southern tribes with our troops in the field; because, I am apprehensive, that their passion for war will constrain them to join the other side, if they do not ours. However, both the paint of time, and the characters you propose for running the line, will be left to your discretion.

.... We have been surprised with a visit of the following Cherokees: *Nenetooyah*, or Bloody Fellow, *Chulloh* or King Fisher, *Nontuaka*, or the Northward, *Teetske*, or the Disturber, *Kuthagusta*, or the Prince, *Schuewegee*, or George Miller, the squaw Jane Dougherty, and James Carey the Interpreter. They have stated the following objects as their business, the most material of which will be complied with, especially the additional annuity.

1. To obtain a higher compensation for the lands they relinquished by the treaty with Governor Blount, on the 2nd July, 1791.
2. That the white people, who are settled southward of the ridge, which divides the waters of the Tennessee from those of Little River, should be removed; and, that the said ridge should be the barrier.
3. That a person of reputation should be commissioned, in behalf of the General Government, to reside in the Cherokee nation, who should at once be their counsellor and protector.
4. That the projected settlement of the Tennessee company at the Muscle Shoals, should be prevented.
5. That the annual allowance of goods should be now furnished, together with some ploughs and other implements of husbandry, as mentioned in the treaty.
6. That James Carey, and such other person as the nation shall hereafter choose, shall be appointed interpreters. They will return in a few days, enriched with presents, personally, and carrying with them fifteen hundred dollars' worth of goods. They will return by the way of Charleston, by which route they came. It would appear, that General Pickens endeavored to prevent their journey, but in vain. They will be accompanied, on their return, by a worthy young gentleman, Mr. Leonard Shaw, who has been educated at Princeton college, and who, from the purest motives, is desirous of being employed in the Indian department. He is to reside with the Cherokees, and correspond with you regularly. I shall broach to the Cherokees the idea of their joining our army, but I have not yet fully done it.

I have been extremely desirous that all the proceedings which have taken place with these Indians, should have been transmitted to you, by Mr. Allison. But the particular circumstances which compel him to return by a given day, will prevent. But I shall do it, as soon as possible. You will then find, what you will always find, that although this particular affair has been, and others which may occur hereafter may be, transacted separately from you, yet, that the whole affair will tend to induce a more perfect confidence on the part of the Indians, in your character, and, of course, will confirm you in an entire reliance upon the candor and uprightness of the Executive of the United States.

I have the honor to be, &c.

Document 16
Hanging Maw's Talk. From a Knoxville, TN paper of 20 October 1792. In *Kentucky Gazette,* 17 November 1792.

Friends and brothers the Printers, I HAVE no money to send you, but I will give you two pounds of Beaver Fur if you will put this TALK on paper, like William Cocke's that it may be heard a great way off, as well as his. HANGING MAW.

{Addressing William Cocke of Mulberry Grove, TN.}...

What have you to talk about treaties? You know nothing about them – I have heard your talks about them – I have heard your talks before; they are all like nothing

You suppose the goods given at the treaty, and those which were to be paid every year to my people, were given to buy our friendship. I told you that you knew nothing about the matter; they were the price of our lands, promised in fair and open treaty. You got a great quantity of good lands, worth an hundred times as much as you gave for them.

You have a heart like a Squaw, and talk like one – You say fear is the best and only assurance of friendship of an Indian. This is the language of a bad heart; why say Indian? The great Man above made us all of the same clay, both red people and white people, and gave to some the hearts of men, and to others the hearts of squaws. Yours is of the latter sort, or you would not talk such hard talks, and say all the Cherokees must be killed; because some of them are bad men and go to war.

You tell the little talks of your bad men, who talk when they ought not, as you do, to make themselves great men, as if they were the headmen and council of your whole nation; and you add a number of lies to your talks, out of your own head, and you have them put on paper and sent a great way off, to make our Father the President and all his beloved men think that the Cherokee, men, women and children are bad, and ought to be laid on the ground.

You are not a man and a warrior – but to make believe you are, you boast of having killed K—you say you did it by good fortune; but remember when it was time of peace, and you did not know but he was a good man when you killed him. You also murdered my beloved brother the Tassel, or some of your people with hearts like yours did it, – in time of peace too – these are not the action of men and warriors.

I suppose you will put more of your talks on paper. I will not answer them any more. You are but a boy, and talk for yourself. Our great Father; the President did not tell you to speak to us, and he will not hear your talk, nor will I hear them any more, they are like the talks of a muse man.

We understand that your government was a good one, and your laws just, and that your Father the President, and the men whom he appointed as warriors and councilors, were to see those laws executed. We never heard that you, William Cocke have been chosen a warrior or a councelor, since the battle of the Long Island, and I know he will not listen to any of your talks. He has sent a Beloved man to hold talks with us. This man is like himself [GW] and has a good heart, and I know our great Father will listen only to his talks, nor doe he allow me to hear any other.

This talk I have delivered in the beloved town of Chota. {no date} October 1792 Hanging Maw.

Document 17
Memorial from the Widow of a Cherokee Chief, submitted to House of Representatives, 4th Congress, 2d session, 17 January 1797.
ASPIA I:621.

Mr. Dwight Foster, from the Committee of Claims, to whom was referred the petition of the widow of the late Scolacuttaw, or Hanging Maw, one of the chiefs of the Cherokee Indians, reported:

That she complains against the conduct of one John Beard, and a number of armed men, who, she states, in the year 1793, contrary to law and the good faith of Government, attacked the dwelling house of the petitioner, and her husband; killed and wounded a number of well disposed Indians; burnt and destroyed and carried away their property, and wounded the petitioner. She now prays, that some provision may be made for her.

After examining the statement by the petitioner, and the facts upon which she rests her present application, the committed have found some difficulty in deciding what measures would be most advisable for the House to adopt.

Previous to the attack on the Hanging Maw, the frontier settlers of Tennessee, and the Indians in that quarter, had been guilty of mutual acts of aggression and hostility. A party of the Indians had killed some settlers; their trail was discovered, conducting across the Tennessee; this circumstance induced a belief in their pursuers, that the Hanging Maw had been concerned in the business, and occasioned his being wounded, and the misfortunes complained of by his widow. The general opinion, however, represents the Hanging Maw as having been uniformly friendly to the settlers, as vigilant to apprize them of the approach of banditti, and constant in his exertions, on all occasions, to compose differences between them and his nation, and... as possessing considerable influence over the Indians. The same disposition is also attributed to his widow, the present petitioner, who, instead of exciting her people to acts of retaliation, has abated nothing in her friendship to the white people.

All these circumstances seem to countenance, if not to require for her, a pension from the Government, or some other relief from the Legislature. Such a provision might also be considered as extending its influence beyond the particular object, or, as an inciting cause to other Indians, to pursue a similar line of conduct, under circumstances alike cruel and distressing, should they happen.

But, on the other hand, it is to be considered, there are citizens on the frontiers, who have suffered injuries as cruel, and deprivations as severe, by the Indians, and who have been thereby left in situations of distress, that would equally call for assistance from the Legislature. Questions arise, whether both descriptions of sufferers ought to be provided for? Whether the abilities of Government would be competent to meet all possible claims of this nature? And, whether help can be extended, by law, to the one, and consistently refused to the other?

It may be said, that those who settle upon the frontiers, voluntarily assume all the risks and dangers attached to that position, and therefore, can have no just claim upon Government, for consequences resulting from their choice; whilst, on the contrary, policy requires that the minds of Indians, who may be roused to hostility by acts of the settlers, should be quieted by small pecuniary interpositions.

Under these views of the subject, the committee have hesitated what report to make; but, upon the whole, as the authority vested in the Executive Department is competent to meet this claim, and should the petitioner, from her sufferings and her attachment to the United States, appear to the Executive to be entitled to any annual relief, as it may be afforded out of the appropriations for contingent expenses in the Indian Department, without an interference of the Legislature, and, as this mode will probably involve the fewest difficulties, the committee think she should apply to that department; and that the prayer of her petition ought not to be granted.

Document 18
Piomingo in the Chickasaw Nation to General James Robertson, 17 June 1793.
ASPIA I:466

Dear Old Friend:

I have received several letters from you since I was able to answer you, owing to matters being unsettled, as they are here at present. I received the corn, and other articles, by your son Randolph, for which I thank my brothers, the Americans, for considering us in so great need. Our situation has been such, that we could not pass to you as usual. I have sent one man with your son, as he requested, and hope shortly to come in myself. Whether this will ever reach you, is uncertain, for I hear the path is watched by Creeks and Cherokees, in order to intercept all messages passing, and I fear your son will never reach Cumberland; but if he should be so fortunate as to get in, he can inform you the circumstances of all matters, as I have made him fully acquainted with all within my knowledge. His being a woodsman, and going on foot, gives me hope he may get in safe. He can inform you of my unsettled situation, which, as soon as I can alter, and get my business arranged, you may be sure of seeing me. I endeavored to prevail with your son to wait longer, until he might go safer, but in vain, as he was anxious to get in., to let you know how matters were, that you might inform Governor Blount, so that he prefers going at the risk of all. I have often told you of the bad doings of the Creeks and Cherokees, which I am sure they will not cease... till they feel the weight of the white people, which, I hope will not be long. Surely, my friend, if you knew how lightly and despisingly [sic] they speak of you and your friends, you could not bear it, as you do. If we did not know you to be warriors, we should not know what to think of you calling them friends, and treating them as such, when they are continually killing your people, and taking your horses. We, the Chickasaws, that are but one very small house in the great city, the United States, could not bear to throw away, and let the blood of one man pass without retaliation. The Creeks were the aggressors, and asked for a cessation of arms of us, as your son can inform you. If you would treat them so, they would not think as little of you. There are very bad talks going on at this time, of which I shall be better able to inform you hereafter. Your son can tell you of seeing Cherokees coming in, which he saw with scalps and war instruments, to invite us and the Choctaws to join all other Indians to war against the United States. The Spaniards are getting all the Indians they can, to a treaty at the Walnut Hills. What their intentions are is uncertain; but I apprehend nothing to your advantage, which you will be better able to judge when I arrive; it will then be in my power to inform you of all that is of consequence. I intend to visit the president when I come in – your son has promised to go with me. I hope you will not be against it. Please to let Governor Blount know of it, which will be about four or five weeks. I want you to get Simson to make me a gun like Colonel Mansker's. I hope you will take great care of yourself, as both the Creeks and Cherokees will try to get you. Keep out your scouts at a great distance, it will be the best for safety, and not let them hunt near you, as they always do you mischief when breaking up to go home. I am very glad to hear you say, that the President has sent a greater warrior to command the army against the Northern tribes, if they do not treat. But, my brother, I hardly know what you mean by treating with tribes that are always at war with you, and will be, until you whip them; perhaps you may then have a treaty with them that may keep peace. Did I not tell you how the Creeks and Cherokees would behave when they treated? I said they would pay no regard to what they did; so you found it. If we confirm a treaty with the Creeks, they will be told every injury done us will be retaliated for, and we will observe to do it.

I am, and will be, your friend and brother,

PIAMINGO.

Document 19
Front page, from Savannah, GA, dated 14 July 1800.
Kentucky Gazette, 1 September 1800.

We are informed by an indisputable authority that the Governor of the Province of West Florida, Lieut. Col. don Vincent Folch, at the head of an expedition composed of nine gallies, retook a few days since, the fort of St. Marks on Apalachee, sunk a small vessel, and captured another in which the English adventurer and notorious vagabond William Augustus Bowles, after finding the Chactaw Indians inclined to favor the Interest of Spain, had made his escape up the waters of that river. Also, that the officers who so shamefully surrendered that strong fortification to the crazy winds of the renowned director general of Muskogee, are placed under arrest to be tried by a regular court martial. And that the Spaniards are full in hopes of putting out of the world that common enemy of peace (Bowles) by the offer of great presents to the Indian who will deliver him dead or alive, in Pensacola or St. Augustine.

Document 20
President Jefferson to Governor William H. Harrison of Indiana Territory.
The Papers of Thomas Jefferson, vol. 39, 13 November 1802–3 March 1803, ed. Barbara B. Oberg. Princeton, NJ: Princeton University Press, 2012, pp. 589–593. [Paragraph breaks added for clarity; edited for length.]

Washington, 27 February 1803. "PRIVATE"

DEAR SIR, –...

...this letter being unofficial and private, I may with safety give you a more extensive view of our policy respecting the Indians... Our system is to live in perpetual peace with the Indians, to cultivate an affectionate attachment from them, by everything just and liberal which we can do for them within the bounds of reason, and by giving them effectual protection against wrongs from our own people.

The decrease of game rendering their subsistence by hunting insufficient, we wish to draw them to agriculture, to spinning and weaving.... When they withdraw themselves to the culture of a small piece of land, they will perceive how useless to them are their extensive forests, and will be willing to pare them off from time to time in exchange for necessaries for their farms and families. To promote this disposition to ex-change lands... we shall push our trading uses, and be glad to see the good and influential individuals among them run in debt, because we observe that when these debts get beyond what the individuals can pay, they become willing to lop them off by a cession of lands....

In this way our settlements will gradually circumscribe and approach the Indians, and they will in time either incorporate with us as citizens of the United States, or remove beyond the Mississippi. The former is certainly the termination of their history most happy for themselves; but, in the whole course of this, it is essential to cultivate their love.... [Yet] Should any tribe be fool-hardy enough to take up the hatchet at any time, the seizing the whole country of that tribe, and driving them across the Mississippi, as the only condition of peace, would be an example to others, and a furtherance of our final consolidation.

... to be prepared against the occupation of Louisiana by a powerful and enterprising people, it is important that, setting less value on interior extension of purchases from the Indians, we bend our whole views to the purchase and settlement of the country on the Mississippi... that we may be able to present as strong a front on our western as on our eastern border, and plant on the Mississippi itself the means of its own defence....

We wish at the same time to begin in your quarter, for which there is at present a favorable opening. The Cahokias extinct, we are entitled to their country by our paramount sovereignty. The Piorias [sic], we understand, have all been driven off from their country, and we might claim it in the same way; but as we understand there is one chief remaining, who would, as the survivor of the tribe, sell the right, it is better to give him such terms as will make him easy for life, and take a conveyance from him. The Kaskaskias being reduced to a few families, I presume we may purchase their whole country for what would place every individual of them at his ease, and be a small price to us, – say by laying off for each family, whenever they would choose it, as much rich land as they could cultivate, adjacent to each other, enclosing the whole in a single fence, and giving them such an annuity in money or goods forever as would place them in happiness; and we might take them also under the protection of the United States.

… Of the means, however, of obtaining what we wish, you will be the best judge; and I have given you this view of the system which we suppose will best promote the interests of the Indians and ourselves, and finally consolidate our whole country to one nation only…The crisis is pressing: whatever can now be obtained must be obtained quickly. The occupation of New Orleans, hourly expected, by the French, is already felt like a light breeze by the Indians. You know the sentiments they entertain of that nation; under the hope of their protection they will immediately stiffen against cessions of lands to us. We had better, therefore, do at once what can now be done.

I must repeat that this letter is to be considered as private and friendly, and is not to control any particular instructions which you may receive through official channel. You will also perceive how sacredly it must be kept within your own breast, and especially how improper to be understood by the Indians. For their interests and their tranquility it is best they should see only the present age of their history.…

Document 21
Tecumseh's speech to Governor Harrison, 20 August 1810.
Messages and Letters of William Henry Harrison, vol. I, 1800–1811. Logan Esarey, ed. (Indianapolis: Indiana Historical Commission, 1922), 463–468. [Edited for length.]

… You ought to know that after we agreed to bury the Tomahawk at Greenville we then found their new fathers in the Americans who told us they would treat us well… I want now to remind you of the promises of the white people. You recollect that the time the Delawares lived near the white people and satisfied with the promises of friendship and remained in security yet one of their town was surprised and the men and women and children murdered [a reference to Gnadenhütten].

The same promises were given to the Shawonese [sic], flags were given to them and were told by the Americans that they were now the children of the Americans. Their flags will be as security for you if the white people intend to do you harm hold up your flags and no harm will be done you. This was at length practiced and the consequence was that the person bearing the flag was murdered with others in their village. [A reference Moluntha's murder.] Know my Bro. after this conduct can you blame me for placing little confidence in the promises of our fathers the Americans.

Brother. Since the peace was made... you have taken our lands from us and I do not see how we can remain at peace with you if you continue to do so....

You want by your distinctions of Indian tribes in allotting them to each a particular track [tract] of land to make them to war with each other. You never see an Indian come and endeavor to make the white people do so. You are continually driving the red people when at last you will drive them into the great lake where they can't either stand or work.

... *Brother.* This land that was sold [at Fort Wayne] and the goods that was given for it was only done by a few.... The treaty at Fort Wayne was made through the threats of Winamac [a Potawatomi allied with Harrison] but in future we are prepared to punish those chiefs who may come forward to propose them it will produce a war among the different tribes and at last I do not know what will be the consequence to the white people.

Brother. I was glad to hear... you said if we could show that the land was sold by persons that had no right to sell you would restore it... These tribes set up a claim but the tribes with me will not agree to their claim... We shall have a great council at which all the tribes shall be present when we will show to those who sold that they had no right to sell the claim they set up and we will know what will be done with those Chiefs that did sell the land to you. I am not alone in this determination it is the determination of all the warriors and red people that listen to me.

... I am a Warrior and all the Warriors will meet together in two or three moons from this. Then I will call for those chiefs that sold you the land.... If you do not restore the land you will have had a hand in killing them....

I wish you would take pity on all the red people and do what I have requested. If you will not give up the land and do cross the boundary of your present settlement it will be very hard and produce great troubles among us. How can we have confidence in the white people when Jesus Christ came upon the earth you kill'd and nail'd him on a cross, you thought he was dead but you were mistaken. You have shakers among you [Shakers – a millenarian Protestant sect] and you laugh and make light of their worship.

... *Brother.* I hope you will confess that you ought not to have listened to those bad birds who bring you bad news. I have declared myself freely to you and if you want any explanation from our Town send a man who can speak to us.

If you think proper to give us any presents and we can be convinced that they are given through friendship alone we will accept them. As we intend to hold our council at the Huron Village that is near the British we may probably make them a visit. Should they offer us any presents of goods we will not take them but should they offer us powder and the tomahawk we will take the powder and refuse the Tomahawk.

I wish you *Brother* to consider everything I have said is true and that it is the sentiment of all the red people who listen to me....

{In his response, Harrison insisted that the U.S. had always treated Indians justly, at which point Tecumseh stood and called him a liar, and a melee nearly ensued.}

Document 22
Lydia Bacon's journal, 30 November 1811 [Vincennes]. Boston-born, she was the wife of Lt. Josiah Bacon, Quarter Master for Col. John P. Boyd of the 4th U.S. Infantry Regiment, who accompanied Harrison's army to Tippecanoe.
From Lydia B. Stetson Bacon, *Biography of Mrs. Lydia R. Bacon* (Boston: Massachusetts Sabbath School Society, 1856), 31–34.

I do not regret that Josiah was in this Battle, for I trust the kindness of God in thus sparing his life, has left impressions on his mind, that will not readily be effaced... While bridling his Horse a Ball hit his hoof & his own boot & at another time his hat, the Army was encamped in a hollow square on a rising piece of ground, the tents all facing outward beyond which a guard was placed....The Indians attacked them a little before day which is their usual method. The first gun was heard, and the regulars were at their post in a moment. The enemy had their faces painted black, which is their usual custom in an attack. This our troops could only see by the light afforded at the flashing of the guns, but accompanied by their tremendous war-whoop and the groans of the wounded, it rendered the scene terrific indeed. Yet amidst it all our troops never faltered, but answered the whoop with three hearty cheers. This dreadful battle lasted until daylight, when the Indians were completely routed and compelled to retire with great loss.....

Oh, what a day was that when we at Vincennes heard of this battle of Tippecanoe. Receiving at first a mere report of the attack and victory without any official communication, and of course without any official communication, and of course without any details, each of us expected to hear sad news from our dear ones, and for hours our souls were harrowed to the quick, and agonized with suspense and dread. At length the express arrived with letters, yet his feelings were so excited, that he could not select and deliver them, but poured them out indiscriminately into my lap. I was so overcome with apprehensions for my husband that I could neither see nor read, and passed them into the hands of a lady who stood by me. Her husband not being in the war, she was more calm and composed, and soon was enabled to find me my letter. When told that the address was in Josiah's own hand-writing, I could hardly believe it. My bodily weakness was great, being just recovering from the ague and fever, and this, aggravated by my intense anxiety respecting my husband, caused me to sink fainting upon the nearest chair. Recovering soon, however... I opened the letter and began to read [with three of her women friends around her] it out loud.... and found that my beloved husband (now more dear than ever) and those whom we most valued had escaped without serious injury. There were but two married men killed from our regiment, and they were soldiers.... How often I have heard or read of Indian fights until my blood chilled in my veins, without thinking that I should ever be so personally interested in one.

Our situation at Vincennes was very much exposed while the troops were absent, for every body left that could handle a sword or carry a musket, and we women remained without even a guard. Mrs. W[hitlock][2] and myself had loaded pistols at our bedside, but I very much doubt whether we should have had presence of mind enough to use them, had we found it necessary. If the Indians had been aware of our situation, a few of them could have burnt the village, and massacred the inhabitants. But a kind Providence watched over us, and kept us from so dreadful a fate.

Another letter brings intelligence of the death of Capt. Bean who was tomahawked in a shocking manner. It is thought by the distance at which he was found from camp that the Indians attempted to take him prisoner, and that he chose death rather than submit to what he knew would be prolonged torture. He was a man of great personal beauty, and a most excellent officer, and commanded the love and esteem of his brother officers in an eminent degree. It was my husband's painful duty to see him interred. This he did, and disguised the grave that his poor body might not be disturbed, and his bones left to bleach upon the plain. The others who died during this murderous attack were all buried in one grave. But the Indians dug up the remains and left them a prey to the beasts of the forests, who by the way, are scarcely more savage than themselves.

Document 23
Indian Removal Act, 28 May 1830.
United States Statutes at Large, vol. IV. Richard Peters, ed. (Boston: Little, Brown & Co., 1846), 411–412.

---

2   The wife of another Army officer, staying in Vincennes.

CHAP. CXLVIII. – An Act to provide for an exchange of lands with the Indians residing in any of the states or territories, and for their removal west of the river Mississippi. Be it enacted by the Senate and House of Representatives of the United States of America, in Congress assembled, That it shall and may be lawful for the President of the United States to cause so much of any territory belonging to the United States, west of the river Mississippi, not included in any state or organized territory, and to which the Indian title has been extinguished, as he may judge necessary, to be divided into a suitable number of districts, for the reception of such tribes or nations of Indians as may choose to exchange the lands where they now reside, and remove there....

SEC. 2. *And be it further enacted*, That it shall and may be lawful for the President to exchange any or all of such districts, so to be laid off and described, with any tribe or nation within the limits of any of the states or territories, and with which the United States have existing treaties, for the whole or any part or portion of the territory claimed and occupied by such tribe or nation, within the bounds of any one or more of the states or territories, where the land claimed and occupied by the Indians, is owned by the United States, or the United States are bound to the state within which it lies to extinguish the Indian claim thereto.

SEC. 3. *And be it further enacted*, That in the making of any such exchange or exchanges, it shall and may be lawful for the President solemnly to assure the tribe or nation with which the exchange is made, that the United States will forever secure and guaranty to them, and their heirs or successors, the country so exchanged with them; and if they prefer it, that the United States will cause a patent or grant to be made and executed to them for the same: Provided always, That such lands shall revert to the United States, if the Indians become extinct, or abandon the same.

SEC. 4. *And be it further enacted*, That if, upon any of the lands now occupied by the Indians, and to be exchanged for, there should be such improvements as add value to the land claimed by any individual or individuals of such tribes or nations, it shall and may be lawful for the President to cause such value to be ascertained by appraisement or otherwise, and to cause such ascertained value to be paid to the person or persons rightfully claiming such improvements. And upon the payment of such valuation, the improvements so valued and paid for, shall pass to the United States, and possession shall not afterwards be permitted to any of the same tribe.

SEC. 5. *And be it further enacted*, That upon the making of any such exchange as is contemplated by this act, it shall and may be lawful for the President to cause such aid and assistance to be furnished to the emigrants as may be necessary and proper to enable them to remove to, and settle in, the country for which they may have exchanged; and also, to give them such aid and assistance as may be necessary for their support and subsistence for the first year after their removal.

SEC. 6. *And be it further enacted*, That it shall and may be lawful for the President to cause such tribe or nation to be protected, at their new residence, against all interruption or disturbance from any other tribe or nation of Indians, or from any other person or persons whatever.

SEC. 7. *And be it further enacted*, That it shall and may be lawful for the President to have the same superintendence and care over any tribe or nation in the country to which they may remove, as contemplated by this act, that he is now authorized to have over them at their present places of residence: *Provided*, That nothing in this act contained shall be construed as authorizing or directing the violation of any existing treaty between the United State and any of the Indian tribes.

SEC. 8. *And be it further enacted*, That for the purposes of giving effect to the provisions of this act, the sum of five hundred thousand dollars is hereby appropriated, to be paid out of any money in the treasury, not otherwise appropriated.

Document 24
Baltimore Patriot, 21 July 1831.

> THE INDIAN DISTURBANCES. – *The St. Louis Beacon* of the 7th inst. says – We are happy to announce that Generals Gaines and Atkinson, with the regular troops, have arrived from the Upper Mississippi, having accomplished, with the aid of the Illinois mounted men commanded by General DUNCAN and accompanied by Gov. REYNOLDS, the peaceable removal of the Indians, and dispersed a confederacy which has been forming for *two* years with incredible secrecy, under the famous Sac chief, BLACK HAWK, and the WINNEBAGO PROPHET, who have been endeavoring to revive the designs of the famous *Shawnee Prophet* and *Tecumseh*.

Document 25
On "the Late Indian Disturbance"
Pittsfield Sun (MA), 4 August 1832, from the *St. Louis Beacon*.

Anonymous [near St. Louis]
Black Hawk and his band were determined to remain until expelled by force – and their continued residence would have kept that part of Illinois in a constant state of alarm and danger – force must have been resorted to eventually – and perhaps the decisive

blow inflicted on them at this early period, has prevented an extensive confederacy of the Indian tribes throughout our line of frontier, with another Tecumseh at their head. Jefferson Barracks, July 6.

Document 26
New Hampshire Sentinel, 11 February 1836.

> A second Tecumseh. – *The St. Augustine Herald* of the 13th inst. has the following statement of POWELL, the Seminole Indian Chief. As he is the head and front of that tribe in their late and present depredations and murder, this account of him may not prove uninteresting to the reader: –
> The character of this chief is but little known, and not sufficiently appreciated. He is represented to be a savage of great tact, energy of character, and bold daring. The skill with which he has for a long time managed to frustrate the measures of our Government, for the removal of the Indians beyond the Mississippi, entitle him to be considered as superior to Black Hawk. Charley Omathla [Emathla], chief of the friendly party, interposed difficulties to the execution of his plans, and he at once shot him. He bore an inveterate hatred to *Gen. Thompson*, and yet he concealed his antipathies so skillfully as to deceive the agent, and to induce him to consider POWELL as personally friendly. Gen. Thompson fell by the hands of Powell. This warrior chief was present three days after, at the battle of Withlacochee. It is proper to observe that he ought not to be called POWELL, as that is only a nick name. His Indian name is 'Oseola,' [sic] and by that should be distinguished. It is apprehended that he will give the Government much trouble, if they do not act with that decision and energy that becomes the power and force of the country. The devastation and ruin that he has already caused, will not fall short of a million dollars.

Document 27
The Floridian (Tallahassee, FL), 21 May 1836.

> A proposition has lately been made to introduce the Cuba BLOODHOUND. – The necessity of having recourse to this ferocious animal is to be deplored, but whatever may be the issue of the present war, that necessity will still exist. – Should the Seminoles be obliged to submit, they will not be allowed to carry with them the slaves which they have captured. – The country will still be left infested with [black] banditti, which can hardly be exterminated by any other means. – While the war lasts the employment of this animal would effectually deter the enemy from separating into small parties. – We should have no scruples in calling to our aid a brute as ferocious and blood-thirsty as the enemy we have to contend with.

Guide to Further Reading

In addition to the works listed in the bibliography, students wanting to delve deeper into the history of conflicts with American Indians in early American history may benefit from the following, selected works, divided by type.

Published/accessible Primary Sources

Doing archival research with unpublished manuscripts can often be out of reach for undergraduate (and sometimes graduate) students. For early American history, however, there are a number of outstanding transcribed/published primary sources available, and a growing number of excellent ones online, often for free. Among the former, the 13 volumes of the *Papers of Sir William Johnson*, edited by James Sullivan and Alexander C. Flick and published by the University of the State of New York between 1921 and 1951, provide exceptional, well-indexed resources into one of the most important British colonial officials. They are exceedingly valuable, as a terrible fire destroyed many of the original manuscripts. Most early American presidents, including George Washington, Thomas Jefferson, James Madison, and Andrew Jackson, have had large edited collections of their papers published as well, sometimes online. Clarence Edwin Carter's *The Territorial Papers of the United States* (Washington, D.C.: Government Printing Office, 1934–1975) offers 28 volumes of equally valuable correspondence, largely between appointed territorial officials and presidents and cabinet officials. Parts are also available from some online vendors, including HathiTrust.

Online accessible sources. *The American State Papers, Indian Affairs* – 2 vols. – was originally published by Gales & Seaton in Washington, D.C., in 1834, at the behest of the Congress. Now available online through the Library of Congress, the *ASPIA* contains many fascinating documents regarding Indian relations in both peace and war, from the late 1780s through the 1820s. The Library of Congress website also maintains the *Annals of Congress*, the *Senate Journal*, and other

Guide to Further Reading 149

outstanding public documents. Charles Kappler's *Indian Treaties, 1778-1883* [see References] is also available online through the Oklahoma State University Library. Period newspapers are a terrific source, and Readex's *Early American Newspaper* databases offer wonderful, digitally scanned and term-searchable newspapers. **Documents 24–27** may be found there.

Syntheses

Unlike a *monograph*, which utilizes previously unpublished primary source historical research as well as secondary sources, a synthesis is an account drawn almost exclusively from pertinent secondary sources. A synthesis can be an excellent choice for introducing oneself to a topic, as the author has typically read most of the latest and classic works on the topic to create the synthetic narrative.

For a general overview of early American history until the early nineteenth century, one cannot do better than Alan Taylor's beautifully written and admirably thorough *American Colonies: The Settling of North America* (New York: Penguin Books, 2002). Fine general accounts of confrontations with Indians include R. Douglas Hurt's *The Indian Frontier 1763–1846* (Albuquerque, NM: University of New Mexico Press, 2002), which gives an excellent overview of conflicts with Indians from Pontiac to the eve of the Mexican War. The Indiana University Press series on the American frontier offers readable, informative narratives of several frontier regions. In addition to John Finger's *The Tennessee Frontier* (2001) noted in the bibliography, see R. Douglas Hurt's *The Ohio Frontier: Crucible of the Old Northwest, 1720–1830* (Bloomington, IN, 1996), Andrew R. L. Cayton's *Frontier Indiana* (Bloomington, IN, 1996), Craig Thompson Friend's *Kentucke's Frontiers* (Bloomington, IN, 2010), and Paul E. Hoffman's *Florida's Frontiers* (Bloomington, IN, 2002).

Sociologist Stephen Rockwell offers a trenchant analysis of U.S.-Indian relations in his *Indian Affairs and the Administrative State in the Nineteenth Century* (New York: Cambridge University Press, 2010). Reviewing how consistently incompetent the administration of Indian affairs has been in U.S. history, regardless of political regime or era, he comes to the depressing conclusion that it must be by design. A well-run Indian department which met the needs of its native charges – in terms of promised food, housing, and education – did not serve the ultimate imperial goals of the U.S.

Monographs

Historians of the early American frontier owe Reginald Horsman a considerable debt, particularly for his *Expansion and American Indian Policy, 1783–1812* (East Lansing, MI: Michigan State University Press,

1967), which methodically examined the chasm between Americans' stated desires to treat Indians fairly and their actual behavior. A number of books examine Americans' process in taking Indian lands. One of the better ones is Stuart Banner, *How the Indians Lost Their Land: Law and Power on the Frontier* (Cambridge, MA: Belknap Press, 2005). Though I cite Anthony F.C. Wallace's *Jefferson and the Indians* in the text, Bernard Sheehan's *Seeds of Extinction: Jeffersonian Philanthropy and the American Indian* (Chapel Hill, NC: University of North Carolina Press, 1973) remains worthy of its reputation as a classic.

Cynthia Cumfer's *Separate Peoples, One Land: The Minds of Cherokees, Blacks, and Whites on the Tennessee Frontier* (Chapel Hill, NC: University of North Carolina Press, 2007) explores the cultural landscape of that region in the late eighteenth and early nineteenth centuries. Joseph T. Glatthaar and James Kirby Martin's *Forgotten Allies: The Oneida Indians and the American Revolution* (New York: Hill and Wang, 2006) provides an in-depth examination of how some Indians chose to help the rebels during the Revolution and how quickly Americans forgot that. The theme of the U.S. quickly forgetting the contributions of native warriors is also addressed in John W. Hall's *Uncommon Defense: Indian Allies in the Black Hawk War* (Cambridge, MA: Harvard University Press, 2009). Alfred Cave's *Prophets of the Great Spirit: Native American Revitalization Movements in Eastern North America* (Lincoln, NE: University of Nebraska Press, 2006) examines religious visionaries from several Indian nations, including Delawares, Red Sticks, Shawnees, and Kickapoos.

Notable Biographies

Reginald Horsman also wrote what remains the best biography available of the important figure *Matthew Elliott, British Indian Agent* (Detroit, MI: Wayne State University Press, 1964). Larry L. Nelson's *A Man of Distinction Among Them: Alexander McKee and British-Indian Affairs along the Ohio Frontier, 1754–1799* (Kent, OH: Kent State University Press, 1999) details the long career of perhaps the most important agent and cultural broker in the Ohio country. His only serious competition would be the subject of Nicholas Wainwright's *George Croghan: Wilderness Diplomat* (Chapel Hill, NC: University of North Carolina Press, 2012). Isabel Thompson Kelsay details the fascinating career of the bilingual Mohawk chief in *Joseph Brant, 1743–1807: Man of Two Worlds* (Syracuse, NY: Syracuse University Press, 1984).

In addition to authoring the most thorough biography available of Tecumseh, John Sugden also wrote *Blue Jacket: Warrior of the Shawnees* (Lincoln, NE: University of Nebraska Press, 2000). He argues convincingly that it was Blue Jacket, rather than the Miami

Little Turtle, who was the overall military leader for the Northwestern Confederacy in the early 1790s. J. Leitch Wright's *William Augustus Bowles: Director General of the Creek Nation* (Athens, GA: University of Georgia Press, 2010) provides a thorough, somewhat sympathetic account of the Tory adventurer. William Heath's *William Wells and the Struggle for the Old Northwest* (Norman, OK: University of Oklahoma Press, 2015), offers the most detailed account available of the Miami warrior-turned-Indian agent. Colin G. Calloway's *The Indian World of George Washington: The First President, the First Americans, and the Birth of the Nation* (New York: Oxford University Press, 2018) is the first effort to analyze the centrality of Indians and Indian affairs to Washington's entire career.

Regional/area Studies

The best narrative account of Spain's efforts in North America is David J. Weber's *The Spanish Frontier in North America* (New Haven: Yale University Press, 1992). Gregory Dowd explores the role of rumors and panics in frontier politics and violence in *Groundless: Rumors, Legends, and Hoaxes on the Early American Frontier* (Baltimore, MD: Johns Hopkins University Press, 2016). Michael N. McConnell explores the pre-Revolutionary Ohio Valley in *A Country Between: The Upper Ohio Valley and Its Peoples, 1724–1775* (Lincoln, NE: University of Nebraska Press, 1992). Jim Piecuch's *Three Peoples, One King: Loyalists, Indians and Slaves in the Revolutionary South, 1775–1782* (Columbia, SC: University of South Carolina Press, 2008) analyzes the alliance of Tories, slaves, and Indians in the South, from their perspective. David Andrew Nichols explores the diversity and resilience of the Anishinabeg and other Indians of the Great Lakes in *Peoples of the Inland Sea: Native Americans and Newcomers in the Great Lakes Region, 1600–1870* (Athens, OH: Ohio University Press, 2018).

Essay Collections

Edited essay collections offer multiple contributions from various scholars concerning a general topic or theme. Essentially academic all-star teams, excellent examples include: Frederick E. Hoxie, Ronald Hoffman and Peter J. Albert, eds. *Native Americans and the Early Republic* (Charlottesville, VA: University of Virginia Press, 1999); Andrew Cayton and Fredrika Teute, eds., *Contact Points: American Frontiers from the Mohawk Valley to the Mississippi, 1750–1830* (Chapel Hill, NC: University of North Carolina Press, 1998); and Daniel P. Barr, ed., *The Boundaries Between Us: Natives and Newcomers Along the Frontiers of the Old Northwest Territory, 1750–1850* (Kent, OH: Kent State University Press, 2006).

Military Histories

Additional work on the Florida conflict can be found in Joseph Knetsch, *Florida's Seminole Wars, 1817–1858* (Charleston, SC: Arcadia Press, 2003). Francis Paul Prucha's *Sword of the Republic: The United States Army on the Frontier, 1783–1846* (Lincoln, NE: University of Nebraska Press, 1987) offers a comprehensive account of the U.S. Army during this critical era. Howard T. Weir III's *A Paradise of Blood: The Creek War of 1813–14* (Yardley, PA: Westholme Publishing, 2016) provides the most comprehensive narrative of the first Creek War available. Patrick Bottiger's *The Borderland of Fear: Vincennes, Prophetstown, and the Invasion of the Miami Homeland* (Lincoln, NE: University of Nebraska Press, 2016) looks at the Tippecanoe campaign from the perspective of French settlers and Miami Indians in Indiana, arguing that they exaggerated the threat of the Shawnee Prophet to a receptive Governor Harrison. Roger L. Nichols' *Warrior Nations: The United States and Indian Peoples* (Norman, OK: University of Oklahoma Press, 2013) examines eight armed conflicts between Indians and Americans from 1786 to 1877. Nichols argues that while Americans indeed bullied and abused native peoples, Indians' own warrior ethos also contributed to what was an exceptionally violent period in history.

References

Alden, John Richard. *John Stuart and the Southern Colonial Frontier: A Study of Indian Relations, War, Trade, and Land Problems in the Southern Wilderness, 1754–1775.* New York: Gordian Press, 1966.
Anderson, Fred. *Crucible of War: The Seven Years' War and the Fate of British North America, 1754–1766.* New York: Alfred A. Knopf, 2000.
Atkinson, James R. *Splendid Land, Splendid People. The Chickasaw Indians to Removal.* Tuscaloosa: University of Alabama Press, 2004.
Axtell, James. *The Indian Peoples of Eastern North America: A Documentary History of the Sexes.* New York: Oxford University Press, 1981.
Barksdale, Kevin T. *The Lost State of Franklin: America's First Secession.* Lexington: University Press of Kentucky, 2009.
Belko, William S., ed. *America's Hundred Years' War: U.S. Expansions to the Gulf Coast and the Fate of the Seminole, 1763–1858.* Gainesville, FL: University Press of Florida, 2011.
Bickham, Troy. *Savages within the Empire: Representations of American Indians in Eighteenth-Century Britain.* New York: Oxford University Press, 2005.
Blackmon, Richard D. *Dark and Bloody Ground: The American Revolution Along the Southern Frontier.* Yardley, PA: Westholme Publishing, 2012.
Boulware, Tyler. *Deconstructing the Cherokee Nation: Town, Region, and Nation Among Eighteenth-Century Cherokees.* Gainesville: University Press of Florida, 2011.
Bowes, John P. *Land Too Good for Indians: Northern Indian Removal.* Norman, OK: University of Oklahoma Press, 2016.
Braund, Kathryn, et al., eds. *Tohopeka: Rethinking the Creek War and the War of 1812.* New York: Pebble Hill Books, 2012.
Brown, Dee. *Bury My Heart at Wounded Knee: An Indian Account of the American West.* New York: Holt & Rinehart, 1971.
Brown, Meredith Mason. *Frontiersman: Daniel Boone and the Making of America.* Baton Rouge, LA: Louisiana State University Press, 2008.
Buss, Jim. *Winning the West with Words: Language and Conquest in the Lower Great Lakes.* Norman: University of Oklahoma Press, 2013.
Calloway, Colin G. *Pen and Ink Witchcraft: Treaties and Treaty Making in American Indian History.* New York: Oxford University Press, 2013.
_____ *The American Revolution in Indian Country: Crisis and Diversity in Native American Communities.* New York: Cambridge University Press, 1995.

_____ *The Indian World of George Washington: The First President, the First Americans, and the Birth of a Nation* New York: Oxford University Press, 2018.

_____ *The Scratch of a Pen: 1763 and the Transformation of North America*. New York: Oxford University Press, 2007.

_____ *The Victory with No Name: The Native American Defeat of the First American Army*. New York: Oxford University Press, 2014.

_____ *The World Turned Upside Down*. New York: Bedford/St. Martin's, 2016.

Campbell, William J. *Speculators in Empire: Iroquoia and the 1768 Treaty of Fort Stanwix*. Norman: University of Oklahoma Press, 2012.

Caughey, John Walton. *McGillivray of the Creeks*. Norman: University of Oklahoma Press, 1959.

Cleves, Rachel Hope. *The Reign of Terror in America: Visions of Violence from Anti-Jacobinism to Antislavery*. New York: Cambridge University Press, 2009.

Conley, Robert J. *A Cherokee Encyclopedia*. Albuquerque: University of New Mexico Press, 2007.

Corkran, David H. *The Creek Frontier, 1540–1783*. Norman: University of Oklahoma Press, 1967.

Din, Gilbert C. *War on the Gulf Coast: The Spanish Fight Against William Augustus Bowles*. Gainesville: University Press of Florida, 2012.

Dixon, David. *Never Come to Peace Again: Pontiac's Uprising and the Fate of the British Empire in North America*. Norman, OK: University of Oklahoma Press, 2014.

Dowd, Gregory Evans. *A Spirited Resistance: The North American Indian Struggle for Unity, 1745–1815*. Baltimore: Johns Hopkins University Press, 1992.

_____ *War Under Heaven: Pontiac, the Indian Nations, and the British Empire*. Baltimore: Johns Hopkins University Press, 2002.

Duval, Kathleen. *Independence Lost: Lives on the Edge of the American Revolution*. New York: Random House, 2015.

Edmunds, R. David. *The Shawnee Prophet*. Lincoln: University of Nebraska Press, 1983.

Ellisor, John T. *The Second Creek War: Interethnic Conflict and Collusion on a Collapsing Frontier*. Lincoln: University of Nebraska Press, 2010.

Ethridge, Robbie. *Creek Country: The Creek Indians and Their World*. Chapel Hill: University of North Carolina Press, 2003.

Fenn, Elizabeth A. "Biological Warfare in Eighteenth-Century North America: Beyond Jeffery Amherst." *Journal of American History*, 86 no. 4 (Mar. 2000), pp. 1552–1580.

_____ *Pox Americana: The Great Smallpox Epidemic of 1775-1782*. New York: Hill and Wang, 2001.

Ferguson, Gillum. *Illinois in the War of 1812*. Urbana: University of Illinois Press, 2012.

Finger, John R. *Tennessee Frontiers: Three Regions in Transition*. Bloomington: Indiana University Press, 2001.

Gaff, Alan D. *Bayonets in the Wilderness: Anthony Wayne's Legion in the Old Northwest*. Norman: University of Oklahoma Press, 2004.

Glatthaar, Joseph T., and James Kirby Martin. *Forgotten Allies: The Oneida Indians and the American Revolution*. New York: Hill and Wang, 2006.

Griffin, Patrick. *American Leviathan: Empire, Nation, and Revolutionary Frontier*. New York: Hill and Wang, 2007.

Hatley, Tom. *The Dividing Paths: Cherokees and South Carolinians through the Revolutionary Era*. New York: Oxford University Press, 1993.

Haveman, Christopher D. *Rivers of Sand: Creek Indian Emigration, Relocation, & Ethnic Cleansing in the American South*. Lincoln, NE: University of Nebraska Press, 2016.

Hinderaker, Eric. *Elusive Empires: Constructing Colonialism in the Ohio Valley, 1673–1800*. New York: Cambridge University Press, 1997.

Holton, Woody. *Forced Founders: Indians, Debtors, Slaves, and the Making of the American Revolution in Virginia*. Chapel Hill, NC: University of North Carolina Press, 2011.

Howe, Daniel Walker. *What Hath God Wrought: The Transformation of America, 1815–1848*. New York: Oxford University Press, 2007.

Ingram, Daniel. *Indians and British Outposts in Eighteenth-Century America*. Gainesville: University Press of Florida, 2014.

Jefferson, Thomas to William Duane, 4 August 1812, in *The Papers of Thomas Jefferson*, Retirement Series, vol. 5, 1 May 1812 to 10 March 1813. J. Jefferson Looney, ed. Princeton, NJ: Princeton University Press, 2008, p. 293.

Jung, Patrick J. *The Black Hawk War of 1832*. Norman: University of Oklahoma Press, 2007.

Kappler, Charles J., ed. *Indian Treaties, 1778–1883*. Mattituck, NY: Interland Publishing, 1972 [1902].

Keeley, Lawrence. *War before Civilization: The Myth of the Peaceful Savage*. New York: Oxford University Press, 1997.

Kelsay, Isabel Thompson. *Joseph Brant 1743–1807: Man of Two Worlds*. Syracuse, NY: Syracuse University Press, 1984.

Lepore, Jill. *The Name of War: King Philip's War and the Origins of American Identity*. New York: Knopf, 1998.

Linklater, Andro. *Measuring America: How an Untamed Wilderness Shaped the United States and Fulfilled the Promise of Democracy*. New York: Walker Books, 2002.

Martin, Joel W. *Sacred Revolt: The Muskogees' Struggle for a New World*. Boston: Beacon Press, 1991.

Merrell, James H. *The Indians' New World: Catawbas and Their Neighbors from European Contact through the Era of Removal*. Chapel Hill: University of North Carolina Press, 1989.

_____ *Into the American Woods: Negotiators on the Pennsylvania Frontier*. New York: W. W. Norton & Co, 1999.

Millett, Nathaniel. *The Maroons of Prospect Bluff and Their Quest for Freedom in the Atlantic World*. Gainesville, FL: University Press of Florida, 2013.

Missall, John, and Mary Lou Missall. *The Seminole Wars: America's Longest Indian Conflict*. Gainesville, FL: University Press of Florida, 2004.

Morris, Michael P. *George Galphin and the Transformation of the Georgia-South Carolina Backcountry*. New York: Lexington Books, 2014.

Mueller, James E. *Shooting Arrows and Slinging Mud: Custer, the Press, and Little Big Horn*. Norman: University of Oklahoma Press, 2013.

Nichols, David Andrew. *Engines of Diplomacy: Indian Trading Factories and the Negotiation of American Empire*. Chapel Hill: University of North Carolina Press, 2016.

_____ *Red Gentlemen & White Savages: Indians, Federalists, and the Search for Order on the American Frontier*. Charlottesville: University of Virginia Press, 2008.

Onuf, Peter. *Statehood and Union: A History of the Northwest Ordinance*. South Bend, IN: University of Notre Dame Press, 2019.

Owens, Robert M. *Mr. Jefferson's Hammer: William Henry Harrison and the Origins of American Indian Policy*. Norman: University of Oklahoma Press, 2007.

_____ *Red Dreams, White Nightmares: Pan-Indian Alliances in the Anglo-American Mind, 1763–1815*. Norman: University of Oklahoma Press, 2015.

Owsley, Frank Lawrence Jr. *Struggle for the Gulf Borderlands: The Creek War and the Battle for New Orleans, 1812–1815*. Gainesville: University Press of Florida, 1981.

Perdue, Theda. *Cherokee Women: Gender and Culture Change, 1700–1835*. Lincoln: University of Nebraska Press, 1998.

_____ et al, *The Cherokee Nation and the Trail of Tears*. New York: Penguin Books, 2007.

Waselkov, Gregory A., Peter H. Wood, and Tom Hatley, eds. *Powhatan's Mantle: Indians in the Colonial Southeast*. Lincoln: University of Nebraska Press, 2006.

Prucha, Francis Paul. *American Indian Policy in the Formative Years: The Indian Trade and Intercourse Acts 1790–1834*. Cambridge, MA: Harvard University Press, 1962.

Putnam, A. W. *History of Middle Tennessee, or Life and Times of Gen. James Robertson*. Knoxville, TN: University of Tennessee Press, 1971 [1859].

Rafert, Stewart D. *The Miami Indians of Indiana: A Persistent People, 1654–1994*. Bloomington, IN: Indiana University Press, 1999.

Sadosky, Leonard. "Rethinking the Gnadenhutten Massacre: The Contest for Power in the Public World of the Revolutionary Pennsylvania Frontier," in *The Sixty Years' War for the Great Lakes, 1754–1814*. David Curtis Skaggs and Larry L. Nelson, eds. East Lansing, MI: Michigan State University Press, 2001, pp. 187–213.

Saunt, Claudio. *A New Order of Things: Property, Power, and Transformation of the Creek Indians, 1733–1816*. New York: Cambridge University Press, 1999.

Sayre, Gordon M. *The Indian Chief as Tragic Hero: Native Resistance and the Literatures of America, from Moctezuma to Tecumseh*. Chapel Hill: University of North Carolina Press, 2005.

Schmidt, Ethan A. *Native Americans in the American Revolution: How the War Divided, Devastated, and Transformed the Early American Indian World*. New York: Praeger, 2014.

Silver, Peter. *Our Savage Neighbors: How Indian War Transformed Early America*. New York: W.W. Norton & Co, 2007.

Sleeper-Smith, Susan. *Indigenous Prosperity and American Conquest: Indian Women of the Ohio River Valley, 1690–1792*. Chapel Hill: University of North Carolina Press, 2018.

Snyder, Christina. *Slavery in Indian Country: The Changing Face of Captivity in Early America*. Cambridge: Harvard University Press, 2010.

Steele, Ian K. *Setting All the Captive Free: Capture, Adjustment, and Recollection in Allegheny Country*. Canada: McGill-Queen's University Press, 2013.
Sugden, John. *Blue Jacket: Warrior of the Shawnees*. Lincoln: University of Nebraska Press, 2000.
———. *Tecumseh: A Life*. New York: Henry Holt, 1998.
Sword, Wiley. *President Washington's Indian War: The Struggle for the Old Northwest, 1790–1795*. Norman: University of Oklahoma Press, 1985.
Taylor, Alan. *American Colonies: The Settling of North America*, Vol. 1. New York: Penguin Books, 2002.
———. *The Internal Enemy: Slavery and War in Virginia, 1772–1832*. New York: W.W. Norton, 2013.
Tucker, Robert W. *Empire of Liberty: The Statecraft of Thomas Jefferson*. New York: Oxford University Press, 1990.
United Nations Office on Genocide Prevention. *When to Refer to a Situation as Genocide*. https://www.un.org/en/genocideprevention/documents/publications-and-resources/GuidanceNote-When%20to%20refer%20to%20a%20situation%20as%20genocide.pdf
Wallace, Anthony F.C. *Jefferson and the Indians: The Tragic Fate of the First Americans*. Cambridge: Belknap University Press, 1999.
———. *King of the Delawares: Teedyuscung, 1700–1763*. Philadelphia: University of Pennsylvania Press, 1990.
Ward, Harry M. *The American Revolution: Nationhood Achieved, 1763–1788*. New York: St. Martin's Press, 1995.
Waselkov, Gregory A. *A Conquering Spirit: Fort Mims and the Redstick War of 1813*. Tuscaloosa: University of Alabama Press, 2006.
Weber, David J. *The Spanish Empire in North America*. New Haven: Yale University Press, 1992.
White, Richard. *The Middle Ground: Indians, Empires, and Republics in the Great Lakes Region, 1650–1815*. New York: Cambridge University Press, 1991.
Willig, Timothy D. *Restoring the Chain of Friendship: British Policy and the Indians of the Great Lakes, 1783–1815*. Lincoln: University of Nebraska Press, 2008.
Wright, J. Leitch Jr. *Creeks and Seminoles: The Destruction and Regeneration of the Muscogulge People*. Lincoln, NE: University of Nebraska Press, 1986.
———. *William Augustus Bowles: Director General of the Creek Nation*. Athens, GA: University of Georgia Press, 1967.

Index

Amherst, Jeffrey *xix*, 13, 29, 61; and biological warfare 19; and gifts 14–15, 123; recalled 20
Attakullakulla (Little Carpenter) *xix*, 20, 30, 32, 126

Beard, John *xiii*, 72
Bird, Capt. Henry 39–40
Black Fish *xix*, 37–38
Black Hawk *xxiii*, 106–109, 146; portrait, 107
Black Hawk War 106–109
Bloodhounds: proposed to fight Indians and maroons 18, 42, 113–114, 147
Blue Jacket *xx*, 67, 110; at Greenville, 77
Blue Licks, battle of 43–44, 52
Boone, Daniel *xx*, 26, 36; at Blue Licks 43–44; capture & escape 37–38; in Dunmore's War 26–27
Bouquet, Henry *xx*, 19, 123; and biological warfare 18–19; recovers prisoners 23–24
Bowles, William A. *xx*, 55–56, 74, 78–79, 139; portrait 55
Brant, Joseph *xx*, 34
Britain's influence on Indians 30, 33–36, 37, 39, 41, 42, 43–44, 45, 46–47, 60, 63, 69, 75–76, 79–80, 85–87, 92, 97–98, 101, 108
Burnt Corn Creek, battle of 95–96
Bushy Run, battle of 19, 23
Butler, Richard *xx*, 48, 51, 66; death of, 68

Catawbas *xvii*, 13, 30
Cavett's Station 73

Cherokees *xvii*, 13, 19, 21, 27, 30–31, 35, 47, 53, 56, 57, 70, 73, 78–79, 89, 90, 123–131, 133–139; Chickamauga/Lower Cherokees 31–32, 41–42, 56, 59, 73, 130–131; and Creek War, 96–97; make peace with U.S., 77; Overhills 31, 41, 58–59, 62; Removal 105–106, 114; and Treaty of Hard Labor, 25–26
Cherokee War 13, 19
Chesapeake-Leopard Affair 85–86
Chickasaws *xvii*, 21, 53–54, 56, 60, 72, 74, 79, 89, 129, 138
Choctaws *x, xvii*, 19, 21, 25, 32, 54, 56, 72, 74, 79, 89, 99, 127, 138
Clark, George Rogers *xx*, 40, 41, 44; executes prisoners at Vincennes 38–39; at Piqua 40; as treaty commissioner 48, 53
Coacoochee 112–113
Cocke, William 57, 134, 136
Crawford, William *xxi*, 43
Creeks *xvii, xxxii*, 25, 30, 32, 35, 47, 53–56, 60–61, 70, 72–73, 100, 126–127, 129, 131, 138–139; and Bowles 78–79; civil war, 89–92; Creek War 91, 95–97; and First Seminole War 101–102; Removal 105; and Second Creek War 111–113
Croghan, George *xxi*, 15–16, 25, 123

Delawares *xviii*, 13, 16, 17, 18, 32, 36, 77, 84, 141; and Gnadenhütten 42–43; and Northwest Confederacy 67, 70; and Pontiac's War 21–23, 47
Dragging Canoe *xxi*, 30–32, 41, 44, 56, 72, 110

Index 159

Ecuyer, Simeon *xxi*, 18

Fallen Timbers, battle of 74–76, 79, 84
Franklin, state of *xxx*, 56–59, 130

Gage, Sir Thomas *xxii*, 20, 23, 25, 29
Galphin, George 35, 126
Girty, Simon *xxii*, 43, 47
Gnadenhütten Massacre *xxix*, 42–43, 141

Hamilton, Henry *xxii*, 38–39
Hanging Maw 72, 135–137
Harmar, Josiah *xxii*, 63–65, 70
Harrison, William Henry *xxii*, 77, 118; as Indian commissioner 82–84, 85–86, 106, 139, 141–143; and Tippecanoe campaign 87–89; in War of 1812 94–95, 100
Hawkins, Benjamin *xxiii*, 53, 60, 78
Hokoloesqua/Cornstalk *xxiii*, 28, 52; murdered, 36–37
Horseshoe Bend/Tohopeka, battle of 96–98, 105–106

Indian Removal 114–115
Indian Removal Act 106; document, 146
Iroquois Indians *xviii*, *xxxi*, 5, 13, 17, 23, 26, 30, 33–36; and Treaty of Fort Stanwix 26

Jackson, Andrew 11, 92; desires to invade Creek Country 92, 96, 97; invades Florida 101–103; and New Orleans 99; portrait 98; and removal 104–106, 114, 118
Jefferson, Thomas 92; Indian policy of 49–50, 69, 77, 81–83, 139–140
Johnson, Sir William *xxiii*; portrait 15, 16–17, 19–21, 25–26, 123–124
Junaluska *xxiv*, 97, 106, 114

Kentucky militia 43, 52–53, 59, 64–66, 71, 94–95
Knox, Henry 51, 60, 70, 72–73, 133

Little Turtle 63–67, 71, 77
Logan, Benjamin *xxiv*, 40, 52
Logan, John *xxiv*, 26–27
Lord Dunmore's War *xxi*, 26–28
Loyalists/Tories *xxxi*, 31, 33, 55–56, 60, 78

Martin, Gen. Joseph 32, 57, 129–130; wife Betsy murdered 72
McCrea, Jane *xxiv*, 33
McGary, Hugh: at Blue Licks 43–44; murders Moluntha 52
McGillivray, Alexander *xxiv*, 35, 54–56, 58–61, 71, 72, 74, 79, 110, 127–128
McIntosh, Chief William *xxv*, 102, 104
McKee, Alexander *xxv*, 39, 47, 52, 141
Miamis 17, 70, 77, 115; and Kekionga 63–64
Moluntha *xxv*, 52

Neolin *xxv*, 16, 84, 124–125
Nicholls, Edward *xxv*, 101, 103
Northwest Confederacy *xxxii*, 63–72, 74–77

Old Tassel/Corn Tassel 57, 59; murdered, 130–131
Osceola *xxvi*, 109–112, compared to Tecumseh 146–147; murders Charley Emathala 110, 146; portrait 110
Outlaw, Alexander 57, 59, 130–131

Pan-Indianism *xxxii*, 19, 21, 25, 31–32, 44, 47, 48, 54, 59, 61, 70–74, 78, 80, 84, 88–90, 108, 111, 124
Paxton Boys *xxvi*; murders of Conestoga Indians, 22–23
Pickens, Gen. Andrew *xxvi*, 53–54, 127–128, 134
Piomingo *xxvi*, 60, 72, 74, 137
Pontiac *xxvi*, 16; death of 24; speech of 124–125
Pontiac's War 17–24, 29. 47
Proclamation of 1763 *xxxii*, 20, 25, 30
Propaganda, American use of 36, 49
Prospect Bluff, maroon fort *xxv*, 101–103

Red Stick Creeks 90–92, 95–98, 101, 103, 118
Robertson, James *xxvii*, 41, 137
Ross, Chief John *xxvii*, 97, 105, 114

Saukenauk 107–108
Scalping 7, 57, 67, 68; bounties for 23, 31, 91

Seminoles *xix*, 100–105, 109, 129; and First Seminole War 102; Second Seminole War 109–114, 147; Third Seminole War 116
Sevier, John *xxvii*, 41, 56–58, 73
Shawnees *xix*, 13, 17, 18, 23, 25, 26–28, 31, 36, 42, 43–44, 48, 52, 53, 67, 70, 77, 105, 124, 141
Slavery: cotton agriculture and growth of 102, 105, 111; and fears of pan-Indianism 111; maroons *xxxi*, 101–103, 147; Nat Turner rebellion and 111
Spain: influence on Indian affairs 12, 14, 55–57, 60–61, 78–81, 126; in Florida 79–81, 98, 100–104, 138–139
St. Clair, Gen. Arthur *xxvii*, 65–66, 69–70, 72, 76, 116
Stuart, John *xxvii*, 20, 25, 35, 125

Tecumseh *xxviii*, 27, 84–85, portrait 85, 89, 93–95, 106, 108, 117, 146; and British alliance 86, 87; spares prisoners 94; death of 95; speech of 141–142
Teedyuscung *xxviii*, 21–22
Tenskwatawa/Shawnee Prophet *xxvi*, 83–87, 146; and Prophetstown 84, 87–90

Thompson, Wiley 109, 147; murdered by Osceola, 111
Tippecanoe, battle of 88–89, 143–144
Treaties: Fort Finney 48, 51; Fort Jackson 98; Fort McIntosh 48, 51; Fort Stanwix (1768) 25–26, 47–48; Fort Stanwix (1784) 48; Fort Wayne 86–87, 141; Ghent 100–101; Greenville 76, 77, 79–80, 83, 106, 141; Hopewell 56; Holston 78; John Jay's 76, 79; Moultrie Creek 104; New Echota 114; New York 60; Paris (1783) 45–46; Payne's Landing 109

Wabash, battle of the 66–69, 71–72
Ward, Nancy/Nanyehi *xxviii*, 32, 72
War Hawks 92, 95
Washington, George 35, 43, 58, 61–62, 64–66, 69, 71–73, 117, 135
Wayne, Gen. "Mad" Anthony *xxviii*, 70–72; at Fallen Timbers 74–76; at Greenville 77, 79
Weatherford, William *xxix*, 79, 96, portrait 98
Wells, William *xxix*, 71
Williamson, David *xxx*, 42, 74

For Product Safety Concerns and Information please contact our EU representative GPSR@taylorandfrancis.com
Taylor & Francis Verlag GmbH, Kaufingerstraße 24, 80331 München, Germany

www.ingramcontent.com/pod-product-compliance
Lightning Source LLC
Chambersburg PA
CBHW052121300426
44116CB00010B/1751